GETTING
CLOSER

ELLEN ROSENBERG

GETTING CLOSER

DISCOVER AND UNDERSTAND YOUR CHILD'S SECRET FEELINGS ABOUT GROWING UP

BERKLEY BOOKS, NEW YORK

GETTING CLOSER

A Berkley Book/published by arrangement with
the author

PRINTING HISTORY
Berkley trade paperback edition/October 1985

ISBN: 0-425-08103-6

A BERKLEY BOOK ® TM 757,375

PRINTED IN THE UNITED STATES OF AMERICA

Acknowledgments

So many people made *Getting Closer* possible. A special thank you to the following:

My husband Roger: I could never have completed this book without your continued encouragement, understanding, and especially your love, which I treasure.

My children, Andy and Hillary: Your terrific attitude and willingness to help gave me the freedom to work on this book. Andy, extra thanks for your wise editorial comments and Hillary, your editorial and spirited notes spurred me on.

My agent and manager, George Greenfield: *Getting Closer* is a reality because of your creative efforts and tremendous support. Thank you for sharing my dreams and making them your own.

All the children, parents, and teachers who have participated in my programs: Thank you for trusting me, for sharing so deeply, for teaching me so much.

My dear friend Emma: Thank you for caring so much and for always being there to help.

Gareth Esersky, my editor: Thank you for your enthusiasm for *Getting Closer* and for your wisdom, guidance, support, and friendship.

Roger Cooper, and everyone at the Berkley Publishing Group, including Rick Nayer and Michael Clayton: Thank you for believing in me and working so hard to help *Getting Closer* happen.

Ellen Rosenberg
April 12, 1985

Dedication

To my parents, Shirley and Samuel Greenfield:
For giving so much of yourselves even when times were hard,
For always making the time to listen,
For loving me so much and making family so important.
All that you are and all that we continue to share will remain
a special part of me for the rest of my life.

To all parents:
May the love, understanding and sensitivity you and your child
have for each other continue to strengthen and grow more
meaningful throughout your lives together.

CONTENTS

CHAPTER 1

SECRET FEELINGS

How can I express my feelings to my parents when the words fumble and I'm embaressed?

I am nervous when I have to talk to my parents what should I do

G 7th, grade

I feel a lone.
Because I can not
talk to know one
not even my parents.
I need some one
to talk to.

7G

I want to get closer to my parents it's just
but they're always out either to work or business trips
or carpooling and I can't talk to them, whenever I
have a problem I feel really embarrassed to say anything
what should I do?

B-8

There are many things my parents don't know
about me and I would like to share w/ them
and I don't know how to do it.

Thousands of children have written anonymously and discussed openly with me their innermost secret feelings at the assembly programs I have conducted throughout the United States. It hasn't mattered where I've been, whether it was a small rural town or a large city, the questions, yearnings, frustrations, confusions, and pressures shared by children of all ages have been always the same.

I have walked away from program after program, overwhelmed at the number of unmet and unanticipated needs children have—at home and at school. Whatever we're doing to help children to feel good about themselves and their relationships, and to deal more effectively with day-to-day life experiences, it can't be enough.

The reality is

Many children are lonely and have no idea how to take the first step to try to make a friend;

Many children aren't sure how to let their friends know how they really feel;

Many are using drugs, having sex, drinking, smoking, stealing, and cheating because they don't know how to handle pressure from peers;

3

Many don't feel close to their parents and families and want so strongly to be closer but don't know how;

Many don't understand their physical changes and have difficulty accepting their sizes;

Many children are teased and denigrated unmercifully and don't know how to respond, or realize that teasing doesn't mean they're less special;

Many were never taught how to be sensitive to others and respectful of differences;

Many believe they don't measure up to brothers, sisters, friends, or cousins and don't have any idea how special they really are;

Many feel pressured in school, can't concentrate, aren't motivated, or feel they have to cheat;

Many don't know how to express their feelings about death, illness, divorce, disability, or any other of life's disturbing changes;

Many are taking their own lives.

The tragedy is that so many children keep their feelings and needs secret. Secret feelings are trapped inside even the most popular, verbal, good-looking, and talented children. There is no rule, no absolute guarantee that smiles on the outside aren't covering up tears or confusions within. Surely this has been proven time and again when "bright," "popular," "wonderful," "happy" children have committed suicide for reasons that their shocked families have never figured out.

Even if there are no serious confusions which demand immediate attention, everyday life is filled with experiences that trigger significant feelings and responses: a sister wears *the* sweater without asking; a teacher doesn't call on your son even though his hand was raised the whole class period; all the girls in the locker room have bras and your daughter is not ready for one yet (or you're not ready for her to have one!); your children want to be with their friends instead of visiting relatives with you; your son's girlfriend breaks up with him; your daughter doesn't get the part she wanted in the school play; your daughter's social studies project is due tomorrow and she hasn't started it; your son's school is planning "grandparents' day" and his are no longer alive; your daughter is sick and has to miss the class trip; . . . and other familiar situations. I question whether there is any such thing as an issue-free child. Life is just not issue-free! At what price can any caring parent, teacher, or any adult who is closely involved with children ever be too complacent or too sure that all is understood and at peace.

Naturally, some days will be smoother than others. But, throughout the growing-up years, friends may change and bodies are sure to develop, with no promise of how or when. Your children will be exposed to new experiences, faced with pressures to handle, decisions to make, expectations to meet, and increasing responsibilities. Along with each experience, there will be feelings that may or may not be expressed.

It doesn't seem to be enough for adults to say, "I love you; I care about you; talk with me about anything." Even if children want urgently to respond, they may not know how. They may be embarrassed, or scared, or believe their parents won't understand or listen, or are too old-fashioned and will be angry and won't take them seriously or think they're old enough. Many simply don't know what words to use. The troubling result is that far too many important feelings and concerns remain hidden . . . even when parents and children are close.

The questions and concerns shared by parents and educators attending my programs for adults further confirm the tremendous need for much more sensitivity and skill in dealing with what children might be feeling but not telling.

Misunderstandings, fights, busy schedules, insensitivity, inaccurate interpretations, inability to listen, lack of knowledge, parental sermons instead of dialogues, intimidation, unfair comparisons, unrealistic expectations, and dramatic changes in so many family relationships often strengthen and perpetuate children's need to keep feelings secret from adults, or anyone.

But even when relationships are good, moods are calm, and expectations are in balance; when "quality time" is shared, intimacy is obvious, smiles abound, and adults and children seem able to talk about "everything," those secret feelings live on inside every child. It's just a matter of how many, which ones, and how the silence is taking its toll.

It's essential for us to consider more seriously what our children *might* be feeling, in case they aren't telling us. But, whether or not our children do share their feelings with us, we *must:*

Actively anticipate their concerns,

Teach them what is essential to know to grow up to be responsible adults,

Better prepare them for all the experiences they will have as they grow and change,

Offer a healthier perspective to all that they might feel.

Only with our eyes wide open, our senses more sharply tuned, and our children's needs more in focus can we hope to raise their self-esteem, nurture self-acceptance, strengthen confidence, instill self-respect, and teach them to be sensitive to differences in others. *Getting Closer* is meant to help you "see" your children more clearly and respond to them in a more meaningful way.

If your children don't know how to express what they feel, *Getting Closer* gives you guidelines to help them turn feelings into words. If what they need to say is too embarrassing or uncomfortable, *Getting Closer* provides step-by-step approaches and dialogue that can help ease the discomfort and break through communication barriers. If your own discomfort is getting in the way of dealing openly with difficult and sensitive issues, *Getting Closer* offers more than just encouragement. It's filled with facts, ideas, practical suggestions, perspectives to consider, and specific sentences to help you get started.

Depending upon your own background, you may find some of the topics in this book more sensitive than others. If you find yourself thinking, "Why does she have to be so explicit?" or "That seems so obvious..." or "Why would that even have to be said?", please understand that I have learned it's a mistake to take anything for granted. The information I have included is in direct response to specific questions and concerns children have shared with me.

The more specific we are with our children, the less likely that misunderstanding will cause needless anxieties. Ignorance is not innocence, as many adults believe. Ignorance leaves children prey to misinformation, invalid worries, and inappropriate decisions. Ignorance can also get kids in a great deal of trouble.

Today's children are being exposed earlier and earlier to situations and pressures that they have not been prepared to handle. Elementary school children regularly ask what to say to their friends who have offered them drugs. Seventh- and eighth-grade girls write that they think they're pregnant but haven't told anyone. There are children everywhere who cannot concentrate in school because they're afraid all the fighting at home means their parents will get a divorce. Countless numbers of boys and girls are anxious and confused about their physical changes because no one ever told them what they need to know. Children of all ages get into cars driven by brothers, sisters, parents, friends, or others who have been drinking. Sometimes, the ability to make a split-second decision may make the difference between getting home safely or not getting home at all.

If our children don't have the information, how will they know what is appropriate or inappropriate, healthy and "normal" or dangerous? How will they be prepared to handle and accept the changes that are destined to occur? How will they be able to feel good about themselves? We *must* be specific with our children. The stakes are too high for any parent to risk believing, "Not *my* child!"

If you allow discomfort, feelings of inadequacy, denial, religious beliefs, or perhaps your own more restricted background to get in the way of offering your child all that he or she needs to know about growing up, you'll be leaving his or her learning to chance. It is very important that this teaching come primarily from you. Then you can be sure it's presented accurately, with a realistic and healthy perspective, according to your own sense of values. If you're not comfortable with the information, just go slowly. You and your child can grow more comfortable together.

If you find yourself thinking "That's just plain common sense" about my suggestions and observations in this book, then my practical approach is being taken as it is given. Getting closer doesn't take magic tricks, or mysterious formulas. Just straight, honest talk. It works! Or, at least it *can* work. Add warmth, trust, and a lifetime supply of love, and you've got a chance to relate to your child in a way that perhaps you never did before. If your relationship is already very close, there's always room to get closer, always more to learn.

Keep in mind how you present yourself to your child. How do you imagine your child responds to you? Do you raise your voice much of the time? Do you yell? Do you always lecture or preach? Do you always stand while your child sits so that you tower over him or her? Do you use physical force? If your voice is loud or deep, your stature is large, and your child generally considers you *awesome*, he or she might be very intimidated and feel afraid to share his or her thoughts with you. Think about whether the way you come across makes you more, or less, approachable. If you're not sure, *ask* your child.

Before we move on to the next chapter and plunge into the often uncomfortable, always sensitive topic of physical growth and development, I want to tell you that it means a great deal to me to share my book with you. I hope it will become a special, personal, accessible, on-hand reference that will help enrich your relationship with your child and enhance your ability to understand and respond to your child's needs, feelings, and concerns, even if they remain hidden.

I also want you to know that this book is not a "holier-than-thou" effort. I, too, am a parent, with a son of fifteen and a daughter of thirteen, and although I'm "ultra tuned in" to what's on the minds and in the hearts of thousands of children who have trusted me with their secret feelings, there's always more to know. And, each child is unique. I continue to work very hard to continue to know my own children, anticipate their feelings and needs, be there for them, and keep the lines of communication open. The truth is, regardless of the extent of my professional experience, if my own children decide to keep their feelings secret, I may never know what they are. I'm working at all of this, too.

Together, let's move forward, topic by topic. You might want to keep a notebook handy in case some secret feelings of your own begin to surface.

CHAPTER 2

PHYSICAL SIZE, GROWTH, and DEVELOPMENT

What happens if your parents are divorced and your living with your father and you get your period what should you do?

I am a boy and I have a bigger chest than most girls. I am am embarrassed in to lockroom

I reached pubirty but its growing on the wrong side.

also I had sex with a boy and I'm afraid that I have aids

I'm Scared

My best friend makes fun of me because I'm not developed yet. What should I do about it because it doesn't feel to great

Thousands of boys and girls (including my own) have taught me that no matter how strongly we believe that our children will ask us any question and tell us "everything," the reality is they may not. Even the brightest, most verbal, seemingly most sophisticated children have talked with me about their misconceptions and anxieties regarding physical development—concerns they felt they could not discuss with their parents.

It is not surprising that several mothers have telephoned me to discuss how upset they were to find evidence that their daughters had gotten their periods but had not shared this news with them. Countless other parents have told of not knowing their son or daughter had started to experience physical changes until months, even years after they began.

While there's no mistaking a child's height or weight, darkened hair over the upper lip, or a deepening voice, other aspects of maturation are less obvious. Unless your daughter tells you, you may not know she has started menstruating or that she's concerned about a vaginal discharge. She may think it's too silly to say that she's afraid of being lopsided when one breast has started to grow earlier than the other. So she may remain concerned, silently.

If your son doesn't tell you, you may not be aware that he has begun to have wet dreams and has questions that need answering, or that he's embarrassed to change in the locker room because his chest seems more like a girl's. Unless he tells, you may not realize how much he worries whether or not his penis is growing normally. So he may remain concerned, silently.

If you're waiting for your son or daughter to come to you with questions and concerns about development, you may be waiting a lifetime, even if you're close. A better approach would be to anticipate all your child's physical changes and make sure he or she understands each change *prior* to its occurrence. That way, whether your child is able to come to you or not when the change occurs, at least you'll insure that your child's development will be experienced with proper knowledge and preparation, as well as with a healthier outlook on such change.

If you're saying to yourself right now, "I feel terrible . . . my child has passed the point where I should have initiated such discussions. I figured I'd just wait until my child comes to me," or "I haven't even known how to talk about this," or "Talking about this makes me very uncomfortable," you're not alone. *Not to worry!!* It's never too late to start, even if your child has completely matured.

TALKING ABOUT PHYSICAL GROWTH AND DEVELOPMENT WITH CHILDREN

Well thought-out factual explanations blended with careful considerations of the various possible emotional responses to those facts will help you create a positive foundation for your child's good feelings about growth. Build information slowly. Let one fact be the base for understanding the next. Be careful not to present too much information at one sitting. Allow your child to have a chance to digest what you've explained and your explanations will seem less like a lecture. Be very aware of your child's responses, both verbal and non-verbal.

Use correct terms. If it seems funny or strange to say certain words aloud, admit that. If you sense your child may think certain words are complicated, there will be less confusion if you say, "I know some of the words I'm going to use are very long and hard to say. Don't worry about remembering those words. It's more important that you get the general idea of what I'm explaining to you. If we want, we can figure out ways of remembering them together."

If appropriate, acknowledge that your son or daughter probably knows several slang words for some of the terms you'll use. This can be a good time to discuss your feelings about the use of slang words, and how such usage usually has little to do with the body part the word represents and much more to do with getting back at someone, name-calling, and so on.

Many parents themselves use slang words and expressions for body parts "down there" and biological functions. Not using correct terms can perpetuate avoidance and discomfort. To help ease the discomfort, you might say, "It's really strange to say this out loud. My parents never spoke about this with me."

It may be very helpful (and more comfortable) to give your child a book that explains growth and development in terms they can understand. You might choose to have your child read a particular chapter alone and then talk about it together. Or, especially with a young child who is just beginning to learn about his or her body, read together, a few pages at a time. Be sure to leave ample time for related discussion.

Humor is a wonderful desensitizer. Use it whenever you can. Children are much more responsive and attentive when learning is fun as well as relevant to them. I do a fallopian tube imitation at my growth and development programs and invite children to do the same, not because I like standing there with my arms held out from my sides with my fingers spread apart in a downward direction, but because it gets the children involved, alleviates their anxiety, and adds a fun dimension to learning—not to mention that it clarifies the shape of the tubes!

Interjecting memories of your own frustrations, confusions, embarrassments, and pressures, along with the good feelings that related to your own physical growth and development, can be an excellent springboard for more personal communication with your child. Many children are reluctant to talk about their concerns because they can't imagine that their parents will understand. The realization that you actually had similar feelings and experiences will help dispel this notion.

Children feel terrific when you let them into your past. They feel much closer to you and may even understand you better. Besides, it can be a great relief for your child to learn that he or she is not the only person to have had such feelings and experiences. The more human you allow yourself to be, the more comfortably your child will relate to you, and the more likely he or she will want to talk further.

Besides the smiles and intimacy that can go along with sharing such memories, specific stories can be chosen to correspond with and identify what you sense your child may be feeling but not telling. Taking into account your child's size, stage of development, and how he or she seems to "fit in" among friends and classmates can help you anticipate what these feelings might be.

You might talk about:

Your first bra; stories about stuffing your own mother's bra with socks, etc.,

The first time you realized that you had a wet dream,

Any feelings you had about what to do with your sheets when you knew you had a wet dream,

How you felt changing in the locker room,

How you felt talking with your own parents about development,

How you wished you could have talked with your own parents about development,

Misconceptions that you were sorry you had about development,

Whether you were taller, shorter, fatter, skinnier, more or less developed than your friends while growing up and how this made you feel,

How you felt when your voice changed,

How you felt, where you were, and who you were with when you got your first period,

How you felt about buying sanitary pads,

How you felt about starting to shave, and so on...

Since children's feelings are often skillfully camouflaged, it's very possible you will incorrectly assess your child's concerns and pick the wrong topic for the time. If this is the case, he or she will probably let you know, but don't waste the opportunity. You can talk about related issues and feelings. (It shouldn't be a total loss!)

If you're correct about the concern, your personal story may open a door for discussion that might otherwise have remained locked. As it may be more comfortable for your child to talk about your feelings than his or her own, don't be surprised if your child asks extensive questions relating to you before acknowledging, "That's how I feel" or "That's just what happened to me."

If your child's reaction gives you reason to believe your story has touched a nerve, yet there is no admission of personal feelings, you might simply say, "I know this is hard for a lot of kids to talk about. Is there something you'd like to say but feel you just can't?" Or you might ask, "Has this ever happened to you?" or "Have you ever felt this way?"

If the answer is "No," and you feel a more truthful reply would have been "Yes," then without pushing further for personal acknowledgment, continue to talk about your own feelings, incorporating important information that you sense would be helpful. At least your child will have heard you.

At the end of your conversation, you might add, "You know, I still have a feeling that you can really relate to what I just said. I can understand if you're just not comfortable. But I want you to know it would mean a lot to me if you tried to let me in. I care so much, and I know what a relief it can be to talk about feelings that are hiding inside just wishing to come out. Would you at least think about it? We can talk again in a couple of days."

This approach can help take the edge off the pressure to confront topics and to divulge feelings that your child might not be ready to share. It might help to remind yourself that the lack of response may have little or nothing to do with your relationship or anything you have done. It's just not so easy to share (for adults, either). Building trust and getting rid of uneasiness is a gradual process that requires patience and awareness.

HOW SOON SHOULD YOU BEGIN TO TALK WITH YOUR CHILD ABOUT PHYSICAL GROWTH AND DEVELOPMENT?

At one of my programs, a parent told me she wondered if she should teach her fifth-grade son about physical development yet, since it seemed that he was going to be a "late bloomer." She reasoned that he needn't be told about such things until *he* started to develop. This attitude troubles me.

Even if your child doesn't begin to grow and develop until much later than the average, he or she will most likely have friends and classmates of the same age who will already have started. Girls may begin to develop as early as third grade, sometimes earlier. Boys usually begin to develop a bit later than do girls, but there are always exceptions. Therefore, I suggest that you start talking with your child about development, softly, slowly, and in an age-appropriate way, at the earliest possible time change might begin.

Children who have had little or no explanation about why there are such developmental differences may spend years worrying, "What's wrong with me?" or "How come everyone else is growing and I'm not?" With proper education, this kind of anxiety is unnecessary. Your children may not like their time schedules for growth, but at least they won't worry that something is wrong with them.

If you're wondering whether it could be damaging to explain too much, too soon, your child will likely take in what he or she is capable of understanding and will "file" the rest away. If your information is factually accurate, it won't be harmful. If your explanations are presented with sensitivity to your child's age, level of maturity, and ability to comprehend, then you'll more accurately anticipate what he or she might be feeling but not telling.

HOW MUCH DO YOU NEED TO TELL CHILDREN?

Much more than you might imagine.

After hearing in a male anatomy and physiology lesson that one testicle is slightly lower than the other, one of my male college students blurted out, "Whew! I thought I had arthritis or something all these years. No one ever told me it was okay for them to be that way!" Many more "Whews!" through the years proved that he was not the only one who wasn't told. Many women in my college classes thought the hairs around their nipples meant something was wrong with their development, that they were more masculine than they should have been.

A sixth-grade boy came up to me after a program and whispered, "Will my penis grow normally if I'm not circumcised?" A fifth-grade girl wrote, "Can you still use deodorant if you don't have hair under your arms?" Hundreds of children have asked whether they would have to get pubic hair cuts!

Far too much is taken for granted about what children know about their bodies and development. There are many questions children don't even know to ask. My advice is: Explain even the most obvious information. Be very specific. That way you'll have a better chance to counter unfounded and secret worries.

If your child says, "Oh, Mom [or Dad], I know that already," you can reply, "Indulge me; I'll feel a lot better if I finish my explanation so I can make double sure you understand." Or you might say, "That's great! Then just use this as a review, and you can check that *I've* got the right information."

PHYSICAL DEVELOPMENT— A CHECKLIST FOR DISCUSSION

One seventh-grade boy asked, "How will I know when puberty has struck?" Well, puberty doesn't quite "strike," although the first signs of development may take a girl or boy by surprise. It would help to explain to children that, generally, puberty is experienced gradually, over a period of time. Little by little, each child will notice certain changes. Those changes will let the child know that his or her body has begun to develop.

"When will I develop?" is a question that thousands of children have asked. Be sure to make it clear that each person has his or her own time schedule for development. Explain that growth may start as early as second or third grade or not until the end of high school. Each person's "growth clock" is different. This information will help your child understand why some friends will begin to develop earlier, others later, and younger brothers or sisters may start to grow before those who are older. It will also clarify why it's natural for groups of children who are the same age to be so many different shapes and sizes.

Since it is important to build understanding gradually, you should help your child make sense of the individual physical changes by establishing why they occur in the first place.

You might say: "Development will only begin when a chemical 'signal' from your growth control center (the pituitary gland at the base of the brain) causes special chemicals called hormones to travel around the bloodstream. These chemicals will cause all the physical changes over a period of time. You can't feel the chemicals flowing through your body but you will know they have been released when you begin to grow and develop."

In order to help you to understand your children's feelings and talk to them about specific physical changes, the following section focuses topic-by-topic on those changes and the common concerns of children regarding them. Where appropriate, I have offered sample explanations, scenarios, and dialogue that can be used as guides for presenting information to children for the first time. Even if your child is past the "first-time" stage, you might wish to skim the topics in order to double check any areas you might wish to discuss and clarify further.

This section is designed to be a practical reference. Use it to review what you have already discussed with your child and to enhance any future interaction.

Breasts—Feelings about breasts

It's not enough to explain that each girl will start to grow breasts when her body is ready. Girls are concerned with "when" and "what size will I be." They often wonder, "Am I going to look like my grandmother?", "Will I be like my mother?", "Will I be like my older sister?", "What am I going to do if my younger sister gets breasts before I do?", "What if all of my friends get a bra and I'm not big enough to wear one?", "What if I'm the only one who's wearing a bra?", "How am I ever going to ask my mother or father (heaven forbid!) if I can get a bra?", or "How can I tell my parents to stop bugging me about getting a bra?"

Give your daughter specific information about breast development. Tell her how breasts and nipples can differ in size and appearance from woman to woman and even on the same body, and assure her that there are no "breast size rules" among women in the same family. Reassure her that her body will develop breasts when it is ready, and they will become the size and shape unique for her. Remember to add that one breast "bump" might appear slightly earlier than the other. And, no matter what the size of a woman's breasts, they all "work" the same. (You can bring in the idea that even women who are smaller-breasted can nurse a child after giving birth if they so choose). This will help her understand and feel better about her development. As she grows older you can explain self breast-examination.

Most girls are concerned about breast size, dealing with braless or bra-wearing peers, changing in the locker room, shopping for a bra, breast sensitivity, and "growing pains," but a great many girls have admitted having difficulty initiating or discussing these topics with their mothers. Most couldn't even imagine mentioning breasts and bras to their fathers.

It can be helpful to remind girls that even though fathers don't have breasts like women, they know about them. They're interested in their daughters and understand it can be awkward to discuss personal questions, especially about something like bras. (In fact, it can be awkward for them, too.)

Let your daughter know that *you* realize how hard it can be to talk about these things and confirm your interest and willingness to be open with her. Such an approach will likely encourage her to confront what she needs to share. You might want to suggest actual sentences your daughter can use to start a discussion if she wants to but is not sure how. This may also be a wonderful time for mothers to introduce old bra stories.

Many girls can't imagine what it's like to have breasts. One twelve-year-old girl even asked, "Can I play soccer with breasts?" In addition to explaining that breasts will change a girl's shape and how she might see herself, you can make a daughter feel better if you let her know that breasts needn't change her lifestyle! Remember your sense of humor. She can continue to play soccer, do homework, go to parties, eat pizza, and do anything she did before her breasts appeared. She can even continue to play with dolls and doesn't have to suddenly grow up just because she's bumpier than she was the week before. And, even if a girl's breasts grow to be a fairly large size, she won't topple over when she walks; her body will know just how to keep them balanced.

It would also be important to teach girls at an early age that it doesn't matter what size their breasts grow to be. Besides explaining that they all "work" the same, talk about how breast size has nothing to do with being more or less womanly. Being a woman has to do with who you are "inside." If friends or boys like them only because they have breasts, what kind of friendship is it?

Female genitals

Many women have negative feelings about their genitals, believing them to be unattractive and not really understanding their anatomy. Although this is often an uncomfortable subject for both parents and children, with correct information and an opportunity to talk about this very private area, you can nurture self-acceptance and help your daughter develop more positive feelings at an early age. The very fact that you are willing to talk about this subject is a positive message in itself.

How to begin: The following is a sample presentation you can use to explain information about the internal female reproductive organs to a child for the first time.

Before you begin, cut out a circle with a four-inch circumference. Hold it one inch below your belly button, and start.

"See this four-inch circle? A girl's or woman's inside reproductive (or sex) organs just about fit inside that tiny circle. Isn't it amazing that such special organs with important jobs are tiny enough to fit in that space?

"Let's talk about the organs themselves. Females have one uterus that looks like an upside-down pear. It is the very special place where babies grow and develop when a woman is pregnant. That's when a baby is growing inside a woman's body."

You might say: "Lots of children think that babies grow in the stomach because when a woman is pregnant it looks like her stomach is pushed out very far. Now you know it's not the stomach but the uterus that gives a growing baby a cozy place to develop. When a baby is growing inside, the uterus has the important job of making sure it gets enough food, oxygen to breathe, and the right amount of blood supply. Isn't it amazing how the uterus is able to get bigger and bigger, sort of like a balloon, in order to allow for the baby's growth?

"The correct name for a baby that is growing inside is *embryo* for the first two months of development. After that, while the baby is growing inside, it's called a fetus. When it's born, it's then called a baby." (Your child might not remember these names at first but she will have at least heard the correct terms.)

"The uterus has a neck (called a cervix) that leads into a canal called the vagina. The vagina leads to an opening between a girl's legs. When a woman is going to have a baby, the usual way for a baby to be born is to pass through this vaginal canal or vagina. That's why the vagina is also called the birth canal. The vagina is able to stretch to allow a baby to pass through even though it seems like a very tiny canal. It's very very flexible. Like a rubber band, it can stretch." (Depending on the age of your child, you may wish to explain caeserean operations.)

Lots of kids refer to the vagina as the "V." They will probably welcome an opportunity to get their laughter out, so say "The 'V' is pretty fantastic! Sometimes the inside of the vagina might feel a bit damp, sort of like it's sweating. That's very natural for girls and women."

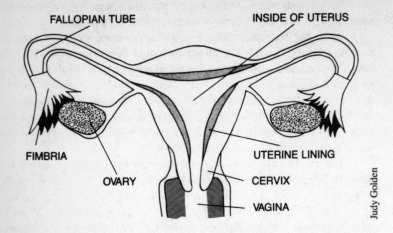

FALLOPIAN TUBE   INSIDE OF UTERUS

FIMBRIA   UTERINE LINING

OVARY   CERVIX

VAGINA

Judy Golden

Continue to explain:

"Some other inside organs are the fallopian tubes. A female has two fallopian tubes, one on each side of the uterus." (This is a good time to do a fallopian tube imitation, such as the one I described on p. 13. Keep your sense of humor, remember?)

"Let's make believe my left fist is an ovary and right arm is a fallopian tube. By spreading the fingers of my right hand over but not touching my left fist I show how the fallopian tube fans around the ovary but doesn't directly connect with it.

"Females have two ovaries, one on the left side of the uterus, the other on the right. The ovaries have two important jobs. One is to provide eggs. Not the kind of eggs that you can buy at the farm or the supermarket, but very tiny egg *cells* that can only be seen if you look at them under a microscope. When a girl is born, her ovaries contain thousands of these little egg cells that will not start to ripen until she begins to mature.

"Besides being the only place in a female body to provide egg cells, the ovaries have the job of releasing important chemicals (or hormones) that will help a girl develop and mature.

"So now you know that, inside, girls and women have one uterus, one neck of the uterus called the cervix, one vagina, two fallopian tubes, and two ovaries. Each inside part has its own important job."

You might not include all of this information in one sitting. How much you present depends upon circumstances, your child's attention span, offshoot discussions, how much time you have together, privacy, and so forth. Although I kept the presentation very simple, the information is comprehensive enough for most young children to be satisfied. Again, the idea is to build information. If your child grasps the relationships of these organs to each other, as well as the simple functions they perform, later explanations of menstruation, conception, and pregnancy will be more easily presented, accepted, and understood.

Follow this up with a conversation explaining the outside genitals, and allow ample time to focus on any feelings your child might have.

Feelings about the genitals

Only one or two students in my twelve years of college teaching experience admitted to knowing that the term *vulva* refers to the entire area between a girl's legs, or simply, to all parts of the outside genitals. The rest thought it was some kind of Swedish car! Only a handful of students said they discussed genital information with either parent. Imagine.

It is no wonder that there are grown women who are uncomfortable about the appearance of their labia, do not know the correct names for their genital parts, are still confused as to where the clitoris is located, and, due to mistaken concepts about cleanliness, douche too frequently, thus removing helpful bacteria and increasing the chance for vaginal infection. We have a responsibility to nurture healthy attitudes and healthy practices among our children. The educational process is best started when they are young.

I have found that when children realize they *can* talk about this subject, they're usually fascinated. One twelve-year-old exclaimed, "So that's what that thing is!" when I identified the clitoris on an anatomy diagram. She was genuinely curious about this part of her body and didn't feel comfortable asking her parents.

Because talk about the genitals characteristically brings with it blushes and embarrassment, it is that much more difficult for young girls to ask questions and share important concerns with their parents.

One of the most frequent secrets girls keep is that of having a vaginal discharge. A girl may worry whether this occurrence is natural and wonder if it means her periods will arrive tomorrow—or maybe this afternoon?—or what's happening? Even if daughters speak with their parents about this, the discussion may not be enough to quiet the concern. I'll never forget the eleven-year-old who waited until everyone cleared away from me at the end of one of my programs so she could whisper privately, "I told my mother about the stains in my underpants. And she told me they were normal. But I'm still worried and I don't know what to do."

No matter what you have already explained to your daughter, it would help to ask periodically whether she has had another discharge. Be sure to give her assurance that discharges are quite normal and remind her to let you know if she notices any kind of a change (in color, if it causes itching, has an unpleasant odor or a significant increase in amount). If there is any question about just how normal your daughter's discharge truly is, ask your family doctor for advice.

Based on the number of stories from women of all ages that confirm a widespread uneasiness about the physical appearance of the labia, I believe it would be helpful to accentuate the positive in your description of the labia to children. You might say:

"Between a girl's legs there are flaps and folds that look like lips. Another name for these lips is *labia*. Some people say that the shape of the labia reminds them of a flower. Just like everyone's nose is different, the labia appear different for each girl and woman. Sometimes, even on the same girl, these flaps can be slightly 'flappier' or larger at times and will then go back to being smaller or less flappy again."

This change can occur if your daughter masturbates or touches her labia in a way that causes a physiological response (the extra blood supply that flows into the area of the genitals during sexual excitement causes the labia to become enlarged). I know masturbation is a very emotional and sensitive issue (see Chapter Seven, page 129). Whether or not your beliefs allow you to mention such a subject to your child, you might wish to be aware that, if your daughter masturbates, her labia may become slightly enlarged in response to sexual excitement. This may or may not cause guilt, confusion, and general concern. Many women have told me they worried for years whether they had caused their genitals permanent damage because the labia seemed stretched after they touched them.

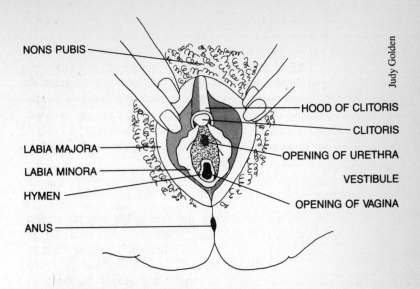

Judy Golden

Many girls do not understand that there are three separate openings between their legs. Starting down from the belly button: the first is the *urethra,* through which liquid wastes pass; the middle is the *vaginal opening;* and the third is the *anus,* through which solid wastes pass. This leads to a great deal of unnecessary confusion and concern, for example, about the ability to be able to urinate if a tampon is in place.

In addition to anticipating feelings and concerns that your daughter might have about her genital anatomy, you should also advise her about hygiene:

It is important to teach girls to wipe themselves from front to back after going to the bathroom because potential bacteria from the anus might cause an infection in the vaginal area (with a knowledge of the three openings, this will be easier for them to understand).

While some physicians are indifferent, many that I have spoken with suggest that wearing cotton underpants, or at least those with a cotton crotch, will allow the area within the vulva to "breathe" and therefore lessen the chance of vaginal infection.

It is important to teach your daughter to wash under the hood of the clitoris as well as the entire area of the vulva.

Once you get past your child's initial uneasiness, you might be surprised at how curious and fascinated she will be about information related to the female genitals. Even more important, sharing such information and offering your child a chance to discuss openly what is so traditionally viewed as "privates" will contribute to your child's self-acceptance, understanding, personal hygiene awareness, and to the quality of the rapport between you.

Menstruation

The number of girls who have admitted to me they have been too embarrassed to talk with either parent about the menstrual period is overwhelming. Many said that even when their parents tried to approach them, they politely listened, held back feelings and questions they wished they could have talked about, and prayed for the conversation to end as quickly as possible.

Many girls have also prayed that there would be some way to prevent their periods from starting in the first place. Said one eleven-year-old, "Do I have to get it?" Well, like it or not, want it or not, girls will feel much better about starting to menstruate if they are prepared.

The more we offer important information and anticipate concerns the more likely it is young girls will experience menstruation with acceptance, understanding, and even a sense of pride for all that starting to menstruate means.

How to begin: Before dealing with all the feelings about menstruation and the practical advice, such as how to take care of getting periods in school or anywhere else, how to use sanitary pads, etc., your child needs to understand what a period is and why it occurs.

The following sample presentation can be used as a guide for introducing the topic of menstruation to a young child for the first time. The presentation is based upon the assumption that parent and child have already discussed the female reproductive organs, even if only to define what they are, any simple functions they perform, and where they are located.

"One of the special changes that happens to a girl is that she'll get what is called her *period*. Another word for getting your period is *menstruation*.

"When a girl gets her period, it's a celebration since it means she is physically on her way to becoming a woman. Lots of girls think it's strange to talk about getting their periods with their mothers or fathers, so it's extra special to me that we're talking about it together right now.

"Before we discuss what you need to do when you get your period, let me explain what a period is and why you'll get it."

Describing the experience of menstruation in a less personal manner may help make your daughter more comfortable with this topic, especially if she is dreading her period. For example, you might say, "A girl will get her period" instead of "You will get your period." This general way of explaining menstruation can be used with boys, too.

"A girl's period will start when chemical messages inside her body let her ovaries and uterus know they have to make some changes. These changes will cause a girl to get her period. A girl won't be able to feel the chemicals, or hormones, flowing around her body giving messages. But when she starts developing, she'll know those chemicals are working to help her grow and change.

"Now about those messages: The message to the ovaries is: 'Hey, please get one of your thousands of immature egg cells to start to ripen and mature.' I told you before that a girl is born with thousands of immature egg cells. They just hang out in the ovaries waiting for this message.

"Remember, these are not the kind of eggs that you can find in the refrigerator. They're tiny cells that can only be seen under a microscope. These egg cells are very special because they're a female's sex cells. I called them sex cells because these are the cells that can become fertilized or entered by a male sperm—the male's sex cell—so that it can grow into a baby.*

"While the egg cell is ripening in the ovary, the uterus gets a message. The message is 'Please make sure that your lining gets

---

*If at this point your child asks you to explain more about making babies, you can say that understanding how babies are made will be easier if you can finish this explanation first.

thicker and richer with an extra blood supply.' This is important in case that ripened egg cell becomes fertilized or entered by a male sperm.

"If the egg cell does become fertilized, it will find a nice spot to plant itself in the cozy thickened lining of the uterus. The extra blood supply built up in the lining will help nourish that planted egg cell so that it can grow into a fully grown baby.

"If the egg cell is not fertilized, the extra blood supply in the lining of the uterus won't be needed, so it slowly passes out of a girl's body. It takes two to seven days, sometimes more, for the lining to slowly trickle out. Then all the messages start over again.

"When the lining of the uterus passes out of a girl's body, it's called having a period! That's right . . . the period is only that cozy old lining that the body didn't need because the egg cell wasn't fertilized." (Using the term "special blood" when referring to the period flow can help take the edge off your daughter's discomfort.)

"Are you with me so far? I know this can be hard to understand. How about if I explain the idea again just to make sure you get it. Be sure to stop me if you don't understand."

After the initial explanation you can go on to discuss related concerns and other important information at a pace that seems comfortable for you and your child. Remember that each "talk" needn't be a formal, sit-down discussion. Talking about these issues bit by bit, during moments when you're naturally together, can help you to casually, and poignantly, build on your child's understanding.

Some of the more important topics you should discuss include when a first period might begin (ages 9–17) and how she might know she has it; how frequent it is; how to keep a calendar; the fact that a period might skip; possible duration of period (2 to 7+ days, including nights); quantity of menstrual flow (usually heavier during first days, lesser toward the end, and approximately four to six tablespoons in total); why and how to use sanitary pads or tampons; playing sports, swimming, and bathing while menstruating; cramps; mood changes; and menopause.

Feelings about menstruation

Even if your daughter has a basic understanding of menstruation, she *still* may feel that getting her period will be scary. This is natural since the experience of menstruation is for her something that never before happened. It's an "unknown." Some parents respond to their daughter's fears by saying, "Oh, that's so silly. Don't be ridiculous. It's not scary at all. After all, I had it, your grandmother had it, your sister has it. We're still here." Or, "It's something that happens to every girl and you'll be just fine."

It would be much more helpful to acknowledge that it's natural to feel a little (or even a lot) scared. You might say: "I can understand why you feel scared, since you never had a period before and it's hard to imagine what it would be like to have it. It also might be strange to think of how it will feel to have that reddish special fluid trickling little by little out of your body. But once you get your period, I just know you'll be relieved to find that having a period is as natural as going to the bathroom . . . just different. I know it's hard to believe that now."

If you're female, you might add, "I had the jitters, too, wondering what it would be like to have my period. In fact, I think I remember praying that I wouldn't get it at all! But when it started, it was no big deal. It just seems like a big deal before you get it. If you want to talk some more about being scared, I'm here to listen."

The thousands of "what-ifs" that girls have asked me over the years are testimony to their great anxiety about knowing what to do about their periods if they're at school, at a mall, on a plane, on a date, at someone else's house babysitting, playing hockey, at the beach, or anywhere. It would likely be a great relief to your daughter if you were ultra-specific with her as to what she could do to take care of her needs in each relevant instance. For example, it's not enough to talk generally about what she can do if she gets her period in school. Girls want to know what they should do in specific situations, such as if they're in the middle of taking a test, if the nurse is not there, if they're on the school bus, if their teacher is a man, and even "if I'm on the stage in the auditorium playing an instrument in the school orchestra concert?"

Any conceivable circumstance that concerns your daughter can be examined to figure out what choices are available, how to be creative until sanitary protection can be obtained (tissues, toilet paper, paper napkins, paper towels), who your daughter can approach and exactly what she can say if she needs assistance, where she can get sanitary pads. From this conversation on, she can always have a packet of tissues with her until she gets a pad. Ask *her* how she thinks *she* would handle each situation. Arming her with choices and the realization that she can take care of herself in just about *any* circumstance (yes, even if there are no bathrooms and she has to temporarily "stuff" tissues into her underpants behind the nearest protected bush) will greatly enhance her sense of confidence and readiness for this special event.

Speaking of special, some parents have told me that they've had special dinners and toasts to celebrate their daughter's first period. One twelve-year-old girl was invited to join her mother's friends for coffee or tea anytime she wished, "now that she was one of them." Another twelve-year-old told me her father celebrated by giving her a cigar (not to smoke, of course)!

Since so many girls are reluctant to tell their parents about their periods in the first place, it's especially wonderful if a parent's reaction can be positive, reassuring, and help confirm that having a period is part of the specialness of being a woman. Enough said.

While some girls have told me about the "emergency—I have my period, please let me go to the bathroom or nurse's office—signals" they have arranged with their classroom teachers, making it comfortable to be excused even during tests, too many others have told of great anxieties about being unable to approach their teacher in the first place.

Teachers could help by having flexible bathroom policies and a backup supply of sanitary pads, and perhaps even by talking privately with all the girls in class. That way girls would know that their teacher will try to help them in any way possible even if the teacher is a man. You might suggest to the principal of your child's school that all classroom teachers receive a memo reminding them of the need to be more sensitive to the feelings girls have about getting their period in school.

Girls are also quite worried about what they'll do if their period stains their clothing while in school. Discuss with your daughter how she can best deal with this situation, like keeping an extra pair of sweatpants in her locker or the back closet.

The parent-teacher association or organization at your school might consider using a portion of their funds to purchase several pairs of sweatpants to be left in the nurse's office in case girls need a backup change of clothing when they have their periods.

Girls who have never had their periods often dread wearing a sanitary pad, anticipating that it will feel "gross." Many imagine that wearing a pad will be like walking around with a volleyball between their legs and "everyone will notice!" It can be a great relief for girls to try on a sanitary pad before their period even begins in order to test what it feels like. You might buy a small box of pads for your daughter and suggest she try one on. If she is reluctant to even consider this idea, you can let her know where the pads will be kept if she changes her mind. More than likely, you'll find a pad or two missing before long.

Many parents are concerned about whether tampons are a safe, appropriate choice for girls who have just started their periods. Most doctors seem to agree that tampons can be used by girls of all ages without any ill effects as long as they are changed according to instructions (each package of tampons contains information about use and toxic shock syndrome). Leaving a tampon in place longer than four to six hours might be unhealthy. (It's even better to change it sooner—every two hours or so.)

If you give your daughter permission to use tampons during the day, have her switch to sanitary pads at night, so the tampon won't be worn for too many hours while sleeping. Girls and women who use tampons would be wise to use a tampon size that is smaller than it need be. Lesser absorption capacity will force the user to change each tampon more frequently, thus reducing the likelihood of leaving it in place too long.

How a girl feels about getting her period will be influenced by what she hears about periods (from her mother, grandmother, sister, aunt, friends, friend's mother or sister, teachers, or anyone else). If an aunt talks about the terrible cramps she gets each time she had her period and her young niece hears, I wouldn't be surprised if her niece might become very scared of having terrible cramps when her own period begins. If a mother curses and complains bitterly about how much of a bother it is to have her period, it would shock me if her daughter were enthusiastic about getting it herself.

Let's face it. If we were really honest, we'd ban periods altogether. Periods *are* a pain. There's nothing to love about having to wear sanitary protection several days each month, being concerned about where and when a period will begin, and so forth. However, it would be unfortunate and unfair to convey these negative feelings since periods, once they begin, are so much a part of a female's life.

The true significance of menstruation, the celebration, lies not in the extra personal care that is required while having a period, but rather in the fact that the menstrual cycle offers a mature woman the capacity to choose if she wishes to bear a child.

Male genitals

As with the subject of female genitals, parents as well as children often are uncomfortable about discussing the penis, scrotum, testicles, and the functions associated with these organs.

We owe young boys the opportunity to learn about their sexual organs and their important functions, and about related personal hygiene. We also owe them a perspective. I've spoken with many a college student who believed himself to be less of a man on the assumption that his penis size was inadequate. Most admitted that they had never talked with their parents about these feelings. They compared themselves to their fathers, brothers, friends in the locker room at school and never felt they "measured up."

With proper information, and a chance to talk about personal concerns and feelings, more boys could feel better about themselves, as they understand that manliness is not measured in terms of genital size. Being a man depends on self-image, and while boys have no control over their genital growth, every boy can work at who he is as a person.

How to begin: The following is a suggested basic way of presenting information about the male genitals to a child for the first time. (You may choose to talk about each of the following topics separately or together, depending upon how much time you have and how your child responds):

"There's a lot of information that I want to share with you about your penis and the sac behind your penis.

"Since so many kids and parents don't talk about these things, it's extra special to me that we're able to talk together right now. If I use any word that you don't understand, please let me know. If what I say doesn't make sense, also tell me and I'll be happy to try to explain it a different way.

"Okay. I'll start by telling you about the outside genitals. They

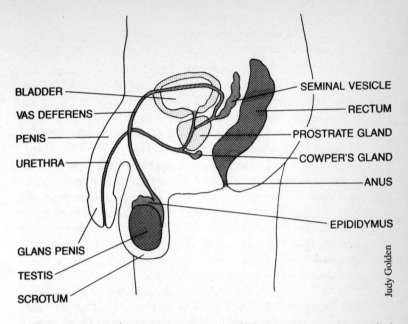

BLADDER

VAS DEFERENS

PENIS

URETHRA

SEMINAL VESICLE

RECTUM

PROSTRATE GLAND

COWPER'S GLAND

ANUS

EPIDIDYMUS

GLANS PENIS

TESTIS

SCROTUM

Judy Golden

can also be called reproductive or sex organs. A male's outside genital organs are the penis and scrotum. The scrotum is the sac that's hanging behind the penis. It has two pouches. Lots of boys call these pouches 'balls.' It's not such a surprising nickname since the testicles inside these pouches are pretty round. Now that you know the area I'm talking about, I'll use the correct word, scrotum, from now on."

(Ordinarily, I don't bother referring to slang words. This is an exception. You may or may not choose to mention this term to your child. As a majority of boys seem to use this slang term, they'll usually know immediately where the scrotum is if you call the area "balls." Identifying this word is also a release from the usual tension that goes along with discussing this topic. The opportunity to let the giggles out will likely be most welcome—by parents as well as children!)

"Inside each scrotum is one testicle. So a boy or man has two testicles, one on each side.

"The penis is the male sex organ in front of the scrotum. The tiny opening at the tip of the penis is the opening of the urethra. The body's liquid waste, or urine, goes through a tube in the middle of the penis to this little opening so it can be passed outside." (If you wish, you might say, "That's what happens when you pee.")

You can look at a diagram with your child and point out the bladder. Explain that liquid wastes are stored there. The urine from the bladder passes out into the urethra, through the penis, and out through the little opening. This will probably be most easily understood if you simply trace the flow on the diagram.

Continue with: "When a boy starts to develop and change, a special kind of fluid called semen develops in his internal sex organs. Although this semen is different from urine, to get out it also passes through the urethra in the center of the penis and through the little opening at the tip. But semen and urine never pass through at the same time. So they never mix. I'll talk more about semen later.

"The tip of the penis is sensitive because it has many nerve endings. Feel the tips of your fingers. They have lots of nerve endings, also. The skin of the penis looks wrinkly and loose, sort of like a glove that's too big. There's a reason for this.

"Did you ever see a person blush? What happens? That's right, his or her face gets red. That's because an extra blood supply flows into the area of the face and stays there for a few seconds, then goes back. The same things happens at certain times with the area of the penis."

Erections. "When a male's body gets a certain signal, an extra blood supply flows into the area of the penis. There are spongy tissues inside the penis that fill up with this extra supply of blood, like a sponge fills up with water. This filling up of the spongy tissues will cause the loose skin of the penis to 'fill in,' making the penis slightly longer, stiffer, and even a bit wider. When the penis becomes stiff like this, it's called having an erection. After a little while, the flow of blood goes out of the spongy tissues and back into general circulation. The penis goes back to being soft again.

"Boys are able to have erections even when they're just born. It's normal for boys and men to have erections every once in a while during the day and night. Lots of men and boys wake up with an erection. Did that ever happen to you?" (If you're a dad, you might say, "That's happened to me many times.")

Circumcision. "All boys are born with a flap of skin at the tip of their penis. This flap is called the foreskin. Some parents decide to have this extra flap of skin removed shortly after birth. Among certain tribes and religions, this is done in a special ceremony. If the foreskin is removed, it's called being circumcised. If the foreskin is not removed, a boy is said to be uncircumcised. It's fine if a boy is circumcised and fine if he's not.

"If a boy is circumcized, the tip, or glans, of his penis will be uncovered all the time and it clearly can be seen. If a boy is not circumcised, the foreskin will cover part of the tip of the penis. A boy can gently roll this flap of skin back when he washes.

"Being circumcised doesn't change how the penis works or how it will develop and grow. If a boy is not circumcised, his regular washing should include the area under the foreskin." (You may or may not want to add at this time: "That's because there are little glands underneath the foreskin that produce a substance that could collect and be unpleasant if it wasn't washed regularly.")

If your son is not circumcised, you might also say: "If your foreskin ever feels tight or uncomfortable to you, or you're having trouble moving it back, please be sure to tell me. Even if you only *think* something is not quite right, let me know."

Penis size. "Some boys and men think the size of the penis is very important. They think that a bigger penis size will make them more manly. But that's just not true. The only thing that a bigger penis means is that it's a bigger penis! Not a bigger man. Not a more manly man. Besides, it would be kind of silly for boys to sit around with rulers waiting to measure how manly they are.

"A seven-foot-tall basketball player with tons of muscles might have a penis that's smaller than a boy who is five feet tall and hardly plays any sports. Penis size has nothing to do with how tall you are or how many muscles you have. A boy's penis grows because of chemicals, or hormones, inside his body. So a person's penis size is up to those chemicals. The same with body size, how tall someone is or how short. Thank those hormones again!

Scrotum/Testicles. "The scrotal sac hangs behind the penis and has the job of holding the two testicles that are inside. You can even check this yourself. You should be able to feel one testicle on each side of your scrotal sac. So, you've got two testicles. (As your son gets older you can explain the importance of monthly self-examination of the testicles.) And if you look in the mirror, you'll see that one testicle is slightly lower than the other. They look kind of lopsided! But that's fine. They're supposed to be that way!

"The testicles have two very important jobs. They release the chemical, or hormone, called testosterone that causes boys to develop and they also produce sperm cells. In fact, the testicles are the only place in a man's body where sperm cells are made.

"Since the testicles are so important and are also very delicate, it's a good idea to protect them as best you can. Like, if you're playing an active sport, wear a jock strap to make sure your genitals stay in place and don't flop around. Many athletes, like wrestlers, baseball catchers, and football and lacrosse players, wear a cup supporter so they can give their genitals extra protection.

"Getting hit in the genitals can really hurt. Did that ever happen to you or any of your friends? If anyone tries to kick or hit you there, tell them to cut it out. And don't hit anyone else there, either.

"You may be wondering what sperm cells are. Sperm cells are a man's sex cells. They're sex cells because these are the cells that are able to mix with a woman's egg cells so a man and woman can create a baby. Egg cells are a woman's sex cells, but they're not the kind of eggs that are found in our refrigerator! They're very small and are released by a woman's ovaries. Men have two testicles and women have two ovaries.

"So now you know that a man's testicles produce sperm cells and a woman's ovaries release egg cells. Later I'll explain more about how babies are created from these.

"Let me tell you more about the sperm cells. They're kind of cute. They look like tiny tadpoles and even have a little tail. The tail helps them swim around in a special fluid called semen. This is the fluid that helps carry the sperm cells out through the opening at the tip of your penis. The way semen passes out of your penis has a name—it's called an *ejaculation*. That's a long word. Let's say it together! Ejaculation.

"Ejaculation only lasts for a few seconds and doesn't happen on any kind of a schedule. I'll explain more about this later. Right now, think about whether you have any questions about your penis or scrotal sac, your testicles, being circumcised, having erections . . . We talked about a lot together. That's great!"

More than likely, it will take several discussions with your child in order to present the various topics set forth in this section. Follow-up conversations can gradually include more in-depth information. Besides explaining the facts, be sure to leave ample time to discuss feelings about the facts.

Feelings about the male genitals

Boys respond with a great deal of interest to explanations about what's inside the penis, how erections happen, and so forth. Although they may be giggly at first, they usually are relieved to have the chance to talk about their bodies and how they work. They *want* to know. The problem is that they're either embarrassed or don't know quite how to tell their parents about such personal questions and feelings.

Aside from needing to understand factual information about genital anatomy, functions, and development, boys need answers to questions that reflect their view of themselves. "When is my turn to grow?" "How big will *mine* be?" "Will mine look like daddy's?" "How will I know that my penis is growing right?" "How will I know if I'm normal?" While your child may have these questions, you'll probably be the one who'll have to initiate discussion.

Last year, a male college student asked, "How does one start to begin to like his or her body? I've always been very uncomfortable with sex for this reason. I always thought my penis was too small."

I cannot emphasize enough how important it is to attempt to give your son a healthy perspective on penis size. The comparisons that are made in locker rooms and bathrooms can be very damaging. Boys *do* "check out" other boy's bodies, if just to have a basis for determining if their body seems to be normal. Unexpressed feelings of inadequacy during the growing-up years can have unfortunate ramifications later on.

Imagine how an uncircumcised boy might feel if his parents never explained circumcision to him and he found himself showering with other boys whose penises appeared noticeably different from his. How comfortable do you think he'd be? How much would he wonder about whether or not he was normal? How much of a chance would there be for other boys to tease and point out the differences, especially if the uncircumcised boy were not part of the "in" or "popular" group. How much whispering would there be?

A boy who is not circumcised may be troubled and confused about whether this will affect sexual relationships or the ability of his penis to grow normally. Make sure your son understands these concerns are unfounded.

There would certainly be less attention paid if all boys, circumcised or not, were informed about circumcision. And differences in size, which are absolutely expected and natural, would not be such an issue, if we would only talk about facts, attitudes, and perspective early.

Even if your son feels so uncomfortable that he won't give you any feedback about his own feelings, it will be helpful to him to hear your thoughts about penis size, comparisons, and manliness.

One of the wonderful questions I've received from children about erections was "What if you're playing baseball, and you're running from first to second base, and you get an erection, should you stop? Should you slide?" Just because boys are capable of having erections from the time they're born doesn't mean we can take for granted their knowledge about the experience.

Boys are often embarrassed by erections that happen at the most inopportune times, like when they're talking to girls or giving reports in front of their classes. While offering boys information about erections won't necessarily take away their embarrassment or the frustration of not being able to "will" an erection to appear or disappear when desired, at least they'll be able to understand that having erections at different times throughout the day and night is normal for all males, and will realize they're not alone in their frustrations.

While some boys purposely wear bikini bathing suits to show off their genital bulges, others are very concerned about the possibility that everyone around them will be able to tell they're having an erection. (It's likely that an erection will seem even bigger to the boy that's having it.)

If your son has worn skinny bathing suits for years while a little boy but decides he'd like to change his style to a suit which is looser and less revealing, you may find this an opportune time to talk about changes and feelings about genitals. Whether or not you choose to confront these feelings, you should be aware that your child's development can affect his self-image, perceptions of how he's seen by others, and emotions in general.

Sometimes a boy may wish to have an erection but finds he can't. This failure could lead him to become anxious about his ability to produce an erection, which in turn could *inhibit* his ability to have one. While the inability to have an erection is a complicated matter best left to later talks, this kind of fear can be allayed by explaining the potential effects of anxiety, fatigue, guilt, alcohol, certain drugs, medications, and illness on the ability to have erections. An erection is a reflex. Sometimes an erection happens when it's least expected; sometimes it won't happen no matter how badly a male might want one. This is common. Please be sure to tell that to your son at the appropriate moment.

Throughout the growing-up years, children need to be reminded and encouraged to let their parents know about any concerns, whether they be about functioning, size, development, appearance, how they *feel*—or anything—no matter how silly the children think their concern is.

Ejaculation/Wet dreams

At every program I conduct for children about growth and development, inevitably there are boys whose eyes get wider and wider as I explain, however softly, that one of the very special parts of growing up for a boy is when he begins to ejaculate. While I have no doubt that there will always be boys present who are hearing this information for the first time, the nature of questions asked by most boys confirms that, even if they have discussed this topic with their parents, there are many concerns and confusions related to ejaculation that are being held back and therefore remain unanswered. One parent told me her son had listened politely to her explanation only to let her know afterwards that he had already been ejaculating for two years.

The more information we give our children about these changes *before* they occur, the more ready and comfortable our children will be about each change. The more we anticipate how our children feel about each aspect of development, the more enlightened we will be about what information and advice will help our children feel good about themselves as they mature.

How to begin: Having already talked about the penis, erections, sperm production, the "special fluid" called semen, and the basic definition of ejaculation, discussing ejaculation in more detail will be a simple matter of reviewing the topics and putting them together. This is an example of how building a strong foundation of basic information makes it that much easier to go forward.

You might wish to use the following presentation as a guide when explaining ejaculation to your child for the first time:

"I love when we have our private talks . . . It makes me feel so good to be able to help you understand all the different ways your body will change when you start to develop. Remember, if I say anything that confuses you, let me know. I'll be happy to say it again and explain it all so you get the idea. Lots of boys think it's strange to talk about ejaculation with their mothers or fathers, so it's extra special to me that we're talking about it together right now."

(Before you begin your explanation, it would be a good idea to double check if your child remembers what you discussed about erections, semen, and sperm cells.)

"One of the special changes that happens to a boy is that he will be able to ejaculate. When this happens it's a celebration of a sort because it means a boy is on his way to becoming a man.

"Although not all erections end in ejaculation, an erection is usually the first step that leads to an ejaculation. So, when a boy's body gets ready to ejaculate, he'll usually start with an erection. Then his inside organs will get a signal telling them it's time to make semen. Sperm cells will mix with the semen and when all the fluids making semen have come together, the inside organs will be ready to wait for the next signal.

"The next signal is the one that will let the semen know when it's time to pass out of the opening at the tip of the penis. When the semen spurts out of the opening, that's called having an ejaculation.

"Ejaculating semen is the way to move the sperm from the inside of a boy's or man's body to the outside through the penis. It's a real celebration when a boy starts to ejaculate. That's because starting to ejaculate means that a boy is physically on his way to being a man.

It's hard to say exactly when a boy will have his first ejaculation. It may start when he is eleven or twelve or not until sixteen or seventeen.

"Boys don't have any schedule for their ejaculations. In fact, an ejaculation only lasts for a few seconds. They may happen a few times on one day, every few days, or not for a few weeks. Each day and week may be different.

"Usually, a boy's first ejaculation will happen while he is sleeping. When ejaculation of semen happens during sleep, that's called having a 'wet dream.' A boy might know he had one because he could notice a little, damp, whitish, possibly sticky spot on his sheet, underwear, or pajamas. Or he might simply notice a dried-up little spot. This is very normal. It not only happens to boys. Men can have ejaculations during sleep, too."

Follow-up discussions can expand on this basic information in order to include: the difference between urine and semen; pleasurable thoughts that relate to wet dreams; control over ejaculation while a boy is awake and lack of control while sleeping; the approximate amount of semen per ejaculation (about one or two teaspoons); the difference between periods and ejaculations; ejaculations continue through man's life; and so forth.

Feelings about ejaculation/wet dreams

One ten-year-old boy responded, "Yick! I don't want a fluid to come out of my penis." This reaction to learning about ejaculation for the first time is very common. Ejaculation is something that they never before have experienced.

Boys are often concerned about what they should do with their sheets if they've had a wet dream. Some boys have even said that they purposely spilled something, such as chocolate milk, on their sheet, to hide the telltale "mark." Anticipating your son's concern, you might tell him that you know many boys think about what they should do with their sheets. You might suggest that he could leave his sheet there and forget about it because parents know about wet dreams and if they discover a slight "spot" on their son's sheets while making his bed, they'll probably feel terrific that he's normal; or that he could make his own bed and change his own sheets.

Boys who don't completely understand the mechanics of ejaculation may well be afraid that the experience will take them by surprise in the middle of a class or anywhere. It is important to be very clear about the fact that a boy will be in control of ejaculation and would be able to feel an ejaculation coming on if he is awake. But he cannot help having wet dreams because he is no longer in control when asleep.

A very common concern of a majority of boys is the amount of semen. Many imagine that they will wake up in a "pool" of fluid. You can have your son measure out a teaspoon or two of water to prove how little this amount really is. It would be helpful to explain that the amount of semen will vary slightly from man to man and even for the same man at different times. You might even mention that the amount and force of the ejaculation will eventually lessen a bit when a man gets older.

Another issue relative to ejaculation is the potential for guilt over having sexual thoughts. If you talk about this kind of guilt with your child (boy or girl) you could help him or her maintain a healthy perspective on what might be natural rather than shameful behavior. This discussion, of course, would be a very personal matter, based on each parent's standards and beliefs.

Swelling in the chest area

Many boys are uncomfortable about the swelling of their chests. The swelling makes them feel like they're growing breasts and, truthfully, it may appear that way to their peers, too. A boy who experiences such swelling might get teased or worry about getting teased, feel terrible about changing clothes in front of others, and often refuse to take off his tee shirt or sweat shirt even in the summer. Understanding that this growth is very common may not completely take away frustration and embarrassment, but it will take the edge off of his concern. At least he can be relieved to know this swelling is normal.

Voice change/Feelings about voice change

A piece of advice: Boys *do not* like to be mistaken for their mothers or sisters on the telephone. If you're not positive about who belongs to the voice at the other end of the wire, *ask* rather than guess.

Boys need to know that they sometimes will simply not be able to trust their voices while they change. It may crack at the most inopportune moments. Teasing from family and friends doesn't promote good feelings. Family members could help by being more sensitive about how a boy might feel at these moments.

Some boys are embarrassed at a sudden inability to reach the notes in their choral section that they had always reached. Instead of moving to a section where the notes are lower, they stay and strain their voices.

Boys and girls should be taught early that a boy isn't more a man because his voice is deeper. Being a man has to do with who a person is inside, *not* what a boy looks like or how he sounds when he speaks. Boys with high or low voices can be very manly!

If your son is continually hoarse, it might be a good idea to check with your doctor.

Pubic hair and body hair/Feelings about pubic and body hair

Many boys and girls have told me stories of how devastated they felt when teased about being the only one with *or* the only one without pubic hair among those in the locker room or in their cabin at summer camp. Depending on where your child's development seems to "fit in" among friends and classmates, he or she may feel indifferent, impatient, confident, proud, or embarrassed. It would certainly help for you to anticipate what your child *might* be feeling in order that discussions be as meaningful as possible.

Here, too, it's not enough to tell children their bodies will eventually grow pubic hair. They're concerned about: "Will I need to get a pubic hair cut?" "What if I grow too much pubic hair?" "When?" "What will it feel like?" "Will it be the same color as the hair on my head?" "Do boys *and* girls grow pubic hair?"

Girls, especially, have expressed the frustration of "only having half" filled in. Many have said that they'd rather have all or nothing, because partial pubic hair looks and feels funny to them.

Some girls have complained about itching in their pubic area as hair grows in. If the itching becomes very troublesome, I suggest you consult your family doctor.

Many boys develop a darkened moustache. Depending upon their coloring, this will be more or less obvious. For some, this is regarded as a sign of maturity; for others, it causes tremendous embarrassment. Since this change is quite visible, you might be watchful for it and initiate related discussion when the time seems right.

Some boys feel more manly because they have a large amount of hair under their arms and on their chests; some don't care if they have a lot of body hair; and others feel embarrassed because they have so little. Here, too, perspective is essential. Children can't control which hairs sprout or don't. What they've got, they've got. Therefore, try to anticipate what your child *might* be feeling with regard to growth of body hair and set aside time for discussion. The lesson here is like all the other "perspective" lessons: More hair doesn't mean more manly, and so forth. More hair simply means more hair.

Some boys desperately rush their shaving experience in order to seem more grown up. Shaving or other methods of removing unwanted hair needs to be discussed with a parent. Some chemical depilatories are irritating and can change the color of your child's hair. Many children sneak and use these chemical hair removers or sneak razors and shave earlier than parents wish to give permission. Children need proper instructions with regard to safety, shaving techniques, and razor cleanliness. Initiate talk about shaving prior to when it is even a consideration in order to make your position clear and offer any appropriate guidelines.

Many girls have spoken with me of their frustrations about wanting to shave their legs or under their arms but not getting permission to do so from their parents. This is a very personal issue. It's also a cultural one, as the decision to shave often is dependent on one's background. If your daughter or son seems extremely upset about not being allowed to shave, you might at least try to find out how intensely they feel about this and why. You may or may not change your mind, but it will help to let your child know that you care enough to reconsider.

One girl was so upset about the hair on her legs that she wore stockings over her legs in gym class so that no one would see how much she had. She told me her mother wouldn't let her shave her legs. Part of the problem was that she never even told her parents how she felt. She never mentioned the stockings to them prior to her conversation with me. How were her parents to even imagine how much her feelings about the hair on her legs affected her on a daily basis? They couldn't. So their daughter suffered, silently.

TEACHING A PERSPECTIVE IS ESSENTIAL

No matter how clearly children understand that differences in size and shape are natural and expected, they still have to deal with the emotions that go along with being bigger or smaller, or more or less developed than most friends and classmates. They still have to walk through the halls at school. They still must sit in their classrooms, walk to the chalkboard, change in the locker room, and walk through lunch lines. The reality is that kids still judge each other by their looks. They still tease unmercifully.

No matter what children understand, how they *feel* about themselves, their body, and their physical development will likely be influenced by how they seem to "measure up" to their peers and whether or not they're accepted or often left out. They may feel very proud, very special, very attractive, very unattractive, very different, very alone, or somewhere in between. Our responsibility is to help each child feel special.

"Be patient about your development." "Just be yourself." "You're special, no matter what size you are." These are tough lessons for a child to learn, especially the child who secretly wishes he or she could hide in the nearest locker and stay there until his or her body begins to develop or everyone else's starts catching up. Helping children accept themselves, their sizes, as well as teaching them to be sensitive to everyone else's need to do the same is a task that must be worked at constantly.

To teach perspective, I have used what I call a "package" concept that has proven very helpful to children, parents, and teachers. You might wish to use it with your own child. The basic concept is that our bodies are like packages. They wrap the person that's inside. Whether a person is tall, short, fat, skinny, more or less developed, able-bodied or disabled, that's all part of his or her outside package. A person is not determined by height, weight, or any other single aspect of development. Size and shape are not "the person." Yet, when people judge others, most often they're judging the "package" rather than who is really inside.

Ask your child if it would make sense to like someone better if that person suddenly lost or gained ten pounds. Would the loss or gain of pounds make someone nicer? A better friend? Would your child invite someone to your house or include him on a team if only that person would grow five inches this week? Would that change *who* the person is? Children need to learn that they don't play ball with inches. They don't share secrets with pounds. They don't call breasts on the telephone, do homework with facial hairs, or dance with muscles. They relate to the person, not the "package."

Considerations that will help clarify perspective include the following: "If someone only likes you because you've started to develop, what kind of friendship do you really think that would be?" "If they don't like you because you've got a few extra pounds on your body, well, maybe they're not such good friends to have, anyway. Maybe it's time to look for other friends who like you for being you, no matter what your size."

Further, you can't just look at someone and know for sure what kind of friend that person would be. You can't know if someone would be fun to be with or someone to trust, or what flavor ice cream she or he loves. *Who* a person is can't be seen until you look beyond the outside package to the person that's inside. Only then can you decide fairly if you want to get to know her or him better.

This concept can be extended to include color of skin (you don't have lunch with a "color," you share your sandwiches with the person inside that skin), clothes (you don't walk home with jackets, you walk with the person inside the jacket), braces and glasses (you don't ask braces or glasses to go with you to the movies), and disabilities (for example, you don't become friends with a leg in a wheelchair; you learn to love the person who is attached to that leg).

Remind children that people cannot control how they look physically or how and when they'll develop. It's not a younger brother's or sister's fault that he or she has started to grow before an older child in the family. It's not a close friend's fault if he or she started to grow earlier or later. If a child is smaller, taller, more or less developed, it's not his or her fault.

It's much harder for children to accept their own time schedules for growth when they're teased, left out, or made to feel so different because of some aspect of their development or appearance that they can't even control.

Perspective. Sensitivity. Respect for differences. These concepts must be taught early on. With increased awareness, we can only hope there will be less judging, less teasing, less cruelty, and more kids giving each other a chance.

"THE TALK," SETTING A TONE, TURNING FEELINGS INTO WORDS

Children have expressed mixed reactions to their parents' "talk" about physical growth and development. While some felt relief and great interest, others were amused or surprised. Many felt that the information was "gross" and embarrassing. Most were generally uncomfortable.

Parent reactions have also been mixed. While one parent may be at ease with this kind of discussion, another may be quite uncomfortable, not infrequently having a feeling of inadequacy, especially if the child concerned is the opposite sex.

At the end of an orientation program at which I explained to parents what I would teach their children the following week about growth and development, a parent came up to me and said, "I dread next week!" This dread is common.

I was talking with a school nurse about school programs about puberty and how parents are often uncomfortable with talking about development to their children, when she shared with me a very revealing personal story. With her permission, and much appreciation, I'll share her tale. It points out beautifully that, no matter what your profession, how much education you've had, how long you've been a parent, or how much knowledge you have, you're still a "human" with your own comfort level:

When her son was fourteen, she wanted to talk to him about masturbation but the topic made her so uncomfortable she was afraid to even mention it. Yet, because she did feel strongly that it was her responsibility to discuss this with him, she did. The entire time she spoke with him, she had a paper bag over her head because she was so embarrassed!

Where is it written that parents must be so comfortable about all of this? It's not!

Don't worry if you're not comfortable discussing physical development. It may not be fair or realistic to expect yourself to be. However, there *would* be cause for concern if your discomfort prevented you from talking about these topics in a way that would be helpful to your child.

Since children usually can sense a parent's strain, acknowledging your discomfort may put you and your child more at ease. Whatever you feel about confronting these topics, you can more effectively, more honestly approach your child if you turn your feelings into words. For example, if you're embarrassed, you can say, "I'm really embarrassed...but it's important for us to talk." Or "It's not so easy for me to talk about this with you. But it's important to me that we deal with it together. Let's try..." Or "I never explained this before. And I'm not so sure I'm going to have all the answers. But we can look them up together."

A more informal approach will be appreciated. Take advantage of the time that you're together. Rather than formally announcing that "the talk" will begin, just ease into conversation. Discussion can be initiated when you're driving in your car, sitting around the living room, preparing food in the kitchen. Take a walk with your child. Sit together on the back steps. Have your son or daughter get into bed a few minutes earlier than usual so you can sit together and talk.

Since children can take in just so much at one sitting, make use of even little stretches of time to discuss difficult topics. You've got much more time than you may think.

DEALING WITH YOUR CHILD'S RESPONSES

Paying attention to your child's reactions while you talk will help you anticipate what he or she is feeling. For example, often when I start talking about breasts at my growth and development programs, I'll notice several girls will immediately cross their arms in front of their chests. While they didn't say anything, their discomfort is quite obvious to me. Sometimes nonverbal signals can be even louder than any spoken words.

If you notice that your child seems uncomfortable or embarrassed, turn feelings into words: "You have a funny look on your face. I wonder if this is embarrassing to you. Is it hard to talk about this with me?" Or, instead of directly calling attention to the fact that your child's not at ease, you might say, "You know, lots of kids are really embarrassed to talk about this with their parents. If you feel kind of funny talking with me, I understand. In fact, I'm not so comfortable either. But maybe we can help each other feel better talking about this." Another approach is to talk about how you felt when your parent spoke with you about these things.

If you're frustrated that your child doesn't seem to be paying attention, you can say something like "It's really frustrating talking with you. I get the feeling you tuned me out fifteen minutes ago. Is this a bad time to talk? Maybe you would be able to concentrate better if we talked later." Be sure to follow through later.

If your child is not responding at all and you get the feeling that you're talking to a cement wall instead of a person, you might say:

"I sense that it's really hard for you to talk about this. It would be so special to me if we could talk together. I know that kids often have lots of questions that they think are too embarrassing or silly to even say aloud. Or maybe they think that their parent will believe they're stupid if they don't already know the answer. If that's what you're feeling, I want you to know that no matter how silly you think your questions are, they wouldn't be silly to me. In fact, the silliest, saddest thing would be if you didn't ask what you want to ask. So, why don't we meet in these chairs in an hour and that will give you a chance to think about what you'd like to ask or what feelings you'd like to share."

You might also say, "Why don't we talk about this again in a few days? That will give you a chance to think about any concerns or questions you might have."

I've had students come up to me in the middle of my programs to hand me their "anonymous" questions. Everyone watched them come up, everyone knew that the question in my hand was from them, and yet, they pleaded with me to answer their question right away. Just the fact that they didn't have to say it aloud seemed to be a big relief. Your child may feel better writing questions down on paper and handing them to you.

You might suggest that your children keep private notebooks for any questions they think of after your discussions. That way they can be sure to remember to ask you later. A question box that could be opened at a specially designated time each day (perhaps before bedtime or right after dinner) might also provide a more comfortable outlet.

If your children still don't respond, at the very least they owe you enough respect to listen. Although their silence may be painfully frustrating and you may wish you could turn them upside down and shake the words out of them, the fact is, you can only do so much. Silence is their choice. You *can* still make sure your children have the information that is so essential for them to know. You *can* still tell them that there are many other kids who feel the same way they do about the facts you're presenting.

With care, you and your child should be able to work out your own ways to become more comfortable together. If you remember to turn your own feelings into words and teach your child to do the same, you may find you can say what you never dreamed possible. You and your child will be that much closer for your efforts and your child will feel that much better.

Keep reminding yourself that becoming less restrained is a process, an unfolding. It may take some time for you and your child to talk more openly with each other about these topics. Be patient and hold on dearly to your sense of humor!

If you never achieve the openness that you want so badly to have with your child, I hope you'll find comfort in knowing that you gave everything that you could give. At least you did your part. You can keep trying to reach out, but you can only do so much. The rest is up to your child.

CHAPTER 3

TEASING
(About Size, Development, or Anything Else)

G 9

Why does everyone laugh at my clothes and hair? I want to be everyones friend.

G

I have a small problem, my chest. its the flatest in the class. Everyone teases me.

I get teased by older kids and I don't know what to say. If I ignore them they keep it up. It makes me feel rejected.

G.8.

My Question is.

Why Do people make fun of me? I cant help it if I'm a little over weight. It's hard because they don't understand it hurts.

Sad

(Lee)

At a recent educational program for teachers I conducted, a teacher said, "The children in seventh and eighth grade are almost inhuman in their treatment of each other. . . . I have trouble sleeping at night when I try to imagine what some of these kids must deal with from their peers." Many other teachers at the elementary and secondary school levels have confirmed the cruelty and lack of respect between students that prevails in their classrooms. Parents cry out wondering how they can help their children deal with this treatment. Children cry out wondering why people think they're so bad, wishing the hurt would go away.

Children are teased about height, weight, breast size, braces, glasses, pimples, body odor, changing voice, whether or not they have begun menstruating, clothing, looks, hairstyle, color of skin, grades, being in a special education class, their name, physical or learning disability, athletic weakness, their home and neighborhood, their parents, whether their family is rich or poor, religious beliefs, or anything else you can think of. Kids tease in ways that can play havoc with self-image. I could probably fill a book if I tried to include all the not-so-loving nicknames that are shouted across playgrounds, lunchrooms, classrooms, hallways, on the bus, walking to and from school, at summer camp, and everywhere.

Whatever we're doing to help children learn to be more accepting of each other, we need to do more. Whatever we're doing to help children respond more effectively to those who don't respect them, we need to do more. And since we probably won't be there to hold our children's hands when someone teases them, we've got to teach them that they have the ability to handle the teasing themselves. We can't do it for them, we can only offer more comprehensive, practical suggestions about "how."

When asked to describe how teasing feels, children at my programs have said, "very embarrassed," "humiliated," "horrible," "low down rotten," "left out," "like no one in the whole world likes me," "like I wish I was never born," "very alone," "dumb," "really mad."

One child in the fifth grade wrote anonymously, "Teesing [sic] make you feel like you do not have nothing to live for." This shared feeling still brings tears to my eyes. It's not fair for children to have to feel this way. Teasing *can* be devastating. If your child has had to stand up to cruel remarks, nasty whispers, and obvious denigration from peers, you know only too well how destructive the effects can be. Encouraging your children to talk about their feelings can help.

If your child has difficulty expressing emotions related to being teased, you can try to help by saying, "Well, if I were teased, I know I'd feel very embarrassed, or I'd be so upset and angry." You can follow with "Is that what you felt?"

Responses from you that acknowledge the validity of your child's feelings can be very supportive. Some examples are:

"That can't make you feel very good."

"I know I would feel rotten, too, if someone teased me. I'd probably wish I could crawl under the lunch table..."

"What an awful feeling! I'm so sad you have to deal with this."

"I'll bet you really felt angry. It's natural to have felt that way. I'm ready to explode just listening to what happened."

"It's so mean for kids to tease and make other kids feel so awful. Isn't it sad that no one ever taught that person how much it can hurt when they say that? I'm so sorry you had to deal with this. It's not fair."

After acknowledging the hurt, support your child's feelings and discuss some of the reasons why other kids tease. (Kids tease in order to get attention, to show off, to be mean, because they're the ones who really feel inadequate, and many more reasons.) The next step is to offer specific sentences and choices that your child can use in order to more effectively deal with any further teasing.

When teased by acquaintances at school or in the neighborhood, your son or daughter might say:

"Cut it out! It really bothers me when you say that. If you don't like me, you don't have to. I'll stay out of your way, and you stay out of mine."

"I don't want to fight. I just want us to leave each other alone."

"You can call me chicken or whatever you want. I can fight if I want to. But I just don't want to. I don't need to fight to show how strong I am. Besides, you might like bloody noses, but I don't. So why don't you just leave me alone and I'll leave you alone. No one ever said you had to be my friend."

After making such statements, your child can just walk away. Or your child can walk the other way in the first place if he or she sees someone approaching that will probably tease and create an uncomfortable situation.

A different approach might be:

"I love it when you call me 'pee wee'! [Or whatever.] Oh please say it again!"

"It's incredible that you want to waste your time calling me stupid names. If that's what you need to do, go right ahead; I've got better things to do than listen."

Several years ago, one twelve-year-old boy told me that he loved to tease. He teased everyone about everything he could think of. And he kept on teasing that person until he stopped getting the reaction he was looking for. He's not alone. Kids do look for reactions, they look to "get" the person that they've teased. A cool, calculated, creative response can effectively ruin the fun and often put an end to the teasing.

If the teasing continues after your child has tried saying what you've suggested, tried walking away, or tried acting indifferent, then it might well be appropriate for you to contact a specific teacher, principal, or guidance counselor, in addition to speaking with the "teaser's" parent, in order to take stronger action.

Boys and girls also need to know that sometimes kids tease because they don't know how else to let the teased people know they like them. They may pull scarves on the playground or act silly in front of their friends, but they're really paying attention in the only way they know how. There's a difference between this type of teasing and that which is meant to be cruel.

When friends tease Friends may kid around and tease without realizing that the teasing hurts. Boys and girls who are teased by friends often keep their feelings inside, unsure whether they should mention how embarrassed or hurt they are. Usually, because kids don't know what to say and don't want to jeopardize their friendships, these feelings are laughed off and incorrectly interpreted as not minding "the fun."

The following sentences, and others like them, can help your child say privately what is important to one or more friends:

"Why did you say that to me in front of everyone? I was really embarrassed. I felt like crawling under the lunch table. Please don't do that again."

"I laughed but I really didn't know what else to do. It wasn't funny. In fact, you made me feel really stupid [awful]. Please don't tease me like that again."

Help your child realize that a sibling or friend *cannot* be expected to stop teasing if he or she is not made aware that the teasing hurts. Explain that you can't expect people to just "know" what you feel; you have to tell them. That is an important guideline for communication in all relationships.

If your child is a teaser If your child is a teaser, it might help to talk some more about the "package concept" in the previous chapter. Remind him or her that someone's height, weight, or development or lack of it is not that person's fault and is not a measure of who he or she is. Reinforce the fact that kids can't help where they live, the color of their skin, their parents' separation, and so forth.

You might follow with:

"If you know deep down what you say doesn't make someone else feel very good, why would you choose to do that? If you don't like someone, it's your right not to have anything to do with that person. That's your choice. But you don't have the right to go out of your way to be cruel. That's unacceptable. I would be very upset if you continued to tease now that you realize how much it can hurt. Please don't *try* to stop. Just stop!!"

Pressure to tease Several children have expressed to me their frustration at being part of a crowd that teases and that has pressured them into doing the same just to be part of the group. This is a difficult situation, especially when children want to belong so badly. If your child is experiencing such pressure to tease others, first explain and talk about what peer pressure means. Follow up with these or other suggestions as alternatives:

> Tell friends they're being mean, and to please stop.
>
> Tell friends you're leaving and you don't like what they're doing and want no part of it.
>
> Tell friends they really should give the kid a chance.
>
> Tell friends you have to go home and will see them tomorrow. Think about how good those friends are if you *have* to do something like tease with them in order to be accepted.

Helping those who are teased Sometimes children who hear others being tormented by groups or individuals wish they could help the person being teased but don't quite know how to go about it. It would be nice to think that such children could simply try to get the others to stop teasing, but such an act could start trouble for them as well. Unfortunately, the teasers are often the school "bullies" or part of cliques that have strength in numbers. Being a "nice guy" could turn out disastrous. So, it may be wiser (and still caring) if your son or daughter went over to the child being teased after the teasing stopped. Statements such as, "I hope you're okay, they're really bullies," or "Don't let them bother you; they think they're hot shots," can be very supportive.

Even if your child is never teased and never teases, your child will benefit from a discussion of what kids tease about, how teasing makes a person feel, and the need for more respect for differences and sensitivity to other's feelings. Maybe your child can help a friend.

When parents tease Many children have revealed to me their feelings about how difficult it is to tell a parent that he or she is "driving me crazy" by teasing. This kind of parental teasing commonly takes the form of using nicknames; kidding about physical development, friends, boyfriends, or girlfriends; and having a "crush" on someone. Most children feel it's pretty bad to be teased privately by a parent, and *awful* to be teased in front of friends.

A girl in the eighth grade told me, "Me and my father are really close but he always twitches my nose or tickles me or calls me little names. I don't mind him calling me my own nicknames as much, but I'm not sure how to tell him to stop it without hurting his feelings."

Most children realize that a parent is trying to be cute or funny, and since they don't want to hurt their parents' feelings, they find it much harder to be honest.

Think about your behavior with your own child. If you tease a great deal, you might talk with your son or daughter about how they really feel about the teasing. If you don't offer them this opportunity, they may well keep their feelings hidden for days, weeks, months, or even years. A teasing parent sets an example that gives children permission to tease others.

CHAPTER 4

FRIENDSHIP AND POPULARITY

G8

why don't people give me a chance to be their friends? I'm nice and I try, but they just won't give me a chance to be a friend. they won't accept me. why?

I haven't Got many friends 66
I'm afraid to talk to My parents

B

I have 3 groups of freinds. I like being
with each group but they don't like me
being with the other groups, and if I still
play with the other grops they won't be
my freinds What should I do?

Wish I was
popular.

Girl   9th Grade

sometimes Iam with a whole bunch
of friends and I feel left out because
I don't quite fit in. sometimes I
laugh with them but inside I really
feel empty and left out.

I have observed again and again that far too many children lack the communication skills, understanding, and confidence to handle successfully the daily ins and outs of their peer relationships.

Even the smoothest friendships can be interrupted or otherwise affected by jealousy, misunderstanding, pressure to be loyal to one person or group instead of another, fights, rumors, who "likes" whom as a boyfriend or girlfriend, competition, disappointments, being left out, pressure to "keep up" or do what everyone else is doing regardless of personal feelings and values, embarrassments, secrets that weren't kept, dishonesty, and developmental and other differences. Popular or not, it is the rare child who is exempt from facing many of these concerns during the growing-up years.

Children who appear to be right in the center of their crowd have admitted how much they worry about being regarded as a "tagalong" and have talked with me about how hard it is wondering from day to day if they'll be included. Thousands of children have asked how they can tell if the friends they believe they have are truly their friends. Thousands more have cried out about the pain of not having any friends.

Those who try to buy friendship, allow others to use them, or feel they have to act in ways that are just not true to themselves in order to "belong" have also expressed their sadness, insecurity, and great yearning to find someone to like them for who they are. At one of my school programs, several of the teachers present literally shed tears as one boy disclosed, "Every afternoon after school, I always have to joke around and try to be so funny. . . . I don't want to have to be so funny every day just so other kids will like me."

Some kids remain loners, unsure of what to do in order to get others to like them. They may have been set apart by their peers for many reasons, such as physical differences; disability; where they come from; their parents; grades; athletic ability; looks; the clothes they wear; how they act in class; and so forth. Or maybe they did something in the third grade that still gets in the way of people accepting them today. Or perhaps they are just plain shy.

Parents and teachers regularly take for granted children's ability to handle day-to-day relationships and interactions. No matter how a child feels about how a peer responds, there is a good chance those feelings will remain unspoken. Many children don't know what to say, even to best friends, when they're frustrated, hurt, unsure, or angry. Those who don't have any friends often have no idea what to say or do in order to try to make a friend. Many children remain alone for years. Many remain lonely even if they appear to be part of a "crowd."

To help your children with friendships, this chapter offers specific approaches and words children can use which will help them communicate their feelings with peers or anyone else. It offers practical suggestions to strengthen their confidence in handling a variety of friendship situations. It also presents a perspective that, once taken, at the very least will encourage boys and girls to like themselves and realize their specialness, no matter what their differences and even if relationships come slowly.

FIRST WE NEED TO REMIND CHILDREN OF THEIR "SPECIALNESS"

If a child doesn't feel good about himself or herself, it will likely be that much more difficult to reach out and establish meaningful friendships. In fact, low self-esteem may prevent a child from even trying to make a friend. Children of all ages must be reminded that they're "worthy." Only with a greater sense of self-worth will they have increased confidence in their ability to relate to one another, as well as a better feeling about themselves.

Maybe your child has friends, or brothers and sisters, who are better looking, get higher grades, are better at sports, are more popular, are more developed, or are often favored by relatives. Such comparisons can make it very difficult for a child to have a positive self-image. Instead, your child might feel, "I'm second-best. If only I could be like——." Even if you do not make obvious comparisons, anticipate that your child might be comparing and responding silently as if you are.

Unfortunately, years of being denigrated by peers, being set apart and left out, laughed at and teased—as well as years of feeling one has never quite measured up to a brother or sister—can make it very difficult for a child to believe he or she is special.

Even if your child already has good feelings inside, it's important to talk periodically about *how* special and unique he or she is. When a child is happily adjusted, popular, and doing well at school, there may be a tendency for parents to become complacent and take their child's uniqueness or individuality for granted. But children are very wise. They are capable of sensing when their "specialness" and their accomplishments are *expected* rather than appreciated. They also have the ability to "see through" unrealistic praise or know when an adult is praising just a bit too much to really mean it.

My suggestions about reminding children of their specialness are not only for the child who seems to need reinforcement because of lack of confidence. *All* children need this reinforcement. *All* children, no matter how seemingly strong and sure of themselves, need to be reminded that each one is special.

To help children of all ages to understand their uniqueness, I suggest to them the following universal perspective: "Did you ever think about how many millions of people there are in this world? Imagine. Millions! Spread over every continent. The amazing thing is that with all those millions of people, there is only one *You*. *You* are the *only You* in the entire world. Think of it! There is no one else exactly like you *anywhere*. In all the years that this world has been in existence, there never was another you. In all the lifetimes that have yet to come, there will never be another you. You're really very special. If ever you find that you aren't sure about being so special, *think again*. Remind yourself. There is something about you that is different from anyone else in the entire world. Look for that 'specialness.' It's there right inside of you!"

It is tragic that many children feel very badly about who they are. It takes a lot of talking in terms kids will understand before they might be ready to accept that each really is special.

If you sense your son or daughter has responded negatively to the peer group at school, or has developed a negative self-image at home, you might say to your child: "I know it may be hard for you to believe me, when so many kids at school have been mean to you all these years, but I hope you realize now that, despite what anyone else says or does, they can't take your specialness away from you. It's always there."

Children need to be free to be who they are. Children are capable of understanding, and respond very positively to the idea, that they not only don't *have* to be like anyone else, but they also *can't* be. They are not their sisters or brothers, not any cousin or friend. They can only be themselves. We need to say out loud, "I love you for who you are. I hope you're not comparing yourself to Richard, or anyone else. That wouldn't be fair. And if you ever feel that I, your teacher, or anyone else in our family compares you and gives you the feeling that you're not as good as someone else, remind them, remind *me,* that you're *not* that someone else. You're *you*. And that's terrific! But first *you* have got to believe it."

A PERSPECTIVE ON POPULARITY

A very wise boy once told me, "I'm very popular in my unpopular group!" How does your child *feel* about being popular? The way children see themselves fitting in among friends and classmates can significantly contribute to, or take away from, their good feelings about themselves.

Some children truly don't care about being popular. The thought of popularity may be "nice" but not necessary for their day-to-day happiness. To others, popularity seems vital, and these kids may mope around (sometimes for years) feeling terrible about themselves because they're not being "let in." And, yes, some of those who are popular often float blissfully through their school years, on top of the world, loving each day and feeling loved by their friends, included, and secure.

While being in the popular group can be wonderful for a child, simply being included doesn't guarantee a sense of security and belonging. One mother told me that she walked into her daughter's room very late one night and discovered her in the act of writing down everything she was planning to say the next day to her new group of friends. Said her mother, "She's been wanting to be part of that crowd for years. They're the most popular group in the school. Now that she's finally 'in,' she seems to feel a great deal of pressure to stay in."

Popular children often worry about staying popular. They worry about who likes who; what it means if all their friends have boyfriends or girlfriends and they don't; which clothes the "crowd" will wear to school; what if no one likes their hairstyles; and what if they're left out of after-school or weekend plans. The pressures of being part of "the" popular clique or crowd can be tough to deal with, especially for a child who is not very self-confident.

Most children, when asked if they would like to be popular, answer yes. But their "yes" usually reflects their opinions of the popular group at the particular school they attend. Some popular groups are "great," but other cliques are considered, by the peers, to be quite spoiled or "stuck up." One fifteen-year-old boy observed that the popular group of boys in his class, "were talking down about a lot of other people not in their group, treating girls as if they were dirt, and generally acting obnoxious." He said, "If that's what it takes to be popular, I'd rather not be."

Since the popular crowd usually represents only a handful of students at any given school, it is even more important to teach *all* children a healthy attitude about friendship.

Children are characteristically concerned about the number of friends they have. As a result, they often forget the true meaning of friendship and the rewards that can come with having even one friend. For children to know who their friends really are, they need to answer the following questions: Can their friends be trusted? Can they depend on friends? Can they honestly share innermost secrets and trust that what is shared will be sacred? Can they be silly and have fun? Can

they be serious, maybe even cry together? Can they forgive each other
for not always knowing what to do or say, for not being perfect, for
making mistakes sometimes?

Whether or not your child is popular, if he or she has even *one
truly good friend,* he or she must realize that friendship is to be
treasured. The number of friends is much less important than who the
friend is and how your child feels with that friend.

WHAT IF YOUR CHILD HAS NO FRIENDS OR WOULD LIKE TO MAKE NEW FRIENDS?

I've never met a child who didn't care about having a friend.
Yet I've met thousands of children who haven't any friends at all,
and don't seem to know the first thing about making a friend.

In every school, there are boys and girls of all ages who walk
through the halls by themselves, sit alone at lunch, and feel ill at ease
in their classrooms. They're the ones who are picked last (or not at
all) when class projects are assigned and who rarely have a partner
for bus trips. They stand apart at recess, watching crowds of other
kids talking, laughing, planning to do homework together or to go to
a party on the weekend. They wish someone would just come over
to them, even to say "Hi." Some children spend years feeling lonely
and rejected.

Try to imagine how a friendless child feels. Think of the tremendous loneliness he or she must encounter. For a child like this,
TV, pets, stuffed animals, computers, electronic games, homework,
housework, and other responsibilities often become "people substi-
tutes." It's a sorry thought. But children don't have to sit and wait
year after year until someone approaches them. Besides, someone
may never come. Lonely children don't have to wait around for anyone. They can learn to make the first move.

A college student once came to me after a class and said, "I
come to school every day, go to all my classes, talk with no one, and
go home. And I come back the next day, go to all my classes, talk
with no one, and go home." Countless conversations with students
from elementary and secondary school to the college level continue

to confirm that we're not doing a good enough job of teaching children about relationships. We can't be if so many children don't even know how to say "Hello."

Unless we teach children how to deal with their loneliness and *how* to take the first step, and give them suggestions on how to make a friend, there will be thousands of children growing into adulthood with very few relationships, minimal interaction, and very negative feelings about themselves.

The following step-by-step approach to making a friend, the "Rosenberg Plan for Friendship," is based not on magic but on common sense. It's a logical, practical approach any child, even a shy one, can use.

1. The Decision:

First, a child must decide that he or she *wants* a friend, is *worthy* of having a friend and is *worthy* of being a friend. If your child is one who has been very lonely and yearns for a friend, tell your child that he or she can decide *this second* if he or she wants to have a friend. Once this decision is made, your child can smile and relax a little, taking comfort in knowing that he or she is going to do something significant.

2. The Search:

Your child's next step is to search the school bus, the classroom, school halls, library, gym class, or anywhere else, and pick out one person that "seems" like he or she might be nice to have as a friend. Please remind your child not to be fooled by outside appearances. The way a person looks, their height, weight, or clothes, tells little or nothing about whether he or she would be a good friend to have.

3. The Approach:

Next, your child needs to go up to the chosen person and "break the ice." Don't assume your child will know what to say. Children need to be prepared for a variety of situations so they will be equipped with choices. Here are some suggestions:

"I always see you on the bus. Do you want me to wait for you at the corner tomorrow morning?"

"I always see you walking home the same way I do. How about if I meet you after school and we walk home together?"

"Do you want to study for the math test with me after school?"

"Do you want to walk into town with me after school?"

"Do you want to come to my house after school?"

"I think we eat during the same lunch period. Do you want me to save you a seat at my table?"

If your child is not quite ready to actually ask someone to spend time at your home, or go somewhere, he or she can simply begin by saying, "Hi!", or by exchanging names, mentioning that they're on the same bus, etc. Or it may be easier for a child to ask the new person what he or she thought of the math test, just to begin a conversation, with no pressure to go further.

Remind your child to approach someone on a one-to-one basis. Many kids have told me about instances where children who weren't part of their group came up to them, in front of their other friends, and asked if they'd like to do something together. Many said that they would have liked to have responded "Yes," but didn't because they didn't want to have to deal with their friends' reactions. So, a private approach may give your child the best chance for a positive reply.

4. The Encouragement:

Encourage your child to get his or her courage up and be confident. Your child may need a little kick in the pants (gentle and loving, but "firm") before he or she will actually take a chance and approach the potential new friend.

Understand that your son or daughter may be very nervous, scared, embarrassed, or unsure, and anticipating these feelings, reassure your child. You might say, "Hey, I'm really proud of you. I know talking to someone for the first time isn't the easiest thing to do. In fact, lots of adults get nervous and scared about this, too. It's really natural and okay to be nervous. I'd be surprised if you weren't. The only thing that's *not* okay is if you let your nervousness prevent you from doing what you really want to do—start a friendship. Just having the guts to go up to someone and start a conversation is terrific, even if they say "No" and fail to react as you had hoped.

You might also say to your child: "Even if your heart is pounding so loud that you think everyone on the third floor of your school will hear it, they really won't. But it's normal to wonder. And it's normal for your heart to pound!"

A harmful response to your child's anxieties about starting a friendship with someone would be: "Oh, don't be ridiculous! What's the worst thing they could say?" Acknowledge that it's tough, but be encouraging anyway. That is more positive than questioning or denying your child's feelings, or telling your child it's silly to feel a certain way.

We'd be lying if we promised kids that any or every approach they make will get a "yes" response. The reality is, of course, that the kid your child asks may or may not say "yes." It can help if your child is armed with a backup question, such as, "Well, if today isn't good, is tomorrow or any other day this week better?" If the response is still "no," your child can move right ahead to "Plan B" (see page 70).

If your child gets frustrated after being rejected and says something like "Oh, I knew I shouldn't have listened to you, I shouldn't have tried, I just *knew* it wouldn't work, nobody wants to spend time with me, nobody will ever say yes," acknowledge the disappointment and tell how sorry you are that things didn't work out. Say that you are proud, and he or she should be too, for the attempt that was made.

There are many important lessons about rejections that you can impart at this time. One or more of these observations could be applied to your child's situation:

"Not everyone relates to everyone else. It would be great, but that's just not the way life seems to be. In fact, I'll bet you have a list of people who for one reason or another you would not want to approach."

"Not every 'No' is a negative statement about you. The person who doesn't want to do homework together, or go home with you after school, may really want to say 'Yes,' but said 'No' because of peer pressure. Even approaching that person alone may not eliminate the pressure if he or she lacks confidence and isn't secure in his or her friendships.

"Maybe the other person's excuse is quite legitimate. 'Today' *really* may not be good, neither might any other day that week. He [or she] honestly may not have been feeling well, or had a dental appointment, or planned to visit a relative, or had prior plans with friends, or may have been upset by a family situation, or something that happened in school, and didn't feel like talking to anybody. But, he [or she] may surprise you next time and ask you to get together next week. There's always that chance."

"Maybe your possible new friend is also shy, unsure, and very uncomfortable about saying 'Yes.'"

"Even if the person said 'No,' I hope you feel more confident and proud for having tried to begin a friendship. Besides, every time you do this, it will get a bit easier."

"You don't lose anything for trying, Yes, you might be dissa-pointed now, or perhaps even embarrassed, but you walked away with everything you had when you first walked up to that other person. Walking away, you still have every part of yourself. You haven't lost a thing; you gained!"

5. "Plan B" and Beyond:

Encourage your child to do everything again. Start all over and look on the school bus, in classrooms, the lunch room, gym class, the library, or anywhere, and pick out Person Number Two who "seems" like he or she might be nice to get to know.

If plan B doesn't work, encourage your child to keep trying until someone finally says "Yes."

6. The Perspective:

Although it might be painful and frustrating, and generally seem awful for your child to experience many negative responses, giving up would be worse. Giving up, making the decision *not* to try any-more, is an unacceptable choice. I truly believe there is someone for everyone. And I'm not just saying that so that kids will feel better.

Children find it frustrating to realize that it is easy for some kids to make friends and harder for others. While some people just seem to "connect," others have to search for or try to create that connection. But that connection exists for all. Kids *must* be encouraged to keep taking chances on themselves.

A child has got to bear in mind that even if he or she approaches twenty people and all twenty say "No," maybe, just maybe, the twenty-first person could be that hoped-for friend. If a kid gives up, he or she may be lonely for many years. No one deserves that.

We need to teach children, early on, that they *do* have choices, *do* have some control over their friendships, and *can* make a *decision* to try to reach out, even if that process may take some time.

Children need to gain confidence but also they must try to be patient. The results will come in time if they keep trying. If they don't try, the rewards and the very things they crave—like friends—may never be theirs.

Many parents have heard their children's hurt and insecurity in statements like the following: "The other kids will probably laugh at me for asking Suzie to come to my house. They'll spread it all around the school. Besides, I'm ugly." "I never know the answer in class and everybody thinks I'm so dumb." "They think I'm so different because I'm in special ed [or come from a different country . . . or wear a hearing aid]." Some kids *will* laugh, some *will* be cruel enough to mock your child and tell others what he or she has said or done, and many will continue to judge by the outside "package." But all the laughter, all the rumors, all the judging, all the disrespect, and all the lack of sensitivity for how difficult trying to make new friends truly is, still doesn't take away from your child's "specialness" or the right to look for a friend. It just becomes harder for your child to believe in himself or herself.

That's why we must work actively and diligently at teaching children that cruelty from someone probably indicates that person wouldn't be a good friend, anyway. We can't leave to chance any child's ability to form relationships, deal with loneliness, and effectively fend off negative reactions from other kids. Of course, it is much easier for an adult to suggest to a child how to start a friendship than it is for children to put this advice in practice. We all need to be patient.

JOINING A CLUB CAN HELP

Aside from offering understanding, a sense of proper perspective, and actual words to help your child approach others, you might suggest that he or she join an after-school activity, for example, sports, a particular club, the Scouts, etc. These activities provide a ready-made social situation in which it can be easier to get to know others who are the same age with common interests. And there is usually a teacher, adult advisor, or leader to oversee and encourage children's interaction.

Some children are more comfortable initiating friendships in the club situation than on their own. It may seem more acceptable and natural to talk with others in the club if they're working or playing together. It's often easier than just saying "Hi" to someone in the halls "with no excuse."

WHAT IF YOUR CHILD MAKES IT DIFFICULT FOR OTHERS TO WANT TO BE FRIENDS?

If you child is unhappy, he or she may broadcast attitudes which turn off other children, even potential friends. Sometimes, a child will act in a way that creates negative attention, like misbehaving in class, being snobbish or obnoxious, pushing others around, or teasing or showing off. Such behavior can make it very difficult for someone to want that child as a friend. You can help your child understand how others might be reacting.

Ask your child to identify what qualities he or she would want to look for in a friend. You can make a list of these "desirable" characteristics and use it to compare the way you see your own child's behavior in relation to peers. Have your own child evaluate whether or not he or she believes his or her own actions would cause classmates to want to be their friend or would cause them to turn away.

This process might very much help children focus on what they're looking for when they begin their search.

WHAT IF YOUR CHILD HAS NEVER ADMITTED LONELINESS OR TALKED ABOUT NOT HAVING OR WANTING ANY FRIENDS?

If your child doesn't communicate feelings to you and you observe that he or she is alone most of the time, and doesn't receive phone calls or mention any friends and prefers to stay home rather than be with friends, you can try to help in several ways.

In all fairness, you should consider that it is possible that your child truly wishes to "hang out" alone after being in school all day with friends. Kids *do* interact before and after classes, during lunch, gym class, and during after-school activities. By the time many children come home, they actually may be tired, having had enough of everyone else. Watching TV, reading, or playing with a pet may be calming for them.

But, if your child has friends, it would be reasonable to assume you would, at least periodically, hear names of classmates in discussions about school or about happenings among friends away from school. If your son or daughter seems to prefer privacy after school during the week, it would be reasonable to assume that he or she would want to spend some time with friends on the weekend.

If you are concerned that your child doesn't have friends, you should speak with your child's teacher(s) in order to discover how much or how little your child interacts with other children. How easily does your child seem to relate to others? Is he or she well liked by classmates? How much time at recess or at lunch does your child spend alone?

If teacher feedback supports your suspicion that your son or daughter is having difficulty interacting with peers and spends most of his or her time alone, it would help your child to talk about loneliness and having no friends.

Since your child has kept this loneliness a secret, keep in mind that the topic will be a difficult one to discuss. Talk to your son or daughter at a time when you have privacy and an open-ended stretch of time ahead, so your conversation can extend, if need be. Here is a sample approach:

"For the past few weeks, I've noticed that you've been staying home after school, watching TV or doing homework. I figured that maybe you've just felt like taking it easy after a busy day at school. But I also figured, if you didn't feel like spending time with other kids during the week, you'd probably be making plans with other kids on the weekends. But the weekends keep passing by, and I still haven't seen you spend time with anybody your age. I'm really concerned that maybe you're lonely and just aren't talking about it.

"Maybe you've really wanted to be able to make a friend but just don't know how. I realize now that every time I've asked you why you're watching TV, especially on days when the weather was nice and I saw other kids playing on the street, maybe you really wanted to go outside with them but were scared they wouldn't include you. Maybe they weren't nice to you at school or the last time you tried to join in. Or maybe you just didn't know what to say to them when you got outside, so it was easier to stay inside.

"I know this may not be such an easy topic to deal with. Even when kids love their parents very much and feel very close to them, it can be hard to talk about certain things. It's hard for parents, too. In fact, it was hard for me to bring up this subject. But I really care about you, so I had to take a chance..."

When and if you do talk with your child about this, remember that your child's nonverbal reactions may be more telling than any verbal response. Please observe carefully.

After you lay the groundwork with your child and identify very clearly what he or she might be feeling but not telling, you can go in a few different directions:

You might talk about how you had those feelings when you were growing up; tell your child how you handled the situation, what worked for you, what didn't, whether or not it was hard to tell your parents how you felt. Then follow with "Have you ever had any of these feelings?"

If the reply is positive, your child will then have an opportunity to tell what emotions he or she needs to share. Then offer your child all the ideas, encouragement, perspectives, and advice that could enable him or her to begin trying to find a friend. At the very least, your child will probably be very relieved to be able to acknowledge these feelings and to learn it's okay to have them.

If the reply is negative and your child tells you that you're way off base about the way he or she feels, or that he or she has lots of friends at school and is really fine, you might say:

"I'm really glad to hear that. I hope you're being honest with me. If you are, great.

"If you're not, I hope you'll at least think about the fact that you don't have to pretend with me. It's not a sign of weakness to feel lonely or wish you could find a friend. It's a super sign of strength to be able even to say you have those concerns.

"I don't mean to pressure you about this. Your answer just leaves me very confused. I think I'd feel much better if you would at least explain to me why your life at home during the week and on the weekend doesn't include anyone I might consider to be your friend. Yet you say everything is fine and you do have friends." (Consider the possibility that your child does have close friends who, for one reason or another, such as a split home, are not available on the weekend.)

Another way you might handle a negative response:

"The last thing I would ever want to do is pressure you into talking with me if you're just not ready or don't feel you want to. But I have a very strong feeling that much of what I say means more to you than you're able to tell me, and that you feel uncomfortable about it.

"Many kids keep their feelings secret because they believe they're silly, or think their parents won't understand. Some kids are afraid they will cause their parents extra worry if they tell the truth. Others might not know what words to use in order to say what they want. I want you to know that nothing you share with me would ever be unimportant. I only feel sad that you might be hiding feelings that really bother you. You don't have to deal with your feelings alone. I really care and I'm here to listen.

"Besides, if you're bothered about any of the feelings I just mentioned about friends, or being lonely—or even if it's just that you'd like to make some new friends—together we can probably figure out some terrific ideas about how you can start changing what doesn't feel good to you."

If your child is not responding, you might say:

"I know I can't shake those feelings out of you, even though I wish I could turn you upside down and have them come out! Would you at least think about what I've said and how it might relate to you? If you can't talk with me alone, you might want to write down how you feel, and we could talk about that."

You might include: "Am I making you uneasy in any way? Is there something I'm saying or doing that is making it hard for you to share your thoughts with me? Do you feel you *can* talk with me even though you're not choosing to do so now?"

You may also wish to add at this point:

"If you feel you can't talk with me—and I hope you'll at least give me a chance to show you that you really can if you try—you might think of talking with someone else." (Suggest your child's father, mother, older brother or sister, grandparent, aunt, uncle, religious leader, friend's parent, trusted teacher, guidance counselor, school psychologist, school social worker, or any adult your child may care for and trust.)

Emphasize again to your child that talking about feelings that are very hard to handle is not a sign of weakness, and that it actually takes some strength to be able to say, "I'm lonely," or "I'm having a tough time being left out by the other kids..."

No matter how sensitive we might be to our children's feelings, or how much we try to promote interaction and help our children respond, there is no guarantee that our children will actually share with us what they need to share. All we can do is try harder to be approachable, reach out to them, and let them know that we understand how difficult it can be for them to talk with us about their innermost feelings.

We can encourage without pressuring and try again in a few days or weeks later, if we sense that our child is still without friends. We can also talk further with teachers, guidance counselors, school psychologists, or others.

BUYING FRIENDSHIP—OR WHAT IF YOUR CHILD ALLOWS HIMSELF OR HERSELF TO BE USED?

Some children are very afraid to take a chance on themselves. Instead of inviting a peer to spend some time together, they try to make themselves more attractive by offering an enticement: "I'll buy you pizza after school." Or "Do you want to come to my house? I'll do your homework for you." Or "I got this great electronic game, do you want to try it after school?"

According to the children's age, the enticements will differ. They may vary from pizza to an invitation to ride a new pony, a swim in the family swimming pool, a ride home from school in the father's or mother's very cool-looking car, help with homework or preparation for a test, a "loan" for something, drugs or alcohol, promised sex, and so forth.

It will not be that easy for your child to take a chance on being accepted by another, especially if he or she is reaching out for the first time in a long while. After suggesting to your child the initial approaches, you might follow with: "Notice I didn't suggest you say, 'Can I buy you a pizza this afternoon?' or 'Do you want me to do your homework?' or even, 'I'll help you with your homework.' That's 'buying' friendship, offering something besides yourself and hoping they'll say yes *because* of the pizza or the homework."

You might continue with: "But how long do you think a person would have to buy pizza for someone else just to get them to be a friend? How much homework would a kid have to do for someone else? And what if they stop? Would that other person continue being a friend? Maybe. Yes, if that person truly liked you for who you are, not for the pizza. No, if they just liked the free slices. But what kind of friendship do you think it would be, if it was only good because of pizza? I hope you realize that you're worth having as a friend and that you don't have to promise anything other than yourself. If someone likes you *only* for what you can give them, then maybe the friendship is not worth it anyway. That could be your signal to think about looking for someone else who can be a better friend.

TURNING FEELINGS INTO WORDS TO MAKE FRIENDSHIPS BETTER

Most children need to learn how to communicate better with, understand more about, and in general, relate more effectively to their friends. Judging from the volume of questions on the subject that I receive from children at my programs, many children do not know what to say or do when difficulties arise between friends.

Some of the most typical difficulties are listed below, with specific approaches, suggestions, and explanations where appropriate, and with suggestions for what your child can say to friends to handle the situations. Teaching children how to turn their feelings into words is a key part of the learning experience in each of these examples.

What if your child is friendly with two different groups and one group is pressuring him or her not to be friendly with the other?
Pressure from either group can cause confusion, frustration, and real fear of loss of friendship.

Children need to understand that each person is entitled to choose his or her friend. No friend has the right to tell another to be unfriendly with a certain person or group. This is an essential issue to discuss with your child.

It is normal for kids to have a couple of different groups of friends. Some friendships may come out of playing sports together, others from attending certain classes, and still others from participation in after-school clubs, drama interests, social interests, or religious groups. Each friendship has its own characteristics and may be more or less intimate than another.

It follows that some friendship choices will exclude certain other people. Prejudice, legitimate gripes, jealousies, grudges, or misunderstandings may influence these choices, or the groups simply may not "connect" with each other. Whatever the reason, some kids will like each other and some won't. They don't have to like each other— that's their privilege. But they *do* have to respect each other's personal rights. Even more important, they must respect your child's right to choose, and understand that such a choice doesn't mean your child cares less about them and more about others but probably likes them both.

Help your child analyze why Group One wants him or her to join. What kind of jealousies exist between Group One and Group Two? Does everyone in Group One share the same feelings or did one person influence everyone else? Is Group One intolerant of differences in others? Are they the "class brains" or does everyone in the group share something else like lower grades, or more money, or better athletic ability or none at all? Are there racial and religious differences between Group One and Group Two? Are there jealousies because Group Two is more popular than Group One?

Help your child explore the differences, jealousies, misunderstandings, and prejudice, if any, and it will add to your child's strength in the belief that he or she has the right to be friendly with anyone.

What can your child say to a friend, or a group, who applies pressure? What does your child feel? Turn the feelings into words. Here's a suggestion:

"I feel really upset when you tell me not to spend time or be close to my other friends. It makes me feel pressured, like I'm in the middle. I'm not asking you to be friendly with my other group. And my seeing them has nothing to do with my friendship with you. I really do like you and it's important to me that we are good friends.

But I like them, too. If you're such good friends of mine, why are you hurting me by trying to force me to choose? My other friends aren't hurting or bothering you. I don't tell you who to be friendly with. Please don't tell me."

If friends are true, they will respect your child's right to choose. If they continue to make it difficult for your son or daughter, remind your child to consider what kind of friends they are. If they won't keep the friendship if your child continues to be friendly with both groups, then perhaps it's time for your child to reevaluate the friendship, disconcerting though it might be.

What if your child feels that one of his or her friends is "two-faced"?

It can be very painful for a child to realize he or she has been maligned behind the back, especially by someone who is considered a good friend. The anger, frustration, mistrust, sadness, embarrassment, humiliation, doubt, and confusion can be tough to handle. Try to help your child understand the motivation behind such a friend's change in behavior as well as how he or she can deal with the hurt.

Children and parents continually ask me how to cope with these feelings and handle this situation. Should your child tell the friend that he or she knows what's happened? At what price would your child remain silent? How do you imagine that broken trust could be built back up? How much resentment would get in the way of continuing with a meaningful friendship? Or will the friendship become superficial anyway?

Encourage your child to tell the offending friend he or she "knows." Your child might say to the friend: "Four people have told me what you said about me this morning. It really hurts to know you said that. I thought we were such good friends." Or "This is really hard for me to say, but . . . I found out that you said some pretty nasty things behind my back. I thought we were good friends. Why did you do it?"

If your child's friend is a true friend, it is hoped he or she will respond honestly and explain what happened and why. Your child may not be happy with that friend, but at least this kind of confrontation can lead to better understanding, and a continuation of the friendship. Even if the friend explains satisfactorily and apologizes, tell your child not to be sruprised if the friendship is somewhat guarded until the trust is rebuilt.

It's also possible that the friend will deny having said anything mean. If the "sources" were reputable, your child may not want to believe the friend's denial. In that case, especially if they've been friends for a long time, your child has a decision to make. Your child might say: "I really want to believe you. But it's hard. I don't think [the source] would have purposely said something that might ruin our friendship. Deep down I wonder if you're afraid to admit what you said because I'll be very mad at you. I'm sad that I even have to ask if you said it, but it's sadder to imagine that you couldn't tell me the truth. It's going to take me a while before I can trust you completely again."

The way the friend responds will give your child a sense of where the friendship stands.

What if a certain friend or friends act nice when alone with your child but differently with other people?

If this happens to your child, he or she may feel sad, left out, embarrassed, confused, angry, and frustrated at being ignored. If you acknowledge that it's natural to feel upset and offer insights about the friend's behavior, your child will most likely appreciate it.

There are numerous, varied reasons why a friend might ignore your child when others are around. If the friend is afraid that someone in the crowd doesn't like your son or daughter, and still wants to be accepted by that crowd, it may not be "cool" to appear your child's good friend. Maybe the friend is totally secure about the friendship with your child and chooses to concentrate fully on impressing the others. This friend may not even be aware that he or she is ignoring your child.

Encourage your child to *privately* talk about the feelings with the friend. Emphasize the importance of turning feelings into words. Suggest your child might say: "Do you have any idea how different you are when we're alone than when we're with other kids? We always get along when we're by ourselves. We can talk with each other about lots of things, and I think you're a good friend. But when we're with anybody else, you ignore me, or act like I don't exist! It hurts me when you do that. Why do you act like that?"

What if a friend hurts or embarrasses your child by telling a special secret, starting a fight, or doing anything else that upsets your child and affects the friendship?

The communication of inner feelings is essential to the development of a positive friendship. Children often repress their reactions towards friends because they're afraid the friends will get angry, or worse, end the friendships. Even when children want to share their feelings with a friend, many have no idea how to express themselves.

The following examples suggest what your child could say to a friend about frustration, anger, or any other feelings that need to be expressed.

If a friend starts a fight:

"It really bothers me that we're such good friends one day, and then, all of a sudden, you're mad at me the next. Most of the time I don't even know what the fight is about! Why do you want to fight all the time?"

Your child can add: "Do you like fighting with me? I don't like it when you start fighting with me. It makes me feel bad. Is there something I do that makes you angry that you haven't told me about? Why do you need to fight with me? I thought we were supposed to be friends."

If a friend hurts or embarrasses your child:

"It really hurt when you said that to me."

"It really hurt when you didn't include me yesterday."

"I felt like crawling into my locker and hiding when you told everyone my secret. I was so embarrassed! Why did you do that to me?" (After the friend responds, your child can add: "Please don't ever tell anything like that again. What I tell you is private.")

"I know I was laughing with everyone when you said that to me at [person's] house. But I was too embarrassed to let anyone know how I felt. So I just made believe I thought it was funny and laughed. Please don't ever say anything like that again."

"It hurt me when I found out that you told so many people about my parents. I thought I could trust you."

Whatever situation you discuss with your child, first identify his or her feelings, then turn them into words. You and your child can adapt the preceding statements or create your own. The more practice your child has, the easier it will be. You can even make up situations in your talks together, just to figure out what could be said. Practicing how to express feelings will help increase communication skills with friends, as well as with parents, family members, teachers, and anyone else.

We need to teach children that an unhappy situation cannot be remedied by silence. Although the fight may blow over, and the hurtful feelings dissipate so the friendship goes on, your child may still feel bad. And what about next time? Children can't expect their friends to be sensitive if they don't let them know how they feel. How could they blame friends for hurting them again if they never told them they were hurt in the first place?

A friendship is not positive if one person can't express what he or she feels to the other, or can't trust that whatever is shared will be taken fairly and with respect.

How can children say "no" to each other without hurting each other's feelings?

They probably can't. Children often ask me how they can deal with kids who are desperate to belong and follow them around, copy how they act, ask if they can come along, and seem more like "leeches" than people! While some kids don't care about other people's feelings, many really do. They don't want to hurt another child but can't stand constant requests to be included. It's very hard to say no, and even harder when a child would actually like to be kind.

Children need to realize that it's perfectly all right for them to say no. Saying no sensitively can take the edge off another person's bad feelings. Your child might say: "Thanks for asking me, and I'm really sorry I keep saying no all the time, but I have many different friends I'm trying to spend time with. It's hard to be free for everyone."

If the persistent one, according to your child, is "not that bad," but your child simply doesn't want to see him or her every day, your child might say: "Maybe we can get together next week some time. I'll let you know." Or "You don't have to ask me every day. If I know I'm going to be free, I'll let you know."

Other ways of handling this situation might be:

"This is really hard for me to say. And I don't mean to hurt your feelings. But it really bothers me when you follow me around all the time. I like you. But it's not fair to think I'm going to be with you all the time."

"Every time I turn around, you're there! It really bugs me when you follow me like that! Please stop!"

Children must realize that there will be times when they will have to hurt someone, no matter how much they don't want to incur bad feelings. This is an important lesson for children, and it's one many adults have yet to learn. There are many kids who keep their feelings silent for fear of hurting their parents or peers. Adults do the same. Many people display false happiness because they don't know how to express feelings that might hurt.

Children need to be able to let someone know if they feel too much pressure, discomfort, frustration or resentment. If an adult acknowledges a child's effort and supports him or her emotionally, a child can learn to express his or her troubles. Remember, it's best to share delicate feelings privately, at a time when neither parent nor child has pressing obligations elsewhere.

To say what needs to be said can be painful for the person who says it as well as those who must listen. While such honesty can end friendships that are not meant to be and can put an end to tagalongs, it can also pave the way for important growth and intimacy.

How can children better handle changes among friends?

Sometimes a child's friend will become distant even if nothing in particular actually "happens" between them. There's no confrontation, no fight. Sometimes friends simply begin to change. They mature, develop new interests, and go off in different directions. A friend's new interest may be something your child isn't ready for— a new boyfriend or girlfriend or experimenting with smoking, drinking, drugs or sex. Even though your child may want to hold on to that friendship, it may be too uncomfortable, too high pressured, and sometimes even dangerous to do so.

As children grow and change, so do friendships. Rarely are children prepared to expect and cope with these changes; rarer still can they express the feelings that accompany all those personal changes. If, for example, your child has had a wonderful friendship with someone since kindergarten but recognizes that he or she has changed and the friendship is just not the same anymore, it may be very sad and painful to realize it's time to let go.

Sometimes children find they don't need to express aloud these specific feelings of growing apart from friends. As they spend less and less time together, there may develop a mutual understanding that requires no discussion. However, one friend may wish to acknowledge this by saying: "I know we're spending less and less time together. I guess we're just growing, or moving, in different directions. But I want you to know I'll always love you and remember the years we spent together. It makes me sad, but I understand."

Throughout the growing-up years, children will have to confront countless friendship situations and conflicts.

The more we talk openly with our children about their day-to-day experiences, the more prepared and confident they will be with their peers. The more we explain, listen, offer encouragement, acknowledge difficulty, and teach our children how to express their feelings, the better they will feel about themselves and their relationships.

WHAT IF YOU DO NOT APPROVE OF YOUR CHILD'S FRIENDS?

If you don't like your child's friend—or the entire crowd your child hangs around with—would you forbid or try to prevent your child from seeing that friend? Would you fabricate reasons why your child can't spend time with a certain friend instead of confronting your true reasons? Would you tell your child the reasons for your disapproval, explaining why you believe the friend is a negative influence, or just not "our kind"? How would you expect your child to respond to these restrictions? How do you think your child would feel?

Many children have indicated how difficult it can be when parents don't like their friends or believe certain friends are a bad influence. It's particularly trying for a child if parents forbid association with a friend who is usually seen at school.

Some kids who are forbidden to see certain friends will listen to their parents and accept that their parents must be right. Many others are resentful and insist that it's their right to choose their own friends. A child may tell a parent: "Okay, so I won't see her [him] anymore," but continue to spend time secretly with that friend at school. A close parent-child relationship and how much a child needs approval from parents can affect a child's reactions to parental restrictions. Most children have said they'd like to have their parents caution them and tell them why they think any certain friend is not a good influence, and then let them make up their own minds. Kids get very frustrated and upset when parents simply announce something like "You cannot see so-and-so" but don't tell them why. Children deserve to understand their parent's reasoning. How else will they learn?

If you believe that your child's friendship with anyone is dangerous, you should discuss this with your child and establish restrictions. For instance, if you're worried about drugs, you might say:

"This is very hard for me to say, because I know how friendly you are with [friend]. But you've come home high every time you've been out together. I don't know who's influencing whom, but I do know that the combination doesn't seem good. Have you thought about what you're doing to yourself? Your behavior really seems to change when you're with him [her]. The changes worry me. I can't let you go out with [friend] anymore."

You might add:

"The last thing I would ever want to do is hurt you or make decisions for you that you rightfully can and should make for yourself, like choosing your own friends. And I would never want to do anything that would hurt our relationship. I know I'm taking a risk by telling you to stop seeing someone you care about. I risked your becoming angry at me; I took the risk that you wouldn't understand that I'm placing restrictions out of serious concern for your well-being. If you're honest with yourself you'll probably admit how different you've been acting lately. Much more irritable. Very into yourself. More pressured, or so it has seemed. I can't stand by and let you do this to yourself.

"If you have any reason why you feel I'm being totally unfair, I can't promise I'll change my mind, but I'd like to listen and consider what you have to say."

Often I've heard, "My mother doesn't want me to hang around with my friend because she knows my friend smokes and thinks I'm going to do it, too," or "My parent's friend saw my friend smoking pot and now they won't let me see my friend anymore." Children get very upset when parents don't trust them. They may understand, but they are rarely happy when parents forbid them from seeing a friend for fear they will imitate their friend's behavior. But how can we be so sure they won't?

Some parents don't open discussions or make any decisions because they don't want to have to deal with their child's reaction to any restrictions. It doesn't feel good when a child slams doors, refuses to come out of the bedroom, and vows not to talk to parents for weeks. It takes guts for parents to hold an unpopular stand that will almost definitely provoke a negative reaction from their child. Parents want to feel loved, too. But refusing to cope with a situation regarding a child's well-being is not wise. Besides, whoever said parenting would feel good all the time?

Children may well keep certain relationships and activities secret if they believe their parents will not approve, so always be prepared to step in as soon as you have the slightest sense that your child's well-being may be in danger. No magic formulas are needed to sharpen your "gut instinct." Use common sense and don't forget that children may *not* have felt that they could tell us what we needed to know to be able to offer help or prevent them from getting involved in something they were not yet equipped to handle.

Here are some guidelines: Confront your child with whatever it is that troubles you. If you have even the slightest question about your child's friendships and activities, ask. If nothing specific has happened but your instinct tells you to be concerned, speak up. Warn your child, offer advice, provide some more specific ways for them to open up and be candid with you, and confirm that your lines of communication are open.

If your worries are valid, yet the situation is not serious enough to warrant issuing an edict regarding how much time your child spends where and with whom, you may want to caution your child anyway. Preventative education never hurts. This way your child will be more aware of dangerous situations and will know how to avoid, or more effectively deal with, such experiences should they arise.

If your instincts are wrong, your child will probably tell you. But, even if you are wrong, talking with your child about friends, pressure and risks, values, decision-making, and self-respect can be an important learning experience for you both. There's always something to gain from such exchanges.

Unless there's a very serious situation which warrants immediate action, it's a good idea to analyze your feelings and personal prejudices carefully before you tell your child not to see a friend. Parental approval is very valuable to most children. If you don't approve, it may dramatically interfere with your child's relationships. But remember that there's a difference between wanting to keep your child away from a potentially bad influence and simply not liking your son's or daughter's friend.

Parents may not always be capable of seeing a friend through their child's eyes. Reactions towards your child's friends probably depend on how those friends act around you. A friend may be shy and hardly utter a sound in your presence but have "personality plus" when with your son or daughter. If the friend has no ill effects on your child and your child seems happy with the friendship, please think twice before teasing or making any negative comments. Children rarely feel free enough to tell their parents they are hurt when their parents tease a friend, even in jest.

If you continually make fun of your children's friends, it may become too frustrating, upsetting, and embarrassing for them to bring friends home to meet you. Every snicker, facial expression, and gesture regarding a friend might be interpreted negatively by your child, whether or not you meant it that way. Be very aware of the verbal and nonverbal messages you send your child. If you think there is even a remote chance your child may feel upset about your reactions to a friend, try to talk about these feelings together. You might say:

"I know I always kid around when you mention [friend] or when I see you with [friend], but I want you to know that I don't really mean it. He [she] seems nice and I don't even know him [her] that well. If you feel he [she] is a good friend, that's what's important to me. I'm sorry if I made you feel embarrassed or upset. Did you ever have feelings about this that you wanted to share but couldn't?"

Children have expressed anxiety about the ways their parents judge friends on appearance, clothes, hair, size and development, athletic ability, jewelry (if they're male and wear an earring, for example), disabilities, grades, special learning problems, parents, religion, race, nationality, where they live, or if they're rich or poor. If you frequently make derogatory comments or otherwise evaluate your child's friends based on these or any other externals and this upsets your child, your child may feel uncomfortable and unable to express displeasure about it. Your child may suffer, silently.

If you have explicitly told your child not to bring home or associate with a certain friend, your child might be too intimidated to let you know how upset he or she is. When barriers between friends are created by parents because of hatred, anger, or a prejudice, children find it particularly difficult. Such ill feelings usually have little to do with the innocent boy or girl who wants to be a friend, and more to do with a deep-rooted bias and animosity which prohibits parents from giving this friend a fair chance.

Even if a parent creates excuses to mask any personal prejudices, children can see through them. While some kids won't be aware of the truths behind their parents' rules, many clearly deduce the source of the restrictions. A boy in the fifth grade recently wrote to me, "What do you do if some person (grown-up) in your family is prejudiced and you are not allowed to see these people or have them over? I've asked but just got yelled at!"

Children may be unable to let their parents know how much these arbitrary rules hurt, frustrate, and anger them. Getting to know your child's friend for who he or she is would be important. Acknowledge this to your child. You might say:

"I've been doing some thinking and it's possible that I've been judging [friend] unfairly. Maybe I let my own prejudices get in the way and they really don't have anything to do with your friend. I'm so sorry. I know now that it's not your friend's fault [what happened so many years ago]. It's just hard for me to separate your friend out. I'm not promising that it will be comfortable for me to give your friend a chance. It may take me a while, but, I want you to know he [she] is welcome in our home. I can at least promise you I'll try to be more open. I know it must have been very hard for you to deal with this. What feelings have you wished you could talk about with me? What did you hold back? It's very special to be able to talk with you like this."

Because parents have usually made up their minds that their children shouldn't associate with particular friends, it is that much more difficult for children to bring up their feelings on the subject. Children deserve to be reminded that parents are worried about their welfare and that's why parents make specific restrictions. Let your children know you love them very much and genuinely wish to protect them from harm.

I hope children will learn that it isn't disrespectful to ask parents why they don't want them involved with particular friends or groups. Parents have a right and responsibility to make rules to try to protect their children, but children have a right to understand why the rules are being made.

Adults who judge others harshly because of prejudices must learn to evaluate children's friends fairly. Every child deserves to be taken for who he or she *is* as an individual. It takes time for some people to get past old "labels" so they can understand that a stereotype or a reputation is not a person. Parents need to teach this to their children.

FRIENDSHIPS TAKE TIME

If your children are frustrated in their attempts to initiate relationships, encourage them to keep trying. Only if they continue their efforts can they expect results. If they become impatient because they want "good friends" to become "best friends" faster, advise them to give the friendship more of a chance. Discuss with your child the strategies for developing closer friendships.

It is essential to remind children that friendship takes time. Getting closer to people is a process that involves many, many steps, including reaching out, saying hello more often, smiling like they've never smiled before, exchanging names, showing interest, letting people know they are cared about, including other people in plans, and maybe even joining an after-school club or two. It also involves gradually "loosening up" with another person and abandoning defenses. It may take years for some people to reach the point where they can just "be" with another person—with no reluctance, without putting on an act or worrying how they're being judged. Building relationships requires patience.

CHAPTER 5

BOYFRIENDS, GIRLFRIENDS, DATING, PARTIES

interested but
afraid to ask out a
girl.

G.6

My best friend is boycrazy. I'm not.
what should I do? She wants me to
have a boy friend

How can I talk about dating ~~comfortably~~ comfortably
with my parents.

Friends:

Why don't boys ask me out. All my other friends go out why won't my mom let me go out with boys? why doesn't my mom trust me

Do you think I should tell my brothers, and father who I like or who I'm going out with. Every time they find out they make fun of me or my girlfriend or a person who I really like.

Boy

I'm under pressure because I don't know if I need a girlfriend or not. Everyone else has one. Do I need one to stay popular.

The subject of boyfriends and girlfriends is a very difficult one for a great number of boys and girls to discuss with their parents. When parents have laid down rules like "wait until you're older," children will hold back their feelings rather than risk their parents' anger or stricter restraints. Even if children have been given permission to "go out," they don't talk to parents about it because they're often embarrassed, afraid of being teased, or don't want to take the chance that a family member might think the chosen person is "ugly," or "a creep." So, it's easier and more comfortable to remain silent.

This chapter will help you better anticipate, understand, and more effectively confront the feelings, issues, and concerns related to boyfriend/girlfriend relationships among children. It is my hope that the earlier we can teach boys and girls what they need to know, the sooner we can strengthen their ability to establish more meaningful relationships not only as they grow up, but also throughout their adult lives.

DIFFERENT RULES, DIFFERENT ATTITUDES, DIFFERENT FEELINGS

My son spent two frustrating hours trying to convince the mother of the girl he liked that her daughter should be allowed to have a boyfriend. He was then in the eighth grade and her mother wouldn't budge! The hard and fast "house rule" was: "No boyfriends until ninth grade." That was that. He went on to someone else who was allowed to have one. My son said, "I felt mainly frustration and anger. I knew a really good girlfriend was slipping away."

When your child is "ready" and you are not

Parents aren't always ready for their children to have boyfriend/ girlfriend relations when the children are. When a child's friends are already involved with who they like today, who they think they'll like tomorrow, if they'll be liked back, or how are they ever going to let someone know they like them, it's probable boys and girls who are restricted from having girlfriends or boyfriends will long to be part of this intrigue and fun.

When parents are saying *"Not yet"* to boyfriends and girlfriends, children who want the freedom to have such a relationship might react in a variety of ways. Some boys and girls will listen without a fuss, but most are upset that they're being deprived of something they believe they ought to be allowed to do. They may listen to their parents, but be very resentful, and feel they're being treated like a "baby." Many will go ahead and have a boyfriend or girlfriend anyway and just not tell their parents about it.

Other children may say they want to have a boyfriend or girl-friend just because their friends do. They may be secretly very relieved about their parents' instructions to wait. Peer pressure in this regard can be very strong. If they're not ready, they may be going along with the crowd anyway, just to feel they belong. Strict parental restraints may be a blessing to them. It's easier to blame parents than to say, "Hey, I really don't even care. Can't you talk about anything else?"

Those children who do go against a parent's wishes may or may not feel guilty. Much depends on the particular child, the nature of the parent-child relationship, and what his or her friends are already doing. One thirteen-year-old boy said, "If my parents told me I couldn't have a girlfriend, I'd really rebel. I'd really dislike that. I can see if they're telling you not to smoke or do something like that, but I'd be really disappointed in them if they told me I couldn't have a girlfriend." A fourteen-year-old girl suggested, "Couldn't parents just set limits? Like, you can talk on the phone with boys, but you can't date."

A mother once admitted to me: "I have a daughter that got to be very boycrazy about the age of twelve. She's fifteen now. How do I deal with that? I'm really not happy with her interest in boys." When I asked what her daughter is doing about such interest and if she had a boyfriend, the mother replied, "No, she doesn't. We don't allow her to date. She talks about boys all the time and she'll comment on boys constantly when we're driving in the car and she sees them on the street. We think she calls boys when she's at her girlfriends' houses."

If the "boycrazy daughter" called boys from her friends' houses, she also might have been spending afternoons with them and even might have had a boyfriend. The way the rules were set up for her, she probably wouldn't talk about any boy-related concerns or activities with her parents. Exactly why was this mother so concerned about her daughter having a boyfriend? What was she trying to prevent by making such rules? Talking to me about this problem, the mother realized she had to do some rethinking. It's natural for kids to be "boycrazy" or "girlcrazy" at a certain point. The issue is how the "craziness" is acted upon.

An attempt at completely eliminating her daughter's interest is unrealistic. Knowing how boycrazy her daughter is, it might be wiser for this mother to allow her daughter to have a boyfriend, and to make clear her constraints, such as how much time she would be permitted to spend with him and under what circumstances. Or, at the very least, the mother could talk honestly with her daughter, and let her know how frustrated and confused she is about how to deal with her daughter's interest in boys.

Parents rightfully have their own feelings about when their son or daughter will be "old enough" to have a boyfriend or girlfriend. Unfortunately, if children know their parents regard them as too young for such friendships, they're much less likely to ask them questions about the boyfriend or girlfriend they're not supposed to have. Instead of approaching parents, sometimes kids will talk with a trusted teacher or a friend's parent, but mostly, they'll turn to friends. Statements such as "If my parents knew I had a boyfriend, they'd *kill* me!" are very common.

I don't suggest that parents give in and change rules just because those rules may be getting broken anyway. Rather, I suggest you reevaluate any guidelines or "rules" you have established regarding boyfriends or girlfriends in light of what actually may be going on. Do your rules need adjustment? Might it help to compromise in order to maintain a comfortable degree of control and be more assured that your ground rules are realistic enough to be honored? Do you need to be stricter?

The freedom that your child's friends have may give you a clue about what your own child may be up to, regardless of your rules. Concentrate on your child's response to your restrictions. If you're not sure what your child feels, *ask*.

When you are "ready" and your child is not

While many children are waiting for the day when their parents get "with it" and allow them to have a boyfriend or girlfriend, others are feeling too pressured by their parents to find one.

Many children have told me of feeling distressed at parents constantly asking, "Who do you like?", and of being embarrassed at restaurants or school events when a parent would say in a too loud voice, "Oh, she [he] is really cute!"

I personally have been frustrated by other adults who, thinking they were very "cool" and funny, asked my daughter, "Do you have a boyfriend? Do you know who you're going to marry yet?"

Be aware that in response to this kind of question a smile on your beloved child's face really could mask daggers of anger aimed towards you! Children of all ages find it hard to tell parents when their kidding remarks are just not funny. Some are afraid of hurting their parent's feelings, others are too scared to say anything that might be taken negatively.

In all fairness, some kidding around *can* be cute and considered funny. It depends who is saying what, how it's said, and who else hears it. If you are not absolutely sure that your child, or perhaps a child's friend, doesn't mind your attempts at humor in this regard, *ask!*

Since each child reaches the boyfriend/girlfriend stage on an individual time basis, try to be very aware not only of what you say, but also the potential effects of your message. Remember, each child will react differently, even in the same family.

Another kind of pressure

Besides being kidded about having a girlfriend, many boys feel pressured, by fathers, brothers, friends, and other male adults, to engage in sexual activities. Questions such as "Did you get anything from her?" or "You mean you never tried anything?" can be very disturbing to a boy who is not yet interested or ready to be even a little sexually involved. He can be intimidated, hesitant to admit that he isn't interested, feel uncomfortable, or even not know what to do! The effect of this kind of urging can unfortunately cause a boy to wonder, "What's wrong with me?" or "Why don't I have these interests or desires?" He may keep his questions and concerns secret for fear of seeming less manly, less worthy. Such influence can possibly contribute to the development of an exploitative attitude towards girls.

"House calls"

Consider this hypothetical situation: Sean gets a telephone call from Jennifer that is answered by his little sister. Little sister then yells loud enough for everyone to hear, "Seannnnnnn, Jennifer is on the phone!" Sean's little sister immediately starts running around the house yelling, *"Sean loves Jennifer, Sean loves Jennifer..."* Sean's father elbows him as he walks to the phone whispering, "Is that *her*?" or "Which one is *she*?"

Sean's mother and father roll their eyes at each other making a few more "cute" remarks and follow with "Do we know her, dear?", as Sean emerges from his not-so-private spot at the hall phone, red-faced, annoyed, wishing everyone would leave him alone, and praying Jennifer didn't hear his family's remarks.

Depending on the age of any of the boy's siblings, the response might also have been, "The *fox* is on the phone" or "It's *her*!" I'm sure you can add more to this list.

If even a more subtle type of this teasing takes place in your home, please give your child a break! A little bit of kidding is normal, but be wary of how far you go. Even a little bit of kidding can be a whole lot annoying. Don't be fooled if your child laughs along with you. He or she may truly think you're funny, or may secretly think the teasing isn't funny at all. If you're not sure how your son or daughter feels, *ask!*

Another "no-no" according to kids is eavesdropping by family members on their phone conversations. Eavesdropping may be fascinating and entertaining, but it is definitely an invasion of privacy, as well as a source of embarrassment.

WHEN AND HOW TO BEGIN TALKING ABOUT BOYFRIENDS AND GIRLFRIENDS

Regardless of when you feel your child will be ready to have a boyfriend or girlfriend, mock marriages are taking place on elementary-school playgrounds with fourth-graders, and sometimes third-graders, in the "wedding party." Mid to upper elementary school boys and girls pull at each other's scarves, try to act "cool," blush in their classrooms, and play spin the bottle after school or at "boy/girl" parties.

Even if your son or daughter hasn't so much as hinted about "liking" someone, realize that such interest might exist, if not in your child, certainly in friends and classmates at school. Interest among friends who are at the same point of development can be wonderfully supportive, but can also confuse, pressure, and make it very difficult for your child to advance socially at his or her own pace. That is all the more reason to start talking about social relationships *early.*

Early means no later than third, fourth, or fifth grade, depending on your child and the level of sophistication of his or her peers. You might help your third-grade daughter understand that it's normal for her "boyfriend" to act very nice when they're alone but to say, "Get away, get away" to her when he's with a bunch of boys at school. Your fourth-grade son may need to talk with you about the pressure he feels because he's not interested in girls and all his friends are. A daughter in the fifth grade may need to talk about how upset she is that she's taller than every boy in her class.

Talking with children about the feelings and situations that commonly accompany emerging opposite-sex interests is not meant to push them into social action prematurely. Rather, such talk is intended to explore feelings, discuss what social pressures might exist, examine how the pressures can be handled, offer specific comments a child can use to help him or her respond more comfortably in a variety of situations, and teach a child how to relate to the other sex with greater ease and respect. If you anticipate these issues before they are experienced, you can prepare your boys and girls for the natural confusions, pressures, frustrations, and disappointments of boy-girl relations, as well as the social excitement of them.

If your child is not ready to talk about social feelings, he or she will probably let you know. Bringing up the subject won't be a waste because your child will still get the message: "You really can talk with me about this when you're ready." Any advice that you started to give can be "filed away" for future use. If your timing is on target and your child is already dealing with these issues and feelings, you will have opened the door for conversation that is often desired but rarely initiated by the child.

Remember, a child's feelings of embarrassment and fear that a parent will think he or she is too young often adds "bricks" to the wall of secrecy protecting children's private feelings about boyfriends, girlfriends, and related social concerns. The older the child, the more pressure, and the more likely he or she will think, "I shouldn't be so nervous, I should know what to say, I *should* be able to handle this by now. I better not tell anyone I can't." More secret feelings.

If a parent is the one to initiate the discussion, a son or daughter will be more apt to believe, "It's okay to let my mom and dad know how I feel! Maybe they really will listen, maybe they'll at least try to understand."

The importance of talking with your child about social relationships continues long after elementary school. Many college students have told me of their feelings of social shyness, discomfort, and inadequacy. Others have wanted to know how to tell if they're ready to make commitments, how to communicate more comfortably, how to build trust, how to deal with possessiveness, jealousy, sexual pressures and performance, exclusivity, long-distance relationships, and with parents who don't approve of the people they like. Most of these college students did not talk with their parents about such feelings. Most wished they could.

High school students, as well as those in middle school and

junior high school, have their own particular questions and concerns: "How do you know if someone likes you?" "What if I like my best friend's girlfriend?" "How do I handle it if I like someone who goes to a different school or is in a different crowd?" "My parents never let me have boys in my room, even if they're friends." "How do I deal with sexual pressures?" "All my friends have a later curfew." "My parents never give me privacy when I have parties. They're always coming downstairs." "No one ever asks me out. I'll never look as good as the girls in the popular crowd."

No child is too old to benefit from parental input regarding relationships. You will always have new situations and experiences to talk about, communication skills to teach, confidence to strengthen, self-image to nurture, perspectives to offer, and approaches to explore.

Some children don't start to date until they reach their twenties, others have started families by then. No matter how different their social situations, *all* children stand to gain from the opportunity to confront, and learn to deal more effectively with, innermost feelings and concerns about relationships.

The need to learn never stops. All of us need to better understand how to "work" at our relationships: to improve our ability to communicate; and to be more intimate, more sensitive to each other's needs, more realistic in our expectations, better able to adjust to changes, more comfortable reaching out to others, and more courageous in our decisions to show our feelings, even if that makes us vulnerable. Growth and change continue for the rest of our lives. There's always more for your child to learn.

If you have already created an ongoing dialogue with your son or daughter about social feelings and experiences, my suggestions for discussions on the subject can help serve as a guide to becoming even more aware of your child's needs. If you have never talked about these topics, remember that turning your feelings into words will help you get started.

Here are some sample beginnings:

"Steven's mother had lunch with me today and told me that he has a girlfriend. I know how friendly you are with Steven and I just want you to know there are no rules that say you have to have a girlfriend, too. Lots of kids feel pressured to like someone just because their friends do."

"Maybe you haven't talked with me about having a boyfriend because you've been embarrassed or thought I'd say you're too young. But I want you to know it's very important to me that we be able to talk together about those kind of things. I know there can be a lot of feelings and social pressures to deal with. Can we at least try to talk together?"

"I know we haven't talked about this before. But I was thinking maybe it would help to tell you what happened to me the first time I asked a girl out."

"Every time I see that you're staying in on Saturday night, I wonder what you're feeling inside. I know many of your friends are busy with dates."

"When I was in the seventh grade, I had the biggest crush on the boy sitting in front of me in English class. (Your child's eyes might light up at the incredible thought that you were actually ever in the seventh grade, let alone that you had a "crush"!). I didn't tell anyone because I was too embarrassed. But I know it would have been a great relief to be able to admit those feelings to someone. I just want you to know that I'm here for you and I'll be happy to try to answer any questions and talk with you about any feelings you might have about liking someone as a boyfriend."

"I love seeing you. But I've been thinking about how many weekends you've been home since you left for college. It occurred to me that maybe you're really still homesick, which is very normal. In fact, when I first went away to school, it took me at least three months to get used to being there. But, I also wondered about what the social situation is like there. Weekends are usually big party times at school. If there aren't parties, weekends are usually when people get a chance to meet. By coming home, you're not giving yourself much of a chance. It can be scary trying to meet new people, wondering what they think of you, and who you can trust. How about if we take a long lunch break together so we can talk about this?"

(If your son or daughter doesn't respond, a follow-up might be: "Would you at least think about what I've said, so we can talk in a couple of weeks?")

SPECIAL TOPICS
TO DISCUSS WITH YOUR CHILD

Social readiness

Children need to know that each person is different and will develop interests in the other sex on his or her own personal schedule—earlier, later, or just about the same time as friends begin to show interest.

A boy in the sixth grade told me, "I'm under pressure because I don't know if I need a girlfriend or not. Everyone else has one. Do I need one to stay popular?" A fifth-grade girl shared, "My best friend is boycrazy. I'm not. What should I do? She wants me to have a boyfriend." This is a typical quandary.

Many boys and girls of all ages are under pressure to have boyfriend/girlfriend relationships long before they're ready or interested. And many secretly worry, "What's wrong with me? Why don't I have those feelings?" In order to prevent being left out, many children make believe they're interested.

At the younger ages, there is more of a tendency to go out in groups. A child who isn't ready for a boyfriend or girlfriend can still spend time with friends, even if many of them are "going out" with one another. It would help to remind children of this. The worst times for the ones who aren't ready are the parties where most people are paired off and the lights are out—the not-ready kids feel awkward and left out. If those children who aren't interested in boyfriends or girlfriends could understand that they don't have to be, and if those who are could be taught to be more sensitive to those who aren't, it would benefit all children. Greater awareness among children of each other's feelings can reduce the pressure, increase the acceptance, make it easier to keep friends, and help many more boys and girls to feel better about themselves.

**"Everyone" has a boyfriend or girlfriend
and your child wants one**

A boy or girl may feel very pressured, frustrated, unattractive, and left out if all his or her friends have boyfriends or girlfriends and he or she is one of the few without a partner. A fourteen-year-old girl, experiencing this situation, told me she planned to go to school the next day and pick *anyone* she could find just to be able to say she had a boyfriend. It didn't matter who!

Rather than saying, "Oh, it's ridiculous to feel that way," or "You're silly to make having a boyfriend or girlfriend seem so important," please remember it can help your child tremendously if you acknowledge how tough it feels to be left out. While being supportive and sensitive, follow with specific information and suggestions that can help your child feel better and more in control.

Offer concrete suggestions as to how your child might more effectively get "whoever" to notice him or her. Also assure your child that not having a boyfriend doesn't decrease self-worth.

If being the only one who isn't "going with" someone weakens your child's friendships or provokes unkind remarks and teasing, you can encourage your child to express his or her feelings to those friends. Offer words and sentences whenever you sense it might be helpful. Your child could say to the friend: "It really makes me feel embarrassed and *awful* when everybody at the lunch table is talking about who they think I should like." This may also be an appropriate time to help your child figure out just how good those friendships really are.

Friends at home when no parent is

A child can feel humiliated, embarrassed, and "not cool" to have to tell friends they can't come in because the parents aren't home. That's often the reason why kids arrived in the first place!

Your son or daughter should understand fully any rules you wish followed while you're not home. He or she doesn't have to like your rules, but if you explain, your child will understand why they were established. Sentiments about rules such as these are seldom kept secret.

Suggest that your child alert friends of any regulations *before* they appear at your front door expecting to be let in. Your child might tell friends, "My parents laid down the law! From now on, I can't have more than three people over when they're not home. They really mean it, too!" When friends are turned away, they may be surprised that your son or daughter actually listened to you, but at least they won't be surprised at the rule. That goes for boyfriends or girlfriends, too.

The more you and your child explore ways to handle potentially uncomfortable situations and reactions from friends because of the house rules, the better prepared your child will be. Any friend who is truly a friend will respect the rules and not give your child a hard time.

Arming your child with ideas and suggested explanations can help him or her know what to say when and if friends appear: "Hey, don't give me such a hard time! You know how my parents feel." Or "You know my parents' rules. I don't like to have to ask you to leave anymore than you want to hear it. But you wouldn't want to break your parents' trust and I don't want to break mine. I'll call you later."

Allowing a boy in her room, or a girl in his

This can be a delicate issue. Let's be honest. The big concern is *sex!* If parents believed their children would do no more than homework, watch TV, talk, or listen to music *with* their clothes on, there would be little or no issue.

Although daughters who can't have boys in their room and sons who can't have girls in their room often feel their parents are being overprotective and old-fashioned, at least they understand why the rules are made. Children tend to feel very frustrated and resentful when parents extend this rule to include friends of the other sex as well as boyfriends and girlfriends.

If you sense that your child might be resentful of your restrictions, you might say: "It's not so easy for me to be strict about this rule since I know how you feel. But it's really not that I don't trust you. I have to deal with my own feelings. This rule makes me feel much more comfortable." The other side of this issue is a consideration of how much you trust your son or daughter's sense of propriety, self-respect, and respect for you.

Whatever you're trying to prevent from going on in the bedroom might well be happening elsewhere, if the inclination is there. Kids are usually very resourceful if they want to be. Perhaps even more important than making rules (which is every parent's right and responsibility) is the need to talk with your child—and keep talking—about facts, feelings, pressures, values, and what you consider appropriate behavior. Always emphasize how special it is to be able to share feelings so openly and feel that much closer.

With this kind of guidance, your child will be prepared to conduct himself or herself in the way you would hope, whether he or she is in the bedroom, den, basement, or backseat of a car.

Attachments to a person of the same sex

It's possible that your son or daughter will be so "attached" to a friend of the same sex that they will have little or no interest in going out with a member of the other sex.

Strong bonds between children of the same sex are very common during the growing-up years. They may want to spend all their time together and one may even get jealous if the other shows interest in anyone else.

Usually, an interest in the other sex will eventually take attention away from that same-sex friendship. Sometimes, that friendship will continue to grow stronger and extend to other children of the same sex. Your child may feel very good about these feelings or secretly be confused.

If you believe it's possible that your child has concerns about his or her involvement in any relationship, talk with him or her about those feelings.

Curfews

Many children have talked about feeling very embarrassed or angry when their curfew is earlier than their friends'. Younger children have expressed feelings of envy at older brothers' or sisters' privileges, and older children are sometimes frustrated when younger sisters or brothers are allowed to stay out nearly as late as they are. Consider carefully your children's reactions to this subject.

The decision about an age-appropriate curfew is a very personal one. Rules vary from family to family. You might find it helpful to make a general rule for regular social plans, such as spending the evening at a friend's house or going to the movies, but make situation-by-situation rules for special occasions, such as allowing your child to stay out later for a "Sweet Sixteen" or graduation party. Flexibility is a good idea, and your child will appreciate it.

If your child slams the door or argues extensively about curfew, try to talk about how this behavior makes you feel and how upset you are that he or she is having such a hard time accepting your regulations. Given the situation, you might say:

"First of all, I understand it's probably frustrating to you to have to leave the party while many of your friends are allowed to stay. But I've given your curfew some more thought and I still feel that midnight is reasonable for someone your age, considering how much activity you have the rest of the week. Besides, you and I both know how grumpy you can be when you're overtired ... and you've told me a few times how you've been falling asleep in your first period class. I know you don't like the rules I've set, but at least I hope you understand I made them because I really care about you."

Another choice, of course is to make curfew later!

The need to "check in"

While children may complain about parents who continually want to know "where are you going, with whom, what do you plan to do, when will you be home?", they may be more understanding if they realized why parents really do need to know.

Talk to your child about all the children who are listed "missing" each year, all the alcohol- and drug-related accidents, and all the exploited and abused children. Depending on your child's age, you might stress the need to "check in" at some point during the evening if plans change and he or she is not to be where you expect them to be.

One short telephone call can lessen a parent's worry. We need to remind children to anticipate what *we* worry about and to encourage them to respond accordingly. Parents should also be aware that children are entitled to the same courtesy—for example, if you know you're going to be late, call.

We also must teach our children what constitutes safe versus unsafe behavior, how they might respond to potentially dangerous situations, and how to call for help. They need to know they can count on us to be there for them if there's a problem.

Parties and privacy

Most children really get embarrassed if their parents parade in and out of the party room. Many have even expressed preferences for going to friends' homes for parties so they don't have to worry about parents' interference.

Rather than barging in, you might consider shouting, "Parent alert!! Parent alert!!" Then wait a few seconds for your child to say,

"Come on in." Children appreciate this. If you have any serious worries about what's going on, speak with your child privately first.

Before your child plans a party, and again before friends arrive, talk with your child about "house rules," appropriate versus inappropriate behavior, and how he or she might deal with friends who are not respectful of your home.

If you absolutely forbid your child to have a party when you're not home or don't want him or her to go to friends' homes when no parents are there, make that point very clear. Many older children have admitted they've avoided visiting friends' homes when parents are there. They simply keep checking to see whose parents are out before deciding where they'll go for the evening. If you don't already know how your child feels about this, ask.

An older kid often gets embarrassed when a parent calls a friend's parent to check if that parent is aware a party is being planned at his or her home. If your child is offended by that, maybe you need to be more emphatic about the rules you want obeyed. However, it's much easier for you to call another child's parent beforehand than it is for your child to show up at the party, find that no parents are home, and realize the situation is unacceptable. Talking about these possibilities with your child ahead of time can prevent uncomfortable confrontations.

Reassure your child that taking such precautions does not reflect a lack of trust but is a matter of your being realistic about what can happen when a bunch of kids get together. Even "nice kids" have been known to drink parents' liquor when the parents aren't home. That can lead to broken furniture, and worse, if kids then try to drive home.

BOYS AND GIRLS ARE "PEOPLE," TOO

A male college student once related that he was nervous taking girls out on dates because he was afraid he wouldn't know what to talk about. To make himself more comfortable, he wrote topics on a "secret" piece of paper that he kept in his pocket. He excused himself to go to the bathroom all night long just to be able to check on the next topic!

Boys and girls of all ages have admitted to being very uncomfortable and not knowing what to say or how to act around the other sex. Secret feelings of inadequacy continue to prevent girls and boys from approaching each other, simply because they fear they won't be interesting.

Let's try to remind children that all they have to do is be themselves. If they're not sure what another person's interests are, they can simply ask. As always, turning feelings into words helps. Your child can start a conversation with "I'm not even sure what you like to talk about." Then, he or she could follow with:

"Did you see [recent movie]? What did you think of it?"

"What's your favorite kind of music?"

"Are you taking French?"

"Have you seen that new TV show with [actor]?"

"What did you think of the social studies test?"

"My brother made the basketball team. Do you want to go with me to watch the next game?"

The other person may be relieved because he or she might not have known what to say, either. You and your child can create your own list of ideas.

Long periods of silence are often tough for anyone. Teach children that silence is just fine. In fact, it can be very nice. No one need feel obliged to fill in every minute with conversation. It's even all right to ask to sit without talking and just enjoy each other's company.

GETTING STARTED

Children, elementary school through college age, have expressed reluctance in trying to start a boyfriend/girlfriend relationship because of fear of embarrassment or rejection; and concern about looks, development, weight, height, clothes, popularity, or being in a different crowd. They also worry about "what everyone will think," or they simply don't know what to say.

The same step-by-step approach I suggested for starting friendships works for reaching out to find a boyfriend or girlfriend. Boys and girls can look in their classrooms, in the halls, on the school bus, at basketball games, or in the lunch room, and pick one person out who seems like he or she would be nice to get to know better.

Again, caution your child not to judge others by outer "packages." He or she can't know for sure what someone will be like just by looks, clothing, hairstyle, and so forth. (See Chapter 4 to review the specific step-by-step suggestions.)

Once a likely person is chosen, how does a kid let that person know about the interest? This, along with "how to know if someone likes you," represents a common anxiety. Notwithstanding the tactics most children employ, such as telling someone in a note, or having a friend, brother or sister "check," a direct way is simply to talk with that person. (Most children would cringe at the thought.) Or, for starters, kids can show some interest by saying "Hi," talking about anything, and generally paying more attention to that person.

A girl in the eighth grade told me, "There's a dance tomorrow after school and I want a certain boy to ask me. If he doesn't ask me by tonight, I will ask him but I'm afraid he will go and tell his friends, and all his friends will make fun of me. What shall I do?"

Walking up to someone and asking them out is often regarded as the most difficult choice. There is not only the concern about rejection, but whether the person will turn around and tell everyone in the school, "You'll never guess who asked me out!" As always, turning feelings into words can help. Worried that the boy would tell his friends, this girl could say: "It wasn't so easy for me to call you and ask you to the dance. I knew I was taking a chance and figured I'd try. I hope we can still be friends. Could you at least respect me enough not to tell anyone I asked? I'd really be embarrassed if people at school started talking about it. Thanks."

When I went to my high school reunion, I was fascinated to find out how many people had secret crushes *on each other* in elementary, junior high, and high school but never let anyone know. If they had just been a little adventurous, they might have been very surprised. Instead, they kept their feelings secret and ended up, twenty years later, saying, *"You mean I really could have gone out with you!"*

The more children anticipate concerns and talk openly about them to each other, the greater the chance their feelings will be respected. With an increase in sensitivity and respect for how hard it can be for a child to approach another, more children who are secretly "ready" will be encouraged to reach out and try to start a relationship.

Although parents don't have the power to change social situations at school or anywhere else, they can help their children analyze and put feelings into perspective. They also can reinforce social skills that might help a son or daughter approach others more confidently and comfortably. Conversations with parents about personal hygiene, appearance, clothes, and how to "reach out" and be more friendly can help children become more confident, outgoing, approachable and attractive.

OUTSIDE BEAUTY, INSIDE BEAUTY, AND THE CONFIDENCE TO TAKE CHANCES

It can also help to talk with children about the concept of "inside versus outside beauty." Many people of all ages are fooled into believing that everyone else is more physically attractive than they are: nicer clothes or hair, no braces or glasses, a nose that doesn't call attention to itself, a well-proportioned body, and so forth. Naturally, the belief is that the more attractive people will be asked out on dates, the unattractive ones left out.

Your child might be interested to know that I had a very handsome young man in one of my college classes who talked with me (one-to-one) about feelings of loneliness. He had always been very shy and didn't feel comfortable approaching anyone, even to say "Hi." He thought people were afraid to approach him because he was very good looking and they thought he wouldn't be interested in them. So, people passed him by, and he waited, lonely, secretly yearning for someone to risk starting a conversation with him, because he was too scared to try.

Children are often fooled and intimidated by other people's good looks, abilities, or socioeconomic status. If they learn early that, no matter what a person looks like, or how talented and popular he or she is, the only way to make a fair decision about *who* that person is inside is to try to get to know him or her—even if that person seems aloof and unapproachable. Plenty of secret feelings hide behind a mask of confidence or good looks. Kids have little, or nothing, to lose by taking a chance. And everything to gain.

Outside beauty doesn't guarantee social grace or know-how. Nor does it guarantee that someone will be nice through and through. Wouldn't it be wonderful if kids could learn early that, no matter what people look like, they can become more and more beautiful as you get to know them? All they need is a chance.

When your child understands that looks don't make the person, then he or she will walk tall, having a sense of pride and personal respect in *who* he or she is. Your child will gain confidence when he or she realizes that if people only like you or shy away from you because of your looks, the relationship would be superficial. People can only be themselves. And that's very special.

CHAPTER 6

PEER PRESSURE
(Drugs, Sex, Drinking, Smoking, or anything else)

G6

How do you say no to someone who said they won't be your friend if you don't try drugs,

8th

My 4 friends arnet virgins and I am. And they tease me about it. What should I do?

I Feel uncomfortable when my Friends smoke and Ask me to

@ what do girl
you do if someone
older tells you
to do something
you dont want to
do?

B 7th

Sometimes I get pressured about doing something with a girl and I dont want to.

M

How do you talk to your parents about drinking or smoking if you know they'll get you in trouble or be mad?

Boy

My friend makes me drink and smoke. He is much stonger than me and beats me up if I don't listen to him. what should I do?

It's not enough to tell our children *"Don't."* No matter how much they understand that what they're about to do is wrong, unhealthy, dangerous, and could get them in trouble with parents, school officials, or the law, their need to belong may be so powerful that they may do it anyway.

Pressure from their peers to become involved with drugs, drinking, smoking, and sexual experimentation occurs to children as early as elementary school. Fifth-graders at my programs write questions like "What do I do if my best friend offers me drugs?" Seventh- and eighth-grade girls admit they let their boyfriends push them into "going all the way" sexually. Boys of the same age wonder, "Am I supposed to want to have sex?" Sixth-graders talk about friends who pressure them to smoke. Too many kids in junior highs and middle schools drink a lot of alcohol.

If you're saying to yourself, "My child doesn't have to deal with this yet," understand that peer pressure takes many forms. If it's not drugs, sex, drinking, or smoking, maybe your son or daughter will be pressured into shoplifting. Or maybe a bunch of kids will try to get your son to race down a steep hill on his bicycle by calling him "chicken." Maybe someone your daughter wishes to have as a friend will ask her to copy answers during an exam. Or perhaps your child's popular crowd will make fun of someone in the school yard and your child won't want to go along with it. Every child will probably be tested by peers in one way or another. *Every* child will have to deal with peer pressure. It's part of growing up.

This chapter will help you prepare your child to recognize, understand, and deal with peer pressure.

TALKING WITH YOUR CHILD ABOUT PEER PRESSURE

How can we get children to trust us enough to come to us for help, advice, and support even if they: tried drugs; started smoking; let someone touch them in places that are totally inappropriate; stole something; are too drunk to get home; think they're pregnant; cheated on an exam; trampled through your neighbor's yard with ten friends to use the "forbidden shortcut"; were mean to the disabled child down the block; beat someone up after school; or chased someone home shouting racial insults like the rest of the crowd?

We've got to talk with our children honestly and directly, not in a preachy way nor out of blame, but out of tremendous concern and out of love. We *must* let our children know we're approachable, no matter what.

If we simply tell our children, "I don't ever want you to do that!", without balancing it with the acknowledgment that sometimes circumstances dictate that they will do the forbidden, we're not being realistic. Children are often swept into actions that they never anticipated, can't control, and don't know how to get out of, especially if their self-confidence is shaky and they want very much to keep the friends who pressure them.

We need to approach them with consideration, while still maintaining our sense of values and our belief in what's right or wrong. Letting our children know that *we* know how hard dealing with peer pressure can be is not meant to condone or excuse inappropriate acts with friends. Rather, such an attitude can open the door for discussion wider than a hard-line *"Don't."*

Before children learn what to say or do if friends pressure them, they've got to be able to recognize what peer pressure is. The following suggested approach can guide you in your explanation:

"I know there will be times that your friends will do something that you know is wrong but you'll find it hard to say no because you won't want to be the only one left out, or you won't want to seem like a goody-goody. Maybe you'll be afraid that if you say no, they won't accept you, or won't be your friends anymore. Or maybe you'll think they'll tease you or spread rumors around school.

"Anytime you feel pressured to do what your friends do, even if you don't want to do it but you want to belong and go along with your crowd, that's called peer pressure. Peer is another word for people who are about the same age or grade you are. Pressure is influence, a feeling you have to do something because others are doing it.

"You can also feel this when you are the only one who wants to do something, but you feel silly or dumb doing it because no one else wants to. Or, maybe all your friends are allowed to go somewhere and you're not allowed to go.

"Most kids feel peer pressure at one time or another. So do adults."

Opening the door for talks

After explaining what peer pressure is, ask your child if he or she ever felt such pressure. Let your child offer examples, and share any you remember from your own childhood. Such sharing can make you that much more "human" and more approachable to your child.

You might continue:

"If you ever find yourself in trouble because you allowed yourself to be pressured into doing something that you know I wouldn't want you to do, it would mean a great deal to me if you would trust me enough to talk about it, no matter how wrong you know you were, or how horrible the situation, how deep the trouble, or how much against what I've taught you.

"I'm not promising I won't be upset. I might even be angry. But I promise not to let my anger get in the way of listening fairly, trying to help you handle the situation and deal with your friends or boyfriend or girlfriend, and, especially, helping you to understand why you allowed yourself to be pressured, so there will be less of a chance of trouble happening again."

"Nothing you do could be worse than if you felt you couldn't come to me. Please trust that you can count on me to be there for you."

Unfortunately, no matter how often parents tell their children they can approach them "no matter what," many children will still keep their pressures secret. Secrecy is deepened especially when pressures relate to emotionally charged, troubling situations of which children know their parents won't approve. Even when the pressures concern a friend's involvements instead of their own, children may not tell their parents about their concern for fear that parents will forbid them to see that friend or think that, because the friend is doing whatever, so are they. And, of course, sometimes they are.

In order to confront any feelings and concerns that might prevent your child from coming to you, even if you have already explained that "the door will always be open for you," I suggest you open that door by saying something like the following:

"Lots of kids don't talk with their parents about how they feel or what pressures they're dealing with because they're embarrassed or scared how their parents might react. It's very normal for kids to feel that way, but I hope none of those feelings would ever prevent you from coming to me if you want my help or advice, or merely need someone to listen." (Parents can even share with a child something they kept from their own parents.)

"Can you think of anything you ever wanted to tell me but were afraid or embarrassed or too scared that you kept your feelings to yourself and never told me? I'm not asking you to tell me what it was. It's more important right now to think about what made you not be able to come to me. Is it hard to talk with me? Do you feel I listen? Is there anything I do or say that makes you uncomfortable with me? It would really help if you could be honest with me so I could learn if there is anything I can do to help us get closer with each other."

By asking such questions, you are giving your child permission to say, for example, "Mom [dad], now that you mentioned it, it really bothers me when you raise your voice and interrupt me before I even get a chance to finish." Or "I always worry that you're going to tell [someone] everything I say to you. I wish you would keep what I share private." Or "Every time I tell you something, you say, 'Oh, you shouldn't feel that way!' But I do. Sometimes I get the feeling you just don't understand."

Your invitation to your child to answer such questions presents you as an accessible, caring person whose ego doesn't need to be considered perfect, in spite of the label "mother" or "father." Your child will see that he or she needn't be pressured to be perfect, either.

By showing that you are willing to take criticism, don't pretend to know "everything," realize you may not have been sensitive to your child's feelings, and would be happy to learn from what your child has to share, you are increasing the chance for your child to approach you with secret feelings. (If what your child says shocks or upsets you, wait to respond. Give yourself a chance to react privately. Listen first.)

Helping your child turn feelings into words

Even when kids want to share with parents, they may not know what words to use and aren't sure how to get started. In order to help your child talk about feelings, pressures, and concerns that are difficult to confront, you might say:

"Sometimes kids just don't know how to get started talking with their parents. They're not sure how to say what they feel. In fact, I don't always know what to say when I want to share my feelings with you!

"If you ever find yourself wanting to talk with me but you just don't know how to get started or there are feelings holding you back, try turning your feelings into words. You might say, 'Mom, I really want to talk with you about something, but I'm afraid you're really going to get mad.' Or 'Dad, I don't know how to tell you this, because I know you're going to think that I'm doing what [friend] is doing. And I'm not. [He's] never pressured me to try it so please don't think I shouldn't spend time with [him]. It's just that I'm worried about [him] and I don't know what to do. Could we talk about it?'"

If children are embarrassed, they can start by saying, "This is really embarrassing for me to say." If they're worried that you won't trust them, they can say, "I'm really worried you won't trust me anymore if I tell you what happened." Whatever they're feeling, they can turn it into words.

By offering your son or daughter actual words to say in order to get feelings out, you will help expand and encourage his or her ability to talk with you about pressures that might ordinarily have been kept secret.

HELPING YOUR CHILD
DEAL WITH PEER PRESSURE

Factual information is essential, but not enough

Unfortunately, because children are often reluctant to talk with parents about sex, drugs, drinking, smoking, and other pressures, too many end up basing serious decisions on the often inaccurate information learned from friends. Serious decisions based on misinformation have a greater likelihood of turning into serious mistakes.

Children need correct, very specific information *prior* to when they might be exposed to certain pressures, for example: the potential effects and legal penalties for using the various types of drugs; how dangerous it can be to mix drugs and alcohol; how judgment and coordination can be impaired by drinking alcohol and using drugs; the long-term dangers of smoking; legal punishments for stealing; how sexual excitement can build and become more difficult to control; how it's possible for a female to get pregnant from having sexual intercourse *or* if a male ejaculates outside the vaginal opening, no matter what position the male or female are in or what time of month; or the possible penalties for being caught cheating. The more you talk with your child, offer important information, explanations, as well as acknowledge the many feelings that might be involved, there will be less risk that he or she will be pressured into decisions that will be unhealthy or dangerous.

But even if parents actively take responsibility to make sure their children understand essential facts, and even if children also are taught correct information in health, sex, and drug education classes at school, facts alone are not enough.

Revealing statements from children, such as, "Yeah, I knew that I could get pregnant. But I didn't want my boyfriend not to go out with me again" or "I know that I shouldn't ride home in my sister's friend's car after she had been drinking, but all my friends piled in and what was I supposed to do?", make it that clear that knowledge of facts is not enough. Many kids *know* the facts. They *know* what they're doing might be dangerous. They just aren't prepared to apply or act upon the facts as they need to.

Not only is a knowledge of facts essential, but also how the facts are used, and whether your child will be able to use that knowledge to make a safe, appropriate decision when the time comes. Those decisions are affected by your child's self-respect, self-confidence, and how strong her or his need is to "belong" and go along with the crowd.

Teaching your child how to make choices

To help children deal more effectively with inevitable pressures from peers, it's vital to teach them how to examine what their choices are, what each choice might mean, what the risks are, and what responses can be useful when pressured.

The following step-by-step approach will break down the decision-making process in a way that is simple for children to learn.

Step 1: Children must be taught they have a choice. They have a right to say yes *or* no. Although this concept might seem very obvious, it would be a mistake to take for granted that children realize it. Many were never taught they have a right to choose.

Children need to learn that while it's fair for friends to offer advice, it's not fair for those friends to expect their advice to be followed as given. Not even best friends have the right to make decisions for each other. Children are entitled to their self-respect and entitled to choose what course of action seems right for them, according to their own standards and sense of values. This respect for themselves and others needs to be taught and reinforced.

By realizing that they're entitled to make their own decisions, children will be encouraged to more actively evaluate each situation, consider the relevant facts, examine personal feelings and values, and arrive at a more reasoned, well-thought-out conclusion.

In all fairness, it's easier for parents to tell children how important it is to follow their own beliefs than it is for children to follow those beliefs. They're often confused and even pained when they feel one way and their friends are pressuring them to feel another. It's also hard for children to determine when to give in to pressure from friends and when to stand firm about their own beliefs.

Ask your child what kinds of situations are more confusing than others. Together, you can examine choices, talk about feelings and reactions from friends, all the while nurturing the attitude that it takes strength to stand up to pressure from friends. Standing up to pressure is a real test of self-confidence but it's also a very good test of the friendship.

You can also talk about priorities, the issue of when it's reasonable to consider giving in to pressure and when it's not. For example, it's not such a big deal to give in to friends who would rather have pizza than hamburgers. But whether to smoke or not because everyone else is, that's a substantial consideration. Each decision carries its own weight with regard to risks.

Step 2: Learning what the choices are. Once your child understands that he or she has a choice, help your child learn how to figure out what choices exist. This can be taught generally, with no particular situation in mind. Or, specific situations can be used as examples for you and your child to figure out choices together.

For choices *in general,* your child might

give in to the pressure and go along with what friends are doing

tell friends what they're doing is not a good idea, will get everyone into trouble, dangerous, scary, mean, etc.

tell friends they really should stop!

leave—walk away from situation

stay—and not give in to pressure

tell someone—call for help.

For choices in *specific situations,* your son or daughter can suggest an example that he or she has already experienced, or you can create one, such as, What choices would your child have if everyone at a party is drinking beer, your child doesn't want to drink, but everyone is saying, "Oh, come on...."

Your child might

give in to the pressure and have a beer

tell them "No thanks, please stop asking"

hold a glass that is tinted so everyone thinks it contains beer

leave the party

tell everyone that they're drinking too much and really should stop.

Perhaps you can add more choices of your own. The idea is to examine as many choices as you and your child can for any given situation. The more practice your child has in determining choices, the better.

Step 3: Learning the consequences of choices. Simply knowing what the choices are is not enough. Your child needs to know what each choice might mean in order that he or she can anticipate the possible results or risks. Using the party example where everyone was drinking beer except your child, you might consider the following choices and their possible consequences.

If your child gives in to peer pressure and has a beer, he or she

might not respect him/herself for giving in to such pressure

might be more accepted by those at the party

could feel sick or high from the beer

might like it. Then what?

might get into trouble because parents will find out

may not drive home safely.

If your child tries to tell friends not to drink, they may

stop and respect your child's word

think your child is a terrible goody-goody

tease and make fun of your child for trying to stop them.

If your child leaves the party, he or she

may be teased and talked about after leaving

may have great self-respect for being confident and strong about making the "right" decision

would be risking losing friendships and acceptance

won't get into any trouble for drinking

will no longer be in an uncomfortable situation

will be understood by friends.

If your child holds a tinted glass to appear to be drinking beer he/she

may be accepted and feel relieved because friends think it's beer

may be embarrassed because some friends might discover it's not beer

may feel privately ashamed to lack the confidence to simply say no.

If your child stays at the party and says "no thanks":

Friends may understand and respect the request

Friends may continue to say, "Oh, come on..."

Friends may tease and not feel your child is part of the crowd

He or she may feel proud to be strong enough not to give in

He or she won't get into trouble

Driving home will be safer.

As your child becomes more aware of how to approach, identify, and examine the consequences of each choice, he or she will have a greater chance of making decisions that are safer, more meaningful, and more appropriate.

If children realize they're going to have to be responsible for any consequences, good or bad, it can make them that much more serious about their decisions.

SAYING "NO" TO FRIENDS
WHO ARE PRESSURING

Children will feel much more comfortable if you offer them specific ways that they can say "No" to friends or anyone who is pressuring, for example:

"No."

"No thanks! If you want to, go ahead. I don't."

"See you tomorrow, I have to go home now."

"I don't think any of us should be doing this."

"It really upsets me when you try to pressure me that way. If you're really my friend, you'll leave me alone and still be my friend no matter what I choose to do."

"If you really like me as a friend, you won't ask me to use drugs, or drink, or anything like that."

"Please take me home right now."

"Please don't touch me like that. Don't touch me there."

"That makes me really uncomfortable. Please stop!"

Nonverbal responses, such as moving a hand away or putting up a hand to signal "stop," can also be very effective. If a friend has not respected your child's *"No"* response, verbal or nonverbal, you can discuss the perspective of "What kind of friendship is it?" and suggest, "Maybe it's time to look for new friends who will respect you."

Acknowledge to your child how hard it might be to say any one of these responses to a friend, especially if your child wants the friendship very badly. Most children feel awkward, embarrassed, unsure, and uncomfortable when they're in a position where they have to tell a friend, boyfriend, or girlfriend, "No."

If your son or daughter assures you that saying "No" won't be difficult, you might say, "I challenge you!" It's much easier for your child to be strong sitting comfortably with you than it would be handling the actual situation. That's why it helps to anticipate pressures and work through several ways to approach and deal with each should any arise.

Parents can also allow children to use their parent's rules as an excuse when they need help in getting out of a difficult situation. Sometimes it's easier for a child to say, "My mom won't let me," or "I have to babysit," than to confront friends directly. I don't suggest parents encourage children to make up excuses on a regular basis, but kids will appreciate having an easy out once in a while.

WHY DOES IT HAVE TO TAKE A TRAGEDY?

To further emphasize how serious certain decisions really can be, you might talk generally about the possible tragic consequences, for example:

"Why does it have to take tragedies? Why does it seem that kids need to wait until a friend gets injured or killed in a terrible drunk-driving accident? Why do kids need to wait until someone they know is rushed to the hospital because he or she has overdosed on drugs before they believe that all of this really can happen to them, too?

"Why do kids seem to have to wait until something terrible happens to people close to them before they believe how serious they must be about their decisions?

"I'm not trying to preach to you. I know you'd probably tune me out in less than a second, if I did. It's just that I really care. I'm concerned about you. I *know* the truth is that no one, not me, not your grandparents, your aunts, uncles, teachers, guidance counselor, religious leader, or any other adult, will be there to hold your hand when someone offers you drugs, or someone says, 'Come on, I can handle driving home. It's only two blocks.' Or someone wants to touch you in places that they absolutely have no business touching you. *You* are going to have to handle the pressure yourself.

"The scary part for me is that, unless you respect yourself and realize that you do have a choice, and unless you're serious about how you make that choice, you may never get another chance to make a safer decision next time. For some kids, there is no next time."

At school assemblies, I always tell children what happened to

Doug, the son of very dear friends. Doug has given me permission to share his experience with as many people as possible, especially kids, in the hope that similar tragedies will be prevented. Time and time again, children have responded to Doug's story with great emotion, and I hope they have become more aware that, if they take their choices casually or give in to pressure, they or the people who love them might regret the consequences for the rest of their lives.

Doug's story:

About three years ago, two of Doug's closest friends were killed. They lost control of their car on a winding road and smashed into a tree after partying and drinking a lot of beer.

Doug and I talked for many hours about this. There's a part of him that will probably never get over this loss. These were his closest friends. They picked each other up for school each morning and spent afternoons and weekends together. I can't imagine how terrible it must be to wake up one day and suddenly find your best friends are no longer alive.

After the accident, Doug and his friends got together and started a "driver doesn't drink" rule. That means that whoever is the driver doesn't even take a sip of alcohol. It doesn't matter if it's New Year's Eve, senior prom, or any other special occasion. The nondrinking driver is responsible for getting everyone home safely. If only Doug and his friends believed the risks involved with drinking and driving *before* the accident took place, maybe his friends would be alive today.

Doug said that, after the accident, his classmates were much more aware of how dangerous it is to drink and drive. But the kids who weren't so friendly with those two boys really didn't learn. They gradually went back to their old habits and continued to take chances. A few months after Doug's friends had died, Doug saw at a rock concert a girl from his high school who was so drunk that she actually was swaying as she walked to her car with car keys in her hand, intending to drive. Doug and his friends ran up to her, took her keys away, and someone drove her home safely. She hadn't learned. Does she have to wait until she loses her best friend to take what she's doing seriously? *Why* does it take a tragedy to make kids believe?

The point here is that children relate much more attentively and with greater concern to personal stories such as Doug's. The students in my assemblies don't know Doug, but they relate very much to the idea of having two best friends die in a way that could have been prevented. Personal stories are more powerful, more sobering than merely saying "Don't."

WHAT IF YOUR CHILD MAKES A MISTAKE?

You should keep in mind that it is hard for children to always make the right choice, especially when they're dealing with friendships, self-confidence, self-image, the tremendous need to belong, and the common belief that "it can't happen to me."

We can give our children information, nurture their self-respect, help strengthen confidence, examine choices, and think through decisions with them in order that they be more prepared. But no matter how much we teach or how much they understand, there are bound to be times when they'll make an error in judgment or give in to pressure.

If our children make a mistake, we need to let them know we love them anyway, but we also need to reprimand them appropriately, examine with them what went wrong or why they were so pressured, and help them learn how to prevent the same thing from happening again. We need to teach them that they can learn from each experience. All of us make mistakes. *No one* is perfect. If we forgive our children for not being perfect, they will learn to forgive themselves. And, as long as they take responsibility for the consequences of their actions, the chances are they won't repeat their mistake next time.

CHAPTER 7

SEXUAL FEELINGS

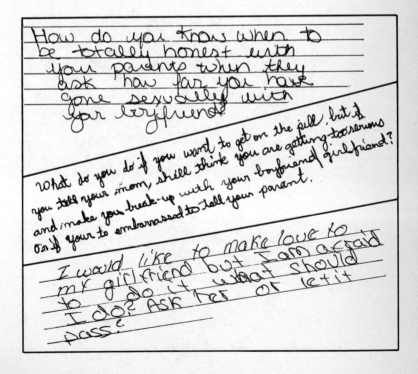

How do you know when to be totally honest with your parents when they ask how far you have gone sexually with your boyfriend?

What do you do if you want to get on the pill, but if you tell your mom, she'll think you are getting too serious and make you break-up with your boyfriend/girlfriend? Or if your to embarrassed to tell your parent.

I would like to make love to my girlfriend but I am afraid to do it. what should I do? Ask her or let it pass?

G-8

When I was 4-10 my grampa molested me. I don't want to be around him. What should I do?

★ PLEASE ANSWER ★

One night I was at my boyfriend's house and he said he wouldn't be my boyfriend anymore unless I went all the way with him. I liked him alot so I did. Now I think I'm pregnant. He dumped me when he found out. I havn't told anyone not even my parents. What should I do?

G   HELP!!!

1st grade)

"I'm afraid of talking about sex with my father because he doesn't understand how I feel. He thinks I'm too young to have these feelings and to like someone. But I'm thirteen and I don't think you have to be a certain age before you can like someone." This concern is typical of those stated by thousands of other boys and girls of varying ages.

Most children find it very difficult to talk with their father, mother, or either parent about sex. As with other sensitive subjects, inhibition is caused by feelings of embarrassment, awkwardness, or guilt, worry that parents will not understand, will be angry, or will think they're too young, and not knowing the words to get started. Many even honestly believe that their parents won't be able to relate to any sexual feelings. A "Not *my* parents!" attitude (perhaps fueled by the mistaken belief that if there are four children in the family, parents must have "done it" four times) is very common.

Personal reluctance to talk about sex is not limited to children. Parents have told me about "dreading" the moment when they'll have to answer their son's or daughter's questions about this subject. Many are embarrassed, uncomfortable, and feel inadequate about trying to explain sex. Many never talked about sexual matters with their own parents or anyone. Parents, as well as kids, don't always know what words to use. But where is it written that parents must be comfortable talking about sex?

There are no rules that say you must be comfortable, yet it would be unfortunate if your discomfort prevented you from discussing important facts and concerns about sex with your child. With children's exposures to sex occurring at earlier and earlier ages, it's important for you to take the responsibility for helping your child understand emerging sexual feelings and related sexual facts, handle sexual pressures, and recognize when he or she is being sexually exploited or abused.

Even if blushing turns you purple and you're worried that you don't have all the answers, it is essential to talk with your child about sex. This chapter will help you better anticipate, understand, and more comfortably talk about important sexual facts, feelings, and concerns that may be difficult for you or your child to express.

DIFFERENT EXPOSURES, PRESSURES, AND FEELINGS ABOUT SEX

Sex talk among friends

If your child constantly hears friends, brothers, or sisters talk about sex, sexual interests, sexual fantasies, sexual acts, sexual plans, he or she might be interested, indifferent, or seriously wondering, "What's wrong with me? Why don't I care about those things? Why don't *I* ever think about those things?"

Pressure to be like everyone else may influence your child to talk about false sexual feelings and trumped-up sexual experiences just to be part of the crowd. He or she may feel inadequate, "out of it," very frustrated, or confused, or may be pressured enough to have a sexual experience just to be able to talk about it.

One of my male college students told the class about how he was pressured into sex. The more his friends had spoken about their sexual experiences, the more frustrated and pressured he had felt. Finally, he hadn't been able to take the pressure anymore and he decided to find someone who would have sex with him. He probably didn't even know her last name—maybe not even her first! How pleasurable could the sharing have been? How intimate? How special?

How much could he have respected himself or the girl? He admitted not having any desire to share himself with her. He simply needed to be able to say that he had a sexual experience. What a shame.

Awareness of individual "readiness"

Children need to be taught that sexual feelings, like other aspects of development influenced by hormones, will emerge for each person on his or her own private maturity schedule. They may be felt earlier, later, or just about the same time as that of friends'. To help children put their feelings in perspective, explain these potential differences in development *before* sex talk among their friends begins.

Since it's very difficult to determine exactly when such feelings will emerge within your child or among friends, you might be wise to approach your child about them as early as third or fourth grade. Why so early? Because that's when many children begin to talk about boyfriends and girlfriends, sexy jokes, sexy movies, sexy magazines, sexy passages in books, and whatever else they've seen or heard about sex. If children aren't taught that it's okay to be or not to be interested in these subjects, worry and confusion about not being like others will potentially play havoc with their self-acceptance and self-esteem.

If you're thinking, "My child just isn't ready yet; why should I even bring up the subject of sexual feelings?", please consider that your child doesn't exist at school in isolation. Unless you figured out a way to insulate him or her in a hermetically sealed iron chamber since entry into elementary school, chances are he or she has at least heard about sex. Even if your son or daughter doesn't have sexual interests, it's possible that friends and classmates do.

If your child isn't ready for your advice, he or she can "file it away" for future use. Remember, children absorb only what they're ready to hear. If you've presented your concerns with sensitivity, in an age-appropriate way, your child won't be harmed by the information. It's better that your child will have "heard" from you about sex early enough so that he or she will not be faced with a sex-related conversation in the locker room or school yard that makes him or her feel pressured and confused.

Children must be taught not only that everyone is different in their development, but also that everyone must be respected for their differences. For example, it wouldn't be nice for them to make fun of someone who is very embarrassed by, or just not interested in, looking at the sexy magazine that "the group" has hidden behind the bush at the tennis court, and that such interest or lack of interest should not interfere with close friendships.

You might suggest a few comments that your child can make if pressured or teased by friends, such as: "It's really fun to listen to you, but cut out the teasing. You know I don't have any stories, so why do you keep asking me?" Or "You know I don't care about that stuff. It really bothers me when you keep trying to get me to look. Cut it out! If you care about our friendship, please stop." Or "It really bothers me when you tell everyone about my magazine. I know you don't care about this yet but I think it's great. I'm not making fun of you, so please don't go around the school talking about me. I thought we were friends."

In your discussion about differences, you should also talk about the possibility that your child may have to adjust to changing interests among friends who have been compatible for years. If friends don't respect your child, it may be very painful to start looking elsewhere for friendships. The more children understand that each person will grow and mature at his or her own rate, the more sensitive they will be towards each other.

When dealing with emerging sexual feelings, consider and discuss with your child the need to develop a sense of self-respect, propriety, and responsibility with regard to sex. Since attitudes are nurtured over time, it might be a mistake to wait too long to begin the teaching process, but it's really never too late to talk. Also, children tend to be less inhibited when they're younger. If you start talking about these sensitive topics early (naturally, in an age-appropriate way), you'll have a better chance of developing a more comfortable rapport with your child.

Sexual pressures while dating

Because boys as well as girls often don't know what to do or say to prevent that other person from touching them and going further sexually than they wish, they may allow themselves to be pressured, secretly.

A girl in the seventh grade wrote me:

PLEASE ANSWER

One night I was at my boyfriend's house, and he said he wouldn't be my boyfriend anymore unless I went all the way with him. I liked him alot, so I did. Now I think I'm pregnant. He dumped me when he found out. I haven't told anyone— not even my parents. What should I do?

HELP!!!

I wish I could say this is my only cry for help from a girl of this age. Unfortunately, it's not. Boys have also asked questions about what they should do if they think their girlfriend is pregnant! Both boys and girls have talked with me about thinking they have to respond sexually, when they aren't really ready to respond, don't know what to do anyway, and truly don't wish to.

Since children have such difficulty coming to parents about pressures and experiences that can lead to pregnancy, sexually transmitted diseases, and other unwanted risks, parents need to approach their children about these subjects even if children seem very innocent—even if they're still wearing braces.

If you're thinking, "Not *my* child!", please realize that denial won't prevent pregnancies, ease anxieties, clarify confusions, or encourage your child to come to you for help. If you won't help your child understand how to handle sexual pressures, who will? Are you willing to leave it to chance that your child will learn?

Situations that increase chances for sexual pressures

Talk to your child about how to anticipate situations which might encourage someone to try to take sexual advantage of her or him. These situations might include being home alone with a boyfriend or girlfriend, walking with someone away from a party to a more secluded area, "parking" on a deserted road or an area that is closed for the night. In order to avoid such situations, your son or daughter might say: "Please don't stop here," or "Please take me home," or "Let's not walk away from the party," or "I'd really rather not do this."

While you are discussing how to avoid someone's trying to take advantage of your child, you might find this an appropriate time to talk about rape. Your child probably doesn't realize that most girls and women who are raped know the person who raped them. The more aware you make your child of sexual risks and the kinds of situations which can increase the risks, the more prepared he or she will be to react in a safe-guarding way.

Children also need to be taught that sexual feelings may be harder to control than they expect, even when they're with a boyfriend or girlfriend whom they trust and even when there's mutual respect. Passion can be very powerful. In the "heat of the moment," the heart and body can more easily be persuaded to go ahead even if the brain says don't.

Children often get indignant about these warnings and say that it's ridiculous to think they can't deal with such a situation. They honestly may believe they can stop if they wish. But the truth is, even nice kids can feel so good touching each other that they'll lose control and won't want to stop. It can happen to anyone. Kids need to be taught, before they find themselves in this siutation, that "stopping" will have to be a personal decision not to allow oneself to go any further, even if it feels good. All children need to be prepared.

Boys and girls also need be taught about the sexual "messages" they give each other. If actions or talk are flirtatious, talk is sexy, and dress is uncommonly sexy, a boyfriend may think a girl is inviting sexual play, whether or not she is conscious of presenting herself that way. Acting as if you're offering a "green light" for sex, with no intention to "go," could potentially be a dangerous game. Messages need to be consistent with intent for boys as well as girls.

TALKING WITH YOUR CHILD ABOUT SEX

No matter what your child's age, it's not too late for you to start talking with her or him about sex. And no matter what you've already discussed, there is always room for further discussion. Most children and parents really wish they could talk with each other about sexual facts and concerns, but often those concerns remain silent.

If you've never talked about sex with your child, here's a suggested beginning:

"I know we never talked about sex before. I guess I've been waiting for you to come to me with questions. But you never came. Maybe you didn't know what to say or were afraid I'd think you were too young. Maybe you've been too embarrassed. I guess I've been a little uncomfortable, myself. But I realize it's possible you may never talk with me about sex if I keep waiting. I finally decided to approach you since there are so many important things that I want to make sure you understand. It means so much to be able to talk with you about this. Let's try..."

Naturally, how you begin will depend on the age of your child. If he or she is younger, you might start: "I know this is a very giggly subject." If your son or daughter is older, you might say: "I know we haven't talked about this for a long time, especially since you're away at school. I'm not looking to invade your privacy. But there are many facts and feelings about sex that I'll feel more comfortable knowing you understand."

If your child is resistant to your approach, remember that being comfortable with the subject is a process that takes time. In fact, your child may never be comfortable talking about sex, but that doesn't mean he or she shouldn't or won't come to you. It simply means it will probably be harder for your child to start talking about sex.

Try to be patient. Initially you can suggest that your child think about what you're saying rather than feel pressured to respond at any particular moment. By saying that you can talk later, you will give him or her some "room" to think. The less pressure to share, the better. Gentle guidance will probably go further than trying to get your child to share on demand.

Helping Your Child Talk with You About Sex

Children want and need to talk about sex, but usually don't know how. Acknowledge that you understand how hard it might be for your child to share sex-related questions and concerns with you. Offer specific suggestions as to how he or she can share more comfortably, or at least know what to say. As always, teaching them to turn feelings into words can help your child get started.

It would be wise to offer examples based on what you think your son or daughter would like to be able to say. By identifying an issue that is relevant at the moment, you have a better chance for a response. You might use the following example to show your child how to express these feelings:

If your child is confused, you might suggest he or she say, "I feel very confused when everyone in the locker room is talking about what they did or what they want to do with their girlfriends. I couldn't care less! I don't understand why I'm so different."

If your child is embarrassed, he or she might say, "Every time my friends tell a joke that's about sex, everyone laughs so hard. And I do, too. But I never understand the joke. I would 'die' if anyone ever asked me to explain what's so funny."

If your child is pressured, he or she might say, "Every time I take my girlfriend home, I get the feeling I'm supposed to make a 'move.' But I don't really want to. And I don't even think I'd know what to do."

You can only go so far. You can talk with your child about the importance of sharing information, feelings, pressures, and concerns about sex. You can even suggest words for him or her to say in order to share more comfortably with you. You can encourage sharing, "be there," anticipate needs, and refer back to your own growing-up experiences to make you that much more human (and to add some humor!), but you can't say the words for your child.

EXPLAINING SEXUAL INTERCOURSE TO YOUR CHILD

Build up to the subject slowly, with sensitivity, and by offering specific explanations in an age-appropriate way. Before explaining sexual intercourse to children, they need to have a good basic understanding of the male and female reproductive systems (see Chapter 2). They need to know what genital part connects to what and which tube leads into where, and to have a basic knowledge of the menstrual cycle, ejaculation, and fertilization.

Once children understand male and female reproductive anatomy, the description of sexual intercourse can be a logical "union" of how male sperm cells "find" female egg cells. Explaining sexual intercourse with a focus on "how babies are made" can take the edge off the potentially emotional issue of "having sex" and can get children involved in figuring out how and where the sperm would have to travel in order to try to fertilize an egg cell.

Looking at a diagram (p. 22) of the female reproductive organs with your child will make it easier for him or her to figure out that the vaginal opening is the only "path" leading toward the fallopian tubes. It will then be much less of a surprise when you explain that the semen containing sperm must be ejaculated into the vaginal opening in order to follow the path to the egg cells. It's the only way in! This logical progression of facts is often greeted with wide eyes and smiles that acknowledge how exciting it can be to be able to figure out and truly understand why sexual intercourse takes place in this way. It makes sense.

You might continue with:

"So, now you know that if a man and woman decide that they would like to try to have a baby, the man needs to ejaculate semen into the woman's vagina. To do this, the man and woman have to get very, very close to each other. They usually like to kiss and hug when they get so close. Sometimes, they might even look like they're wrestling because they might be hugging and loving each other so much that they're curled up together like a pretzel!"

(This recognition will help to allay any potential concern that mother and father are hurting each other if a child happens to "walk in" while his or her parents are engaged in love-making.)

"When they get close enough and feel like they're ready to get even closer, the man and woman move together in a way that will let the man place his penis snugly inside the woman's vagina. Since the walls or sides of the vagina are very flexible, they can stretch to allow this to happen in a comfortable way, sort of like when you put your hand in a glove and the fingers of the glove allow your fingers to move in.

"When ejaculation takes place inside, the sperm cells will start swimming on their way towards the fallopian tubes where they might fertilize an egg cell.

"It's interesting to know that even if a man and woman don't have sexual intercourse, if a man ejaculates just outside the opening of the vagina, the sperm cells still might be able to swim inside to try to fertilize an egg cell."

You might add:

"Egg cells only live for about two days each month. So, just because a man and woman would like to have a baby, and even if the man ejaculates inside a woman, it doesn't mean for sure that the egg cell will be in the fallopian tube to be fertilized. In fact, some couples have to try over a long period of time before the day when the egg and sperm finally meet up with each other."

When parents finally share this "ultimate" information with their child, they might be very surprised to find it is they, not their child, who experiences the emotional reaction. I'll never forget the first time I ever talked with my son about how babies are "made." He was seven or eight years old and I was reading a child's book about reproduction to him. First we read about flowers, then cows, then cats and dogs, and finally human beings. Right after I explained to him how humans reproduce (in very, very simple terms), my heart was pounding, and with my expectations of his reaction mounting, he closed the book and said, "Why didn't they have giraffes?"

While some children might react calmly to this information on reproduction, many others, in their own words feel this kind of sharing is *"gross"* and *"disgusting!"* They can't imagine why anyone would want to do such a thing, and they can't believe their parents could *ever* have done this (or, well, maybe those two or three times, just to have children).

If you notice an awed expression on your child's face, or even if you don't, it would probably help to say:

"I'm guessing that maybe you're having a hard time imagining that anyone would really want to do this! How do you feel about what I explained to you? Well, if you can't relate to this kind of closeness, then please try to understand it's not something you have to relate to. It's not a kid's thing to do. This kind of sexual sharing is for adults. And when you get older, I know you'll find it easier to understand why sexual intercourse can be so special.

"The reason why I explained sexual intercourse to you is because I feel you're old enough to know. And I wouldn't want anyone trying to tell you it's something it isn't.

(Depending on the age of your child, you may wish to include explanations of various methods of birth control, as well as sexually transmitted diseases and their symptoms and treatment, and the importance of notification.)

When you put all the information on sex "together," this is an ideal time to talk about your values with regard to sexual intimacy, the risks and responsibilities involved in sexual intimacy, the decision to become pregnant, teenage pregnancies, and how you feel about the importance of being married if pregnant.

Children need to learn early that sexual intercourse is not something that should be done with just anybody. Such closeness involves intimacy, mutual trust, caring, and respect. And, if a man and woman are trying to have a child, both should be ready to accept that responsibility *together*. Of course, the particulars of this type of discussion depend on the personal values that you wish to impart to your child.

Simply mentioning the word responsibility with regard to having a baby is not as meaningful to children as specifically "spelling out" responsibility by mentioning the needs and demands of a baby, such as clothing, bathing, feeding, diapering, nurturing, and of course, enough money to pay for all of these needs. It's important to remind children that while babies can be cute and fun, they require full-time, twenty-four-hour-a-day care. They can't be put away like dolls. Since the care of an infant comes first, that means there may not be time for homework, sports, parties, dancing, computers, horseback riding, swimming, "hanging out," movies, TV, or anything else.

In addition to talking about sexual intercourse in the context of having a baby, it's fair and important that children learn that parents are able to experience sexual intimacy and gain pleasure from it for all of their lives. You could mention that senior citizens also can enjoy sexual sharing. ("Yes," you might say, "that also includes grandparents!") Kids are usually amazed to realize that there is no cut-off age for sexual sharing as long as people are healthy.

Birth control

Depending on the age of your child and your religious beliefs, after you've explained sexual intercourse, you might wish to discuss methods of contraception, "ways to prevent pregnancy from happening."

If you're thinking, "How can I mention such a subject to my child?", it may help you to know that I regularly receive contraception questions from fourth-, fifth-, and sixth-grade children, such as, "What's the pill?" "What's a rubber?" "How does the pill work?" One of the most wonderful questions was, "What's a condominium?" And you know that child wasn't referring to housing!

To explain what a condom or "rubber" is, you might say that it is a sheath that fits like a glove over the penis. Instead of ejaculating semen into the vagina, the condom will "catch" the semen in the tip. If there are no sperm released in or near the vaginal opening, there is no chance for pregnancy to occur.

The diaphragm can be explained as a dish- or Frisbee-shaped

rubber device that is fitted so that it can be placed in a way to block the sperm from entering the cervix, or "neck" (entrance) of the uterus. A special "sperm-killing" cream is placed around the rim of the diaphragm as extra protection to prevent sperm from passing through towards the fallopian tubes. If the sperm can't get through or are killed because of the cream, no sperm will be able to enter an egg cell. No sperm, no pregnancy.

If you wish to offer a simple explanation of the birth control pill, you might say: "The 'pill' prevents pregnancy because the hormones or chemicals that make up the pill fool a woman's body into believing that the egg cell shouldn't be released that month (during her menstrual cycle). If no egg cell is released, there will be no egg to fertilize and pregnancy won't occur."

Obviously, these are very simple descriptions and you might wish to expand on them. You should explain to your child that these methods aren't absolutely guaranteed and that it's possible they won't work and the woman will still become pregnant. Emphasize that there are risks of pregnancy involved even when a couple tries to take measures to protect themselves against pregnancy. Some methods have higher risks than others. All methods have the best chance of working when the people using them know exactly how to use them properly. Most kids don't have enough information about contraceptives to use them properly.

Talking at length about the serious risks and responsibilities related to sexual intercourse should add to your child's respect for sexual interaction as a sharing experience that is most appropriate for mature people.

For older children, especially those in their late teens and early twenties, you will probably need to be much more specific when presenting contraception information. Even if your child resists and says, "I know that already!", you can respond by saying, "Fine . . . then please just listen and review what you already know. I'll feel much more comfortable knowing that you at least heard me."

The focus for an older child needs to be on the positive and negative aspects of all contraceptive methods that are practical, effective, and safe to consider; and on proper usage, common human failures with regard to use, the importance of *both* male and female to take responsibility for protection, and, especially, the personal feelings regarding the use of one method versus another.

After telling me about her abortion, a female college student told me, "I had a diaphragm. But my boyfriend didn't like using it, so I didn't." Even when contraceptive protection is understood, a contraceptive method may or may not be used properly because of the other person's influence, lack of confidence in the method, feeling that "it won't happen to me," or "just this once" not using a contraceptive method. The more you examine the facts of contraception and explore related feelings with your child, the greater the chance that your child will consider these issues with a healthy perspective.

Many parents have shared their concerns with me about not knowing how to respond to a college-bound daughter who wants a diaphragm or a prescription for the pill. The major questions have been, "If I take her to the doctor, does that mean I'm condoning? Am I encouraging her sexual behavior?"

I feel that we need to be honest, but realistic about our children's sexual behavior. *If* you know your child intends to be sexually active, would you want to know he or she is properly prepared and protected rather than not? If you refuse to be the one to take your daughter to the doctor, will she go to a health-care facility alone or with a friend, anyway? It's your choice. Would you rather be involved in the decision as to which method is most effective and safest to use? You can talk to your son about prophylactics, using this same approach.

You're entitled to say: "I'm really confused. Part of me wants to make sure that you're protected if you're going to be sexually active. But a big part of me doesn't want you to think that I'm agreeing with or condoning your sexual activity. I wish you'd wait. But if you're honestly planning to have sex, I'll go with you. As long as you understand how I feel."

Sexually transmitted diseases (STDs)

Your child should be informed of the risks of sexually transmitted or venereal diseases. Many children will probably recognize the initials "V.D.," even if they have no idea what they represent.

I've received questions from upper elementary school children about herpes and "V.D." For a simple explanation, you might say that these are diseases which can be passed from person to person while having sexual relations, that many of these diseases are very uncomfortable, and if they aren't treated properly, they can result in permanent damage to you.

For younger children, it's not necessary to offer a detailed description of each disease. However, if your child is already in high school or older, you need to be sure that he or she knows the risks, symptoms, and effects of sexually transmitted diseases and the need for immediate treatment, proper reporting to appropriate agencies (as well as sexual partners), and availability of treatment facilities (health-care clinics, hospitals, family physician, family planning clinics, gynecologist, urologist).

TALKING WITH YOUR CHILD
ABOUT SEXUAL ABUSE

We must be aware that sexual abuse is very real, and probably more prevalent than any of us might imagine. An elementary school principal once told me of a mother in his district who, by chance, discovered that her seven-year-old daughter had been abused. The mother and daughter were watching a television program on sexual abuse when the child turned to her mother and said, "_____ does that to me sometimes." The child was referring to her babysitter, a boy who attended the local high school. After much concern by the mother over how to handle the situation, the boy was confronted and he eventually confessed. If the TV program hadn't brought the situation out in the open, the mother may never have known.

I'm not suggesting that you never leave your child with a babysitter. Parents, siblings, relatives, and strangers are also guilty of sexually abusing children. I am suggesting that we must be aware of the reality of sexual abuse and we must find ways to educate our children of that reality and talk to them about ways to prevent it.

The mother was lucky she happened to be watching that program with her daughter. What if she hadn't? How long would the sexual abuse have continued? Would her daughter have ever known to tell? Depending on the nature of the abuse, the mother might have noticed redness, soreness, or infections in the area of her daughter's genitals. Her daughter might have acted unusually upset when the babysitter arrived to take care of her. If a child is being abused by a brother or sister, he or she might also put up a big fuss if the parents are planning to leave them alone together. Or your child may be very upset, moody, or seemingly stressed, have a lot of stomach aches, headaches, and other ailments. These symptoms don't have to mean there has been sexual abuse, but they may.

In order to help children know how to recognize and deal with sexual abuse, we must first make sure they understand what kind of touching is appropriate and what is not. They need to learn that no one has the right to touch them or kiss them in "private" areas of their body. And they have a right to tell anyone, even a parent, to *stop*— even if it's scary, or hard, for them to speak up, and even if that person, parent, or anyone, threatens not to love the child anymore or says, "You would let me touch if you really love me." If we make children more aware of the potential ways they might be bribed or manipulated, we can help reduce vulnerability to such trickery and strengthen their ability to respond.

The age of your child will probably determine how explicit you want to be in the naming of "private areas." For a very young child, you could simply identify the "private areas" as those that are covered up when wearing underwear, a bra, or a bathing suit.

You can offer verbal responses for your child to use if someone ever tries to touch them inappropriately:

"Please stop."

"Don't touch me like that."

"I don't want you to do that; it makes me uncomfortable."

"*Stop!* Please *don't*!"

"I really love you. But please don't do that to me."

Acknowledge to your child that you know how hard it might be to say "Stop" when that other person is a parent, brother, sister, relative, neighbor, babysitter, or anyone. Let your child know *you* know it's even harder for someone to resist if he or she is threatened by the person.

Your child also needs to know not to blame himself or herself for being abused. It's not their fault if someone has taken advantage of them. It's not their fault if they were scared and didn't know what else to do but let someone touch them. It's not their fault if they didn't know how to tell you before. But they can tell you now. Here are some suggestions how they can tell you:

"Mom, it's so hard to tell you this. I'm afraid you won't believe me . . . or, I'm afraid that Dad will hurt me if I tell you."

"Dad, it took me three months to get up the courage to tell you about———. Please listen to me before you say anything."

Please don't wait for a crisis before you start talking with your child about sexual abuse. The earlier he or she is armed with knowledge and an awareness of how to try to respond, the better.

If your child is ever abused or concerned about abuse, you'll be more approachable to him or her if you have already openly discussed sexual abuse and talked about how important it is to you that he or she come to you if there is even a hint of a concern. If you can reassure your child that you will listen and take what is said seriously, no matter who the person is, you'll likely be able to cut through many of the barriers that keep these feelings secret until many years after it's too late.

Children *must* be encouraged to tell—and keep telling until someone believes them—when they think they've been sexually abused. It will help to remind them of the people they might go to, such as parents, grandparents, aunts, uncles, older brothers and sisters, friends' parents, teachers, guidance counselors, principals, school nurses, school psychologists, and local family agencies.

Unfortunately, children may be so guilty, ashamed, scared, humiliated, embarrassed, and scared of the consequences of telling that they may well keep the sexual abuse secret. At least if we discuss abuse with them honestly, with sensitivity to their needs and feelings, in terms they'll understand, there is a better chance that they'll be able to recognize when they're being abused, know it's *not* natural or right, be more prepared to handle the situation, and be more confident of taking a chance to discuss it with us.

Denial won't prevent sexual abuse. Preventative education may. *Every* child must be prepared.

OTHER IMPORTANT TOPICS

Sexual fantasies

Based on the large number of college students who have expressed relief in realizing that they weren't "weird" or "perverted" because of their sexual fantasies, I suggest you discuss with your child how natural it is to have these fantasies—and how natural it is not to have them. If you never discussed sexual fantasies with your child, it's possible he or she might secretly feel guilty and confused for having them.

Children may think or dream about having some sort of sexual experience with a particular person in their class, a teacher, or even a movie or TV star, or anyone else. By helping your child understand he or she is not alone in having such types of thoughts, you can help put the fantasies in a reasonable perspective.

In talking about this topic, what you choose to share with your child in regard to "perspective" depends on your own personal comfort level and standards.

Masturbation

This is a very emotionally charged topic that most children wouldn't dream of discussing with their parents—and vice versa. Children's feelings about touching and stimulating their genital area, breasts, or any other body part that they find responsive, range from satisfaction and stimulation to terrible guilt, confusion, and embarrassment.

Children often have an inner sense that masturbation is something that should not be mentioned. Many are very curious about it and don't quite know what it is. Over the years, I have encountered college students who, upon learning about masturbation, realized they had been masturbating all along but never knew that's what they were doing.

Whatever your beliefs with regard to masturbation, you should help your child gain accurate information about it. Masturbation doesn't cause warts, hair on palms, or failing eyesight. It's not harmful unless it's done unhygienically, and unless sharp, dangerous, or inappropriate objects are used in the process. It does enable a person to learn about how their body responds sexually. It's *not* an indication that a boy is homosexually oriented—a point that would be helpful to mention since many boys tend to tease each other about masturbation and connect it with homosexuality. If the child being teased or hearing such comments has little or no correct information, he or she may believe the connection is true, which potentially could lead to further confusion, worry, and guilt.

Realize that you are teaching your child all the time. Even if you do not say anything aloud, your nonverbal messages can still indicate your attitude, such as if you respond to the revelation that your child is masturbating with stern looks and diversionary tactics, or if you move your child's hand away. That's saying a lot.

Think about what messages, if any, you have given your child with regard to your views on masturbation. Have you ever discussed the subject? If you're uncomfortable or embarrassed and would like to initiate a discussion, here's a suggested opening line: "It's really a little embarrassing to bring up this subject. But I know we haven't talked about it and there's a lot I'd like to share with you," or "It feels very strange talking about this out loud."

Masturbation can be explained as when a person touches his or her own genitals, or other sensitive areas of the body because it feels good.

Homosexuality

It's possible that you will at some time be with your child and see two men or two women behaving towards each other in a way that clearly suggests more than friendly intimacy. The common references in the media to the laws, rights, and attitudes affecting the homosexual population in this country, as well as an increasing number of movie, theater, and television presentations about homosexual relationships, family reactions toward a homosexual member, and the adjustments, acceptance, and the pain of denial of being homosexual, all make it likely that your child has feelings and questions about homosexuality.

You can help your child deal with this subject by creating the chance for your child to express his or her feelings about it and thus allow you to clarify any hidden confusions, dispel misconceptions, as well as offer your personal values and perspectives. If you have difficulty in bringing up the subject, you may wish to use an article in the newspaper, or a TV program that you can watch together as a springboard for more meaningful conversation.

Some common misconceptions include:

Homosexuality is a mental illness, a "sickness."

Someone who is "gay" chooses to be gay.

Because someone is homosexual, he or she will automatically make sexual advances to anyone of the same sex.

Because someone is gay, he or she deserves to be hated, shunned, and feared.

Because someone is gay, he or she won't any longer be able to be a good friend, a good son or daughter, a good parent, or a good citizen.

Parents are to blame if their child is gay.

A simple definition of someone who is homosexual is a man or woman who relates emotionally and sexually to a person of the same sex.

Sexual self-image

It is important to stress to your child that every *body* is different. There are adults who have told me they spent years never quite accepting their body size, and, more specifically, how their breasts or genital organs developed. These feelings significantly affected their general as well as sexual self-image.

Boys and men who feel their penis is too small might question their manliness and sexual attractiveness, and worry that a sexual partner would find them inadequate. Girls and women with smaller breasts might be concerned that they are less sexually appealing and less feminine. These feelings of unattractiveness may also exist in men who are quite short and women who are tall.

My guess is that there are plenty of adults, even those who have been married for years, who still have sex with the lights off—and not necessarily because they believe the dark atmosphere is much more romantic, but because they're afraid if their partner actually sees them nude, they'll be less attractive, a "turn off," and potentially less loved.

If we nurture self-acceptance early, children can learn to accept what they cannot change in themselves and to be sensitive to differences in others. If they can be taught that breasts or penises or height or weight or any other aspect of their outer "package" is not as important as *who* you are, then perhaps they'll feel better about themselves and be less judgmental in regard to others.

Touching

Children need to be taught that touching should not always be interpreted as a sexual "move." A hug, a kiss, or a touch to be close doesn't have to mean an entire sexual interlude may follow. Some adults have told me that they hesitate to get close to their husband or wife to say goodnight because they're afraid he or she will expect more. So they do nothing.

If children learn not to attach inappropriate "labels" and expectations to touching, they'll be able to have greater freedom to physically express themselves in various ways for various reasons.

Even with friends, a hand on the shoulder can be comforting, a pat on the back, reassuring. Touching is a nice way to say, "I care." It doesn't have to be sexual.

Abortion

This is another very personal, emotional topic, but children would certainly benefit by having you explore with them the facts, feelings, and your personal values that relate to this subject. An abortion can be defined as an operation that a woman chooses to have which removes the fertilized egg from the wall of the uterus so it won't develop any further. Children *need* to have enough information, strengthened self-confidence, and an ability to respond to sexual pressure in a safe way, so that girls would never find themselves in a position to have to make an abortion decision. Help them to prevent pregnancy in the first place!

Orgasms

Orgasms can be explained as follows:

"When people are having sex, sexual feelings gradually build up and get tinglier and tinglier. When these feelings are at their strongest, highest point of tingliness, they are usually released by having what is called an orgasm."

"Orgasms can be felt as tingly feelings of warmth, along with flutterings or short contractions in the genital area. They usually last for a few seconds."

"Both males and females are able to have orgasms. Orgasms can be different for each person. They may or may not be experienced each time a person has sex. Not everyone has orgasms."

(Note: You needn't be so "tingly"-oriented with older children. With those who are younger, it's an easier, more comfortable way of dealing with the concept of sexual stimulation and excitement.)

Naturally, you can narrow down your presentation to a basic sentence or two, depending on the age and sophistication of your child. You might mention to an older child that when people do not experience orgasms, it can be because they don't know how their body responds sexually and don't know how to tell the other person what kind of touching will be stimulating. Without adequate stimulation, they never actually reach a point where strong sexual feelings have been built up. Thus, there's no release.

You might explain to them that sometimes orgasms don't happen because there needs to be more time for the feelings to have been built up: the more time spent in sharing sexual pleasure and allowing sexual, "tingly" feelings the chance to build up, the more likely that person will have an orgasm.

Performance pressure might be lessened if your older child can realize there are no rules that state men and women *must* have an orgasm when having sex. Even without reaching the point of orgasm, people can share sexually in a pleasurable, satisfying, and very special way.

FEELING GOOD ABOUT SEXUAL INTERACTION

You have a very special opportunity to offer your child the gift of understanding sexual interaction with a perspective that is sensitive, responsible, respectful, and open to growth and discovery throughout a lifetime.

Children of all ages, even those in their late teens and early twenties, have hidden feelings, questions, and concerns about sex, sexual performance, and sexually related topics. They may worry whether or not they'll know what to do and whether they'll be "good" at "performing" sex, and they may fear what the other person will think of them as a sexual partner, especially if they don't know what they're doing. All too often, these feelings are never discussed with parents, and questions are never asked. And so the children remain uncomfortable, silently.

In order to help your child feel good about future sexual relationships, it is not enough to simply say, "It's natural. You'll know...." Rather, you could help them feel better by acknowledging how common it is to be unsure and even nervous about being intimate with someone for the first time. Children's concerns about sexual relationships can be allayed by helping them appreciate how exciting it can be to share oneself so intimately when the time is right.

Help your child understand that there isn't any "right" way to have sex. It's *not* a performance, not a contest to be graded. No one need judge anyone else. They can start out slowly, testing touches, expressing feelings, and working at the experience in a way that will enable it to grow more beautiful and special in time.

Instead of simply enjoying a sexual interaction as it progresses, many people judge themselves and their partner every step of the way. They question, "Is this good enough? Am I doing it right? What is he [she] thinking?" rather than simply allowing themselves to experience the sharing in a positive way. Tell your son or daughter that there is no rule that states, "No talking allowed during sex!" Tell them they can ask their partner if a touch is too heavy or too light. They can move their partner's hand to the left and say, "That feels so good." They can talk together and teach each other what feels good. They can even laugh. The more honest the experience, the better. And, certainly, afterwards they can discuss any feelings about what they shared.

It would also help your child's peace of mind to tell him or her that many first sexual experiences are bungling, awkward, and not as pleasurable as has been expected after all the years of anticipation. Violins may not crescendo in the background and bells may never ring. But they can ring, in their own way, in time.

Tell your child that just because someone is male doesn't mean he's *expected* to know exactly how to give pleasure to a female and doesn't mean he has to be *ready* for sex any minute the opportunity presents itself. There aren't any rules about these matters. But many people have unfair, unrealistic attitudes and expectations about roles that cause them confusion and feelings of inadequacy.

Since children often see sexual responses dramatically portrayed in movies and books, they may develop wrong standards of what constitutes a "good" or appropriate response and what doesn't. In fact, some people fake excitement during sex just because they think such a reaction is expected. Perhaps it would ease their performance pressure if children were taught that everyone responds in his or her own way: some people are more excited than others when having sex, some are quieter. There need be no universal standard. Only one's own.

Even though there are many statistics about the average frequency of sex in specific age categories, I'd rather teach children that there are no rules about what frequency is normal. It's a personal choice. If both people are satisfied with a relationship, that's all that counts. Tell your child that throughout the years ahead, he or she may prefer to hold a hand or give a kiss or just lie close to someone to feel good. There are countless ways to express intimate feelings and countless ways to share sexually. Sexual intercourse is not the only way.

Remind your children that, if they ever have any questions or secret concerns about sex, you're there to listen, be understanding and caring, and answer their questions. Tell them no question is too silly, and that you would be sad if they didn't feel they could come to you.

CHAPTER 8

COMPARISONS AND COMPETITION

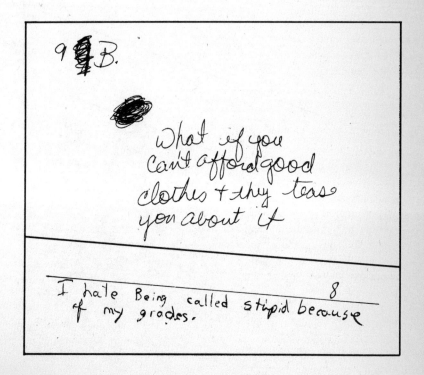

There's always a group of people who make fun of my friends the things I wear, what I do how I look And it really gets on my nerves! I don't want to make fun of them back because I'm afraid I'll lose my friendship with them. What should I do?

I always get compared to my sister "The Brain" by my teachers and parents

While it's natural for children to compare their clothes, looks, grades, athletic abilities, friends, or anything else, many children are not being prepared to put these comparisons into perspective.

All too often, the feeling among children is "better grades, better person," "better clothes, better person," "better looking, better person," and so forth. It's hard for children to feel good about themselves if they never think they "measure up" or they don't feel they "fit in."

Competition is a fact of life that can challenge, inspire, and motivate children to accomplish goals they never thought possible. But it also can cause them to withdraw, hold back, and be so scared that they won't even try to do something.

The explanations and specific perspectives offered in this chapter should help you to more effectively prepare your child to deal with day-to-day competition and comparisons with brothers, sisters, cousins, friends, classmates, or anyone.

CLOTHES

Children who place a great deal of importance on what they wear often believe that certain, often more expensive, clothes with the right labels will be their ticket to popularity. If their parents can't or won't buy them clothes that at least make them look like everyone else, they may feel embarrassed, left out, "different" in a negative way, and less attractive, and they may worry that they won't be accepted.

They may spend frantic hours the night before school trying on every outfit they own, never quite satisfied with a final choice. They might even growl and vow that it's going to be your fault if no one likes them because you wouldn't buy them the particular pair of jeans or sneakers that "everyone" is wearing. If they don't wear the popular clothes, they may worry that people will secretly whisper and make fun about them, and not include them in friendship groups.

Sometimes it works out that the popular people do include a majority who have more expensive clothes. And it may be that those popular people will initially be interested in someone because of how he or she dresses. But after a while, if that person is judged not to be "cool" or nice, or doesn't have whatever qualities that particular crowd is looking for in a member, great clothes or not, he or she might not be included.

You might ask your child if he or she feels people are popular *because* of their clothes. How long does your son or daughter think a person would stay popular if he or she is judged to be not as nice on the "inside" as he or she looks on the outside? Has your child ever passed someone by just because of what they were wearing? Has your child ever not worn something because of what a friend might think? If your child doesn't answer these questions right away, you can suggest that he or she think about them and plan to talk to you later about them.

Many kids judge others by what they're wearing and never even give them a chance to be friends. Children need to be taught that clothes or labels don't make the person. They don't become friends with a pair of jeans, they become friends with the person wearing them. They don't tell secrets to a pair of sneakers, they share secrets with the person wearing them. Whether those sneakers have holes or are brand-new will not necessarily change whether that friend will keep the secret. No matter what someone wears, he or she can be a special person, a special friend.

If your son or daughter blames being left out on old outfits, not enough changes of clothes, hand-me-downs, or the clothes you feel are appropriate, maybe it's time for your child to look for friends who will accept him or her for the unique person he or she is, not for what clothes are worn.

All children need to understand that it's not a kid's fault if parents don't have enough money to buy clothes. Kids can only do their best with what parents provide for them. They can try to be neat. And, even if the same clothes have to be worn every day, it's fair to hope the clothes and the person in them will be clean. (It's very important for parents to make sure that their child bathes or showers every day, even if the child doesn't have a physical-education class. If there is a problem that makes it difficult for your child to bathe regularly at home, such as there are not enough bathrooms for all the children in the family to take frequent turns, most schools will be very cooperative in arranging the use of the locker-room shower or nurse's office facility to help that child stay clean.) If anyone teases or judges your children unfairly for their clothes, they should be comforted by the knowledge that inside beauty is something that not everyone is wise enough to see.

It's especially hard for children who have always been able to wear new clothes to understand that some children feel lucky to be able to wait for hand-me-downs. We need to help children understand and appreciate their situation (what they have and why) as well as put into perspective others' situations. They need to learn that "beautiful" clothes don't guarantee that the person wearing them is as beautiful inside. The more children are encouraged to look inside the outer covering in order to give a person a chance, the more they'll accept others, the less judgmental they'll be about others and themselves, and the better they'll feel.

Your daughter may refuse to wear her new outfit to school a second time if "everyone" or even one person has whispered or hinted that something is "wrong" with it, such as the color is "gross," the shoes don't match the pants, or it looks awful. This reaction is not limited to girls; many boys have also expressed how uncomfortable they have felt when friends teased them about what they were wearing.

You might help your child to deal with friends' judgments by suggesting replies he or she can make to any negative reactions. Your child could say: "Thanks for telling me; I'll be sure not to lend it to you!" Or "Well, sorry you think it's gross. I *love* it!" Your child will probably not be teased anymore by the teaser if he or she doesn't seem to be rattled by the teaser's comment.

It is especially difficult for children to tell parents, relatives, or a friend that they don't like the clothing they received as a gift. Whether it's a birthday or holiday present, or something that was brought home "free" from a family-owned clothing store, children are usually afraid to hurt the gift-giver's feelings, concerned about seeming ungrateful, or guilty because of the money spent. So they wish, silently, that it could be returned.

Children also get very frustrated when their parents give them little or no opportunity for personal choice in clothes. They may feel very stifled, pigeonholed, or bored if pushed or expected to wear the same "look" all the time. They may not feel they can share these feelings with you.

As children grow and change, so do their tastes. They may try to express their changes with different kinds of appearances that may or may not be what you feel is right for them. Many parents wonder when to step back and remain silent about children's tastes and how much interference is reasonable. When many children look in the try-on mirror, they have little voices inside their heads that say, "That's not *you*! Or is it?" It's often hard for them to distinguish between what they know you want them to look like and what they really want to look like themselves.

If your child is picking clothes that are in your estimation inappropriately revealing, not in good taste, making a questionable statement about themselves, certainly you should tell them. Most children do appreciate parental guidance. In fact, those who don't get parental guidance at all might wonder how much their parents really care. But helpful guidance is one thing and telling a child what to wear, without room for discussion, is quite another.

A positive and very much appreciated approach to clothes choices would be to guide instead of "bulldoze," advise where possible instead of dictate, be strong when appropriate but be reasonable and open to compromise. With my own children, I know that if they really don't like something, they'll end up leaving it in their drawer or closet, anyway.

Another reason why it is a good idea to allow children some freedom to choose is to help them develop confidence in making their own choices, which, in turn, can help your child to develop his or her own sense of identity.

GRADES

Kids compare grades. Depending on whether their grades are higher or lower than those earned by classmates, brothers, or sisters, they may feel better or worse about themselves.

When test papers are returned or report cards distributed, there are bound to be voices all around whispering, "What did you get? What did you get?" Those who get the highest grades may be so proud and happy that they'll shout it aloud to anyone who asks. In fact, they may not wait for anyone to ask! Or someone may quickly stuff the paper in a notebook, secretly hoping that no one will find out he or she is one of the "class brains."

Those who earn lower grades may feel embarrassed, worried, frightened, or humiliated if their grade is much lower than parents and teachers expect, much lower than most classmates received, or much lower than they had hoped. They may feel even worse if their teacher reads their grades aloud. They, too, may stuff their papers in their notebooks, praying that no one will ask them what they got.

Often children mistakenly believe that their self-worth is measured by their report card. They feel: "better grades, better person," "bad grade, bad person." They think they will only be considered special and important if their grades are high. This assumption is often reinforced by parents and teachers who continually compare them to brothers and sisters or classmates, and ask why their grades aren't as high. The result of these comparisons is that they may feel they can never measure up. They're scared to bring grades home, scared to approach their parents about any concerns about school. Many protect themselves against the pressure to achieve by not even trying.

Every child is entitled to feel good, each must be encouraged to work at his or her own achievement level.

We need to teach children that the only seat in a classroom they can fill is their own. The only achievement that will be meaningful for them is their own at their own level. They can only be themselves. We need to nurture self-acceptance and work harder to let our children know *we* accept them for who they are.

A person's personality, niceness, dependability as a friend, and specialness have nothing to do with their grades and everything to do with *who* they are. The grade is *not* who they are.

All children can be encouraged to challenge themselves to raise their levels of achievement. That means that no matter what their grades, they can try to study harder, organize their notes better, spend more time getting extra help at school, and generally work to raise their grades on the next test. If a child raises his or her grade from a 70 to a 71 or a 72, hopefully he or she can feel proud of trying. The next time, perhaps the grade can be raised to a 73 or 74, and so on. Who knows how high that grade can eventually be raised! With this approach, a child, instead of being overwhelmed and disappointed every single time a test doesn't come back 100, is being encouraged to work on a gradual scale. Be aware that continued difficulty may indicate a need for evaluation of skills and perhaps new class placement.

Children need for parents and teachers to give them positive feedback, pats on the back, and encouragement. Instead of being punished for getting that 71, imagine the difference in a child's attitude if a parent would say, "I'm so proud of you. You really must have worked hard!" Instead of spending time reprimanding, your time would be better spent in helping that child with study skills and organization of notebooks, and in teaching how to balance work and play time. Instead of parents expecting a child to achieve at a high level, parents can make a child feel much more positive and much less frustrated if they deal with where their child *is* . . . and help him or her grow from there.

Even if you're not comparing your children's grades, your children might think you are

A girl in the eighth grade wrote me, "I feel pressured about my grades because my brother is always getting 100's and although my mother doesn't say anything, I know she's comparing me and I HATE that."

If you know that one of the children in your family is more talented in some area, has higher grades, or is better at sports or anything than another child, try to anticipate that the latter might feel you make comparisons, even if you try to persuade him or her you do not.

You might say, "Every time Steven gets on the honor roll, I wonder if you think I expected you to do the same. I want you to know I'm proud of Steven and I hope you are, too. But I'm also proud of you. I don't expect you to do what Steven does. And I don't expect Steven to do all the special things that you can do. I hope you don't think I'm comparing you because I'm not. I hope you're not comparing yourself. You're you and Steven is Steven."

If you're not sure how your child feels in comparison to other children in your family, *ask*. It's possible that your child is secretly pressured.

"LOOKS"

Children constantly judge each other's faces, noses, bodies, legs, pimples, hairstyles, braces, clothes, glasses, makeup, height, weight, development or lack of development, and so on. Depending on how they see themselves in comparison to everyone else, they may feel very attractive, less attractive, or very unattractive. Many walk around thinking they're so ugly that no one will ever like them—and they have a hard time liking themselves. How do you imagine your child feels about his or her looks?

If your child thinks that everyone else is better looking, he or she may feel inferior, shy, afraid to reach out, jealous, and terribly embarrassed much of the time.

Your child may be surprised to realize that there are people who are very good looking on the outside who don't feel very good about themselves inside. They may be shy and lonely in spite of their good looks, as in the case of that very handsome college student I told you about who remained secretly lonely on the inside and very handsome and envied on the outside. There's more to feeling good than looking good. Good looks without good inner feelings can leave a person feeling very empty.

We need to teach children that everyone can be beautiful. Even if they are overweight. Even if their hair is frizzy. Even if they don't like their nose. Even if they have pimples on their face. Even if they have a physical disability that is hard for others to look at. Even if children *understand* this perspective, it can be hard for them to believe. We need to help them believe it.

Many children spend years being upset about parts of themselves that they cannot control or change. Parents can help them adjust by talking with their children about their concerns, acknowledging their feelings, sympathizing with their anxieties, and offering a perspective to their conceptions.

If you encourage children to make lists of what they wish they could change about themselves, that will help identify exactly what they must work harder to accept and what they might realistically be able to change. You and your child could confront one concern at a time, and explore ways to help your child feel better about it.

For example, if children are unhappy about being overweight, they can exercise and watch their food intake (many children love to plan menus with their parents). If they're unhappy about certain aspects of their general appearance, they might be able to get contact lenses, a new hairstyle, begin to use a tasteful amount of makeup (if appropriate), or perhaps even consider a new style of clothing. Very definitely their efforts to change can make a difference in how they feel about themselves and, potentially, how others see them.

However, they can't switch their legs for new ones. They can't speed up or slow down development, they can't trade in the texture of their hair, they can't change their voice. The sooner children can distinguish between what can or cannot be changed, the sooner they will be able to work at accepting the "can't change" areas and move on to the areas where they can exert some control or change.

It can be very upsetting to know your son or daughter is hurting because he or she hasn't reached the point of being able to accept what cannot be changed. I can only suggest that you continue to offer support and remind your child about perspectives; for example, "If your friends only like you because of your height, what kind of friendship could that be?" Try to strike a delicate balance between comforting them and pushing them towards making the decision to stop agonizing in order to move on to what can be changed or controlled. You might say (in this case, about height, but you could adopt this to other concerns):

"I know you're upset, and I'm frustrated for you. If it was within my power to add five inches to your height this week, I would. But we both know that I can't. You're going to have to decide for yourself how long you'd like to continue being miserable about something you can't change. I wish things were different. But they're not. You have the power to decide to put it behind you and go on to other things."

SPORTS

Some children seem to be "natural" athletes. They love sports, thrive on competition, and are often very popular because of their athletic abilities. Much of the time, it's not a lack of interest that prevents children from signing up or trying out for sports but a feeling of being inferior to others. They may feel that even trying would be too embarrassing, too scary, or too humiliating for them. They don't want to be teased, don't want to be picked last, or don't want anyone at school whispering about how poorly they might play. So they don't even try.

This feeling of inferiority can be especially disturbing or acute to a child who has an older brother or sister who is a good athlete. That child may be concerned that everyone will compare and expect him or her to be as good. Those who are more confident and athletic will be better able to handle such pressure. Those who are less confident and less skilled athletically may shy away, secretly wishing they could play.

It's time for children to be taught that they're entitled to participate, no matter what their level of skill or ability. It's not their fault if they're less coordinated. It's also not their fault if they weren't lucky enough to have a parent, brother, or sister, or anyone to teach them the fundamentals of various sports when they were young.

If your child doesn't wish to participate in highly competitive sports, there are usually less competitive programs offered after school.

If he or she doesn't wish to become involved with team sports, there are many individual sports from which to choose. Everyone has a right to enjoy sports. Everyone has a right to try.

Physical-education teachers and coaches at school have an important opportunity, along with parents, to nurture acceptance of everybody's differences. Rather than comparing unfairly or embarrassing a child because of poor performance, teachers, coaches and parents should encourage all children to challenge themselves to raise their own level of ability.

If children are constantly compared to others, there is a risk that they'll never measure up. The only way they can fairly judge their improvement is by evaluating how far they personally have progressed. That way, no matter what anyone else does, they can be proud of their own accomplishments and development.

Sports are usually quite competitive. It's the rare coach who doesn't emphasize playing to win. Sometimes the parents are the ones who make sports more uncomfortable and competitive for their children. Therefore, it's no surprise that children feel much pressure to perform as others expect, especially when they are not as skilled.

It would help to nurture a positive support system among fellow participants like students in gym classes and players on teams. What a wonderful relief it would be for those who are struggling and nervous if other children could actually say, "Don't worry about it," if a ball is dropped—even if it's the third out. How terrific if teammates could say, "Hey, it's okay. Good try!"

All children would benefit from learning that they needn't be perfect. Those that are afraid they'll strike out, or not catch the pass, could breathe a sigh of relief if they knew they could enjoy the freedom to try without being pressured by expectations of a perfect performance.

Those who are top athletes and know that everyone expects them to achieve would also be able to breathe easier if they were reminded that even the pros make mistakes sometimes. No one is perfect. All children need to go easy on themselves and understand that some days will probably be better than others.

Some children have written to me asking what they should do about the pressure their parents are exerting on them to play or compete in a certain sport. One boy wrote, "My dad wants me to be a great horseback rider and compete. I like horseback riding but I don't want to compete. I want to make my dad happy, but I don't know what to do."

Because children want so badly to please their parents, they may find it difficult to be honest about how pressured or put upon they might feel about their parents' wishes regarding sports activities. They also may not want to hurt their parents' feelings or seem ungrateful. Often parents urge a child in a certain direction because they know he or she has a special talent. Other parents want their children to fulfill the dreams they never were able to satisfy for themselves, and so they try to live through their children and give little or no room for their children to express their own personal feelings about participation in the sport.

Think about the kinds of sports activities you encourage your child to experience. Are there any that may be a source of pressure? Are your performance expectations realistic? Fair? Do you compare one child in your family to another? Could your child only be playing because of you, not because he or she wants it for himself or herself? If you're not sure how your child feels about such activities, ask!

TRYOUTS

Some children think tryouts are fun. They get to see how everyone else does. They're confident enough to know that if they don't make it, it won't change their friendships and won't change who they are, and they'll be proud of themselves for having tried. Others shudder at the thought of testing themselves in front of judges, classmates, and friends, but try out anyway. Still others are so scared that they won't try out at all. Most kids regard tryouts as necessary, sometimes frustrating, sometimes embarrassing experiences that they would rather do without.

Those that stay away from tryouts may appear to be very relieved and yet may secretly feel sad that they didn't have the guts to try. Children need to be taught that trying out at least gives them a chance to make it. Not trying out definitely puts them out of the running. By trying, they have nothing to lose and everything to gain. They *deserve* to give themselves a chance! And, if they don't expect to win, they won't be very disappointed if they lose. In fact, they can feel proud that they got their courage up to try.

You might also suggest that it can be fun watching others try out, interesting to see what the judges are looking for, and a good learning experience that will increase their awareness of what they have to practice in order to do better next time.

Whether the tryout is for cheerleading, sports, a part in the school play, a chance to be a class officer, or anything, more than likely there will be those who are expected to win, others who have a chance, and others who would shock everyone if they made it.

Children who are among those expected to win might feel embarrassed and humiliated if they don't make it, especially if they have bragged to everyone that they would. Those who are picked may have difficulty dealing with friends who are not. Those who are picked mainly because they are a teacher's favorite or happen to be more familiar to the judge than the others trying out might feel happy but embarrassed and awkward.

Children would have a better perspective if you remind them that sometimes even the best athletes perform poorly at the tryouts. It's not fair to expect perfection. In fact, children who are expected to perform very well may be under greater pressure than those who aren't. If you talk to your child about these expectations, how they might affect concentration, and how to put them in perspective beforehand, you can help their peace of mind.

It's also possible that someone who never expected to be picked might perform brilliantly, surprising everyone, especially themselves. That's another reason why children need to be encouraged to at least try. They never know what might happen.

Talk with your child about the fact that judges are only human, which implies they're capable of making errors in judgments. They're also capable of playing favorites, picking someone they know instead of evaluating everyone fairly, or picking someone because of looks or grades.

Arming your child with the knowledge that there are variables that he or she may not be able to control, even if the actual performance goes beautifully, should ease the shock if he or she is not being picked. When children believe the judging wasn't completely fair, they find their failure to be chosen much more painful to accept.

Children often judge each other unfairly, too. Before the competition, discuss the possibility that the child who is more popular or considered better looking or more developed may get the most votes, regardless of whether that child is best qualified for that position. When this does occur, it can be very frustrating and upsetting to those who know their qualifications made them worthy of being picked. But, sometimes, that's the way life is.

Children need to understand that life isn't always fair. But they can learn from every experience. They can do their best and hope it will be appreciated and respected. If they realize that in tryouts, as in other aspects of life, there are certain things that they can't control and others that they can, then we can hope that they will be more prepared to handle disappointments. Boys and girls can try to control how much they prepare beforehand and how they try out. They can't control the judge's decisions.

FINAL THOUGHTS

Children need to learn that they can only be themselves. That is something they *can* control. They can work harder, practice longer, and dream about new goals. But, if they *don't* make a team, don't get a part in the school play, or don't raise their grades as high as their sister's or brother's, they need to understand that nothing can take away from their specialness. It is very sad to think that so many kids spend years wishing they could be like someone else who is "better." They're *not* someone else. They can never be. It's time more children understand that.

CHAPTER 9

PARENTS

> (B)
>
> My dad comes home from a long day's work, changes, watches the news, eats dinner, and watches sports or goes to friends house, then goes to bed I do great in school, sports and my social status is Ace. But I'd give it all up to do something with my dad. Unconsciously, I try to get attention but nothing works. I even ~~GOT SUSPENDED~~
>
> 98

> Sometimes I feel like my parents wouldn't care less if I live or die.

No one likes me
because of my
mother's behavior.
What should I do?

Girl 8

My dad tries to by
me instead of just
~~spend~~ speanding time
with me.
    how can I tell him
how I feal

1. How do I deal with my mom?
She is gone almost all day and
2. When she get's home from
work she is crabby.

G

I have a younger brother. My father
always seems to be loving him more.
I asked my ~~brother~~ mother if he loved
my brother more than me, she said
no but I still think he does.
    What should I Do?

G 7

How can I tell my parents
that I don't want to be juged
by my brother and sisters

This chapter will consider a variety of children's feelings and concerns about their parents that they find hard to share with them. It is my hope that you will take this opportunity to think seriously about which of these concerns might apply to you and your relationship with your child. The more you understand how your child might feel about you, the closer you will be able to be to your child.

Concerns and issues are listed below under general "feeling" categories. You may find that, in your own case, some of the concerns might seem to evoke a different feeling in your child than the one under which it is listed. Most likely, any child's "feeling" about any of these concerns will contain a variety of emotions.

Many of the listed concerns are those that cannot be changed or controlled, such as a parent's age, physical appearance, or foreign accent. While others, such as how a parent acts in front of their son's or daughter's friends, are among those that can be worked at.

As you identify which concerns might apply to your child personally, you might find it helpful to make a list of those which can be changed, those which cannot be changed, and those which you choose not to change, such as curfews or privileges with friends. Such a list will guide you in what you need to teach your child to understand

and accept, as well as what you feel is important to work at trying to change.

SECRET EMBARRASSMENTS

Children often feel embarrassed when:

Parents make them come home earlier than anyone else

Parents don't allow them to go places with friends (especially if "everyone" is going)

Parents tell their friends that their daughter got her period

Parents tell their friends about their son's or daughter's girl-friend/boyfriend, or anything private about friends

Parents try to act "cool" with the children's friends

Parents dress "weirdly" or try to look like "one of the kids"

Parents ask them to perform in front of friends or relatives

Parents brag about their grades to friends or relatives

Parents yell at them in front of the children's friends

Parents are drunk in front of friends

Parents try to talk with them about bras, boyfriends, girl-friends, physical development

Parents are unemployed

Parents are older than most friends' parents

Parents have a foreign accent

Parents have a physical characteristic that makes them look "different"

Parents tease them in public about "liking someone"

Parents forget a friend's name or call them the wrong name

Parents tease them when they get "certain" phone calls

Parents sing in front of friends (worse when they don't know the words!)

Parents make bigoted comments.

Except for issues such as wanting a later curfew, children are reluctant to tell parents how embarrassed they make them feel, because they're concerned about how parents will react and often they simply don't know how to talk about these feelings. First, they must realize it's okay to talk about these things. Then, as in any other case where children have difficulty expressing themselves, they need to be taught how to turn feelings into words.

They also need to know that, while you'll consider their feelings, this doesn't necessarily mean that you'll be able to change some restriction, such as their curfew, or a prohibition on going to the mall or hanging out at the candy store. The embarrassment should lessen as you explain that you're not "out to get them," but rather you're concerned for their well-being. They may not like your "rules," and you may or may not feel there is room for compromise. But you can help them understand and accept what you cannot change, by acknowledging their feelings, trying to be sensitive and caring about their situations, and allowing them the opportunity to air those feelings openly.

If you're not sure how your child feels, *ask*. If any of the above concerns were all too familiar to you, approach your child to clear the way for discussion. For example, with your adaptations, you might say:

"I've been thinking. I know I always kid you when we see your friends in restaurants. And I know we all laugh about it. But maybe deep down you really don't think all the kidding is funny, and maybe you don't know how to tell me that. I never meant to embarrass you, but it would be very important to me if you would tell me your feelings so I'll know not to do it next time."

If you're on target with your child's concern, you will have given your child "permission" to let you know he or she is embarrassed by it and this should pave the way for more open and honest responses about the concern, and other situations as well.

If the particular situation is something you cannot change, such as your accent, you can refer back to the "package" concept in Chapter 2 in order to remind your child about how to put judgments in perspective.

If the issue is something you may not be able to control, such as becoming unemployed due to the closing of a factory, discuss your feelings and the situation with your child. Even a small child can understand that you will make plans to try to find new employment. If you talk to your child about the disappointments and life changes you are confronting, you can help teach him or her about coping, the support family members can offer each other, and making the most of any situation. If your child can understand and learn to respect your strength in the face of adversity, then he or she will be better able to respond to comments made by friends about the situation.

SECRET FRUSTRATIONS

Children often feel very frustrated when:

Parents make dentist/doctor/haircut appointments without telling them and the appointment upsets plans

Parents invite relatives to use child's room or bed without asking or at least without advanced notice

Parent(s) remain on the telephone for a long time even though they know the child is waiting to talk with them

Parents continually tell child, "You're too young to try that," or "You'll never be able to do that..."

Parents constantly nag about cleaning room, homework, combing hair, etc.

Parents rarely allow children to try to make decisions for themselves

Parents constantly tell them to go out and find friends or to invite friends over (especially upsetting when a child doesn't have any but doesn't know how to tell parents)

Parents ask a lot of questions about who they're going to be with, where they're going, what they're going to do, when they'll be back

Parents don't recognize how badly their child needs their attention

Parents interrupt them when they try to speak or never quite hear them

Parents take sides with child's brother or sister without giving him or her a fair chance to be heard

Parents blame them for something they didn't do and deny the possibility of being unfair

Parents read the newspaper or watch TV while the child is trying to talk with them, and parent says, "I can do two things at once!"

Parents lie or simply fail to tell them something important

Parents promise to go someplace with them and then cancel at the last minute

Parents spend time with them but are so preoccupied that they're really "not there"

Parents have red eyes, are obviously upset, or have just responded, "Oh, that's terrible!" on the telephone, and when asked, "What's wrong?", they respond, "Nothing!"

Parents don't have time to spend with them, alone or at all

Parents seem to spend more time with another child in the family than with them

Parents compare them to a brother, sister, cousin, or friend

Parents are not home most of the time

Parents' friends "drop by" very frequently and take away from private time parents could have had with them

Parents don't like and often say nasty things about family members

Parents don't like children's friends

Parents eavesdrop on telephone conversations with friends, boyfriends, or girlfriends

Parents don't believe them

Parents invade their privacy (read diary, notes, look in drawers)

Parents lecture or preach instead of talk

Parents yell much of the time

Parents are overprotective (especially with children who are disabled)

Parents are out of town and babysitter doesn't know what children are allowed to do

Parents don't trust

Parents don't respond in consistent way

Parents won't give them another chance and won't forgive.

Take your time thinking through each of these concerns. Depending on the child and how intense he or she feels about the specific situation, these frustrations may also provoke sadness, anger, jealousy, confusion, and other emotions, for parents as well as children.

Which frustrations might be secretly affecting your child? You could help ease the frustration(s) by creating the chance for your child to talk about them with you.

SECRET PRESSURES

Children often feel pressured when:

Parents expect them to kiss relatives or parents' friends they don't even know or like

Parents compare one child to another (grades, musical talent, sports ability, better helper around the house) which makes the child feel he or she will never "measure up"

Parents compare children to themselves

Parents impose own interests, own dreams on children

Parents have unrealistic expectations about grades, or threaten to punish them if they're not on honor roll

Parents expect child to be a high achiever rather than appreciate what he or she is

Parents want children to physically express affection (kisses, hugs) but children don't want to

Parents want children to share "everything" and get upset when they don't

Parents abuse their child in any way and threaten them not to tell

Parents are very strict

Parents impose too hectic an after-school schedule on child (sports lessons, dancing lessons, Girl Scouts, 4-H club, etc.)

Parents want child to pursue a profession child doesn't really want to pursue but child studies in area to satisfy them

Parents expect son or daughter to go to college

Parents force child to invite "hated" son or daughter of parent's close friend to a party

Parents force children to visit relatives instead of allowing them to be with friends.

Much of the pressure children feel because of parents relates to the feeling that they must measure up to standards that often seem hopeless to reach, and fulfill expectations that seem painfully unrealistic and dreams that aren't theirs.

If you're not sure to what extent your child might feel pressured because of any of the above concerns or others that you have added on your own, please *ask;* then *talk.*

SECRET WORRIES

Children often feel especially worried when:

Parents fight and children fear divorce

Parent(s) smoke, especially if parent has been ill

Parents drink or take drugs

Parents have money problems

A parent is very ill; children fear death of that parent

A parent has to be hospitalized; children fear death

A parent loses job and children don't know whether he or

she will be able to find another one, or if there will be enough money to support the family

A parent no longer lives with them and they don't know if they'll be able to remain close

They have broken something and anticipate their parents will be furious

They are not sure it's all right to spend time with friends instead of family

They did something wrong and fear parent might find out

They think they're getting a low or failing grade and fear parents will "kill" them when they find out.

Some children may be oblivious, but most are quite aware. If there's stress, they'll sense it. Usually they'll think the worst. If children sense there's a problem but don't know what it is, they might worry about money, security, whether a loved one is very ill or has died, or if their parents will divorce.

Imaginary fears and worries can be worse than real ones. Even if an issue is upsetting to children, they will feel more secure by knowing that you will share your concerns with them if there is a family problem. That way they will not have to guess or worry needlessly. They will trust you and feel terrific that you trust them.

Some parents try to protect their child from worries. Such protection will probably do more harm than good. You owe it to your children to help them learn to cope with difficulties. It would be nice if life were problem-free, but that's just not reality.

SECRET SADNESS

Children often feel sad when:

Parents try to buy them with presents instead of spending time with them

Parents won't listen or don't understand when they try to talk to them

Parents must miss or don't feel it's important to attend an event that is special to the children

Parents seem to ignore them

Parents who live away from home don't call or write, don't remember birthdays, and don't seem to care if they see their child or not

They are living with one parent and secretly want to live with the other

Parents don't say, "I love you," or give hugs

Parents work most of the day and evening and very rarely even see their children

Parents punish them and they interpret this as not being loved

Parents don't save artwork or other presents that children made specially for them

Parents don't include children in family plans.

Children have difficulty admitting sadness to their parents for a variety of reasons. They may not feel comfortable crying in front of their parents. They may not want to take a chance that they'll lose control and get very upset while talking. They may not want to get their parents upset. And so they remain sad, silently—sometimes with a mask of happiness on the outside.

Parents also hold back when it comes to revealing sadness. They, too, may be reluctant to cry in front of their child. They may be very concerned that being honest about a situation will make their child even more upset. And yet if they would share their sadness with their children, they might find their children to be relieved, as in the case of a thirteen-year-old girl who once told me her tale of secret sadness. Her mother had been ill for four or five years and in and out of the hospital countless times. In all those years, the girl had seen her mother cry only once. Not wanting to upset her mother, the girl had always cried in her room, burying her tears in her pillow. The one time she did see her mother cry, she was so relieved. She couldn't understand why her mother wasn't crying all the time!

It would have been wonderful if the girl and her mother could have cried together, holding each other. It is very sad they felt they had to hold back. It's stressful to pretend for so long, and it can be such a relief to let feelings out. We need to teach that to our children, and show it by example.

Many parents don't realize that it would ease their son's or daughter's frustration and sadness if they would only be truthful. For example, if a parent returns from a hectic day at the office and "needs space" when he or she walks in, but is greeted by four children wanting instant attention, that parent might say: "It's so good to see you! I can't wait to hear what each of you wants to say! But my head hurts, the traffic was awful, and I just need a little bit of time to myself so I can be ready to listen. How about if we meet in about fifteen minutes and I'll be ready?"

If you say nothing and allow yourself to be pressured, and grit your teeth as you try to look interested in who said what to whom in the lunchroom, your reaction can dampen everyone's good feelings. You deserve some "space." If you're honest and ask for their understanding, you'll probably find that your kids will tiptoe and give you time to relax. But, if you don't explain how you feel, you can't blame your children for feeling hurt or less loved.

"NO MORE KISSES"

It's hard to say exactly what triggers children's pulling back from the hugs and kisses they have readily shared with their parents throughout childhood. Perhaps the resistance can be attributed to a desire to seem more grown up. Each child's reason will probably be a bit different.

Many parents have talked to me about how hurt they felt about having to think several times before trying to hug their son or daughter and then encountering a resistance when they do. It would be a sad mistake for parents to measure closeness by the number of hugs children give at bedtime. Perhaps the quickest and best way to get to the source of the change in your child's reaction is to ask. You might say:

"There are so many times that I have to hold myself back from giving you a hug like I used to. I get the feeling that you just don't want me to do that anymore. You seem tense when I try to say goodnight. Have I done anything to make your feelings change? Does it make you feel less grownup when I show you affection like that?

"I want to respect your feelings and wouldn't want to pressure you. But it's hard for me not to feel hurt when you pull away. And I think I'd feel a lot better if I could at least try to understand the change in you."

Pressuring your child for affection at a time when he or she is trying to figure out just how to "feel" like an adult may be an undesirable approach. "No more kisses and hugs" doesn't necessarily mean "no more love." If you're concerned about this and wonder what has changed, ask your child.

LESS SHARING

As children grow and change, it's very natural for them to seek out their friends for advice. It's also natural for children at some point to want to talk more with friends instead of parents about what happened in school, boyfriends, girlfriends, who did what at the party, or almost anything.

Although such redirection is usually a dramatic change from the constant, expansive "minute-by-minute" reporting to parents about what happened in elementary school, it doesn't necessarily reflect negatively on a child's relationship with parents or either's ability to communicate with each other in a meaningful way.

Such change usually has little to do with distance or how much a child loves a parent, and a lot to do with simply wanting to be involved more with friends. The change is normal. Less sharing doesn't necessarily mean less intimacy, less closeness.

When this change takes place, perhaps the most important issues are whether or not your child can and will come to you when he or she wants and needs to do so, whether or not you still feel comfortable approaching your child, and whether or not you feel close when you're together.

If you truly don't feel as close as you used to, talk about those feelings with your child. If you're not sure how your son or daughter feels about approaching you, ask. If you do feel good about your relationship with your child, it would be wonderful to let your child know.

Many children aren't sure that their parents understand why they don't want to spend as much time with them or talk with them about "everything." You might be able to ease your child's secret concerns if you mentioned how happy you are that he or she has such good friends to talk to, and that, although you would miss the "small talk," you hope he or she knows that you're there when he or she wants and needs to talk with you.

Keep in mind that there is a distinction between constant prying and reasonable questions about "how things are." The more creative you can be with your questions, the greater the chance that your child will actually respond, perhaps even at length. If your questions only require a "yes" or "no" answer, you and your child will probably have a very short conversation!

IT'S NEVER TOO LATE
TO GET CLOSER

A girl in the fifth grade came up to me after an assembly program and said, "My mother doesn't even know how much I love flowers." I said, "Tell her." She replied, "There's so much my mother doesn't know about me." I repeated, "Tell her!"

A boy in the eighth grade wrote to me: "There are many things my parents don't know about me and I would like to share with them and I don't know how to do it." A college sophomore wrote, "I want to get closer with my mother. I want to tell her that I love her but I just can't. I know she loves me a lot, but we don't relate very well. I try to talk with her, to share with her my problems and feelings, and she tries to listen, but she never really hears me. I wish she could understand me."

There's no age cutoff for wanting to get closer to a parent. Just because a child is older, doesn't mean that he or she is more comfortable with you, or readier to acknowledge inner feelings to you. Many parents are fooled into taking their son's or daughter's smiles at "face value" and never imagining there are tears on the inside.

All too often, the people we love the most seem to assume that we should "know" how they feel just by looking at them. Sometimes that is possible, but most of the time, "knowing" is guesswork. The only way we will know definitely how someone feels is when that person tells us. The only way our children will know for sure how we feel is when we tell them. If we leave to chance that they'll "sense" our pressure or sadness or frustration, they may not. As you interact with your son or daughter on a daily basis, consider the many situations that might be triggering a "secret feeling" reaction. Once you have identified a reaction, when a similar situation arises, you can anticipate the feelings that your child *might* have, initiate a discussion, and be closer to your child for your efforts.

No matter how close you already are with your child, there is always room to get closer. You can start right now. To begin, it just takes desire and a recognition that not only is it possible to work at your relationship, but it's critical.

CHAPTER 10

FAMILY RELATIONSHIPS

> I've got a sister who everyone likes and people thinks shes wonderful and you feel like your nothing. What do you do?
>
> Grade 9.   Girl

How do you tell your family that you love them?

G 8

I dont have a very good relationship with my family members, yet I wish I did but I dont know how to become closer to them.

G

I dont live with either of my natural parents. How can I feel like I belong + belong just as much as their 2 real kids

There are vast numbers of children walking around secretly feeling sad, lonely, unwanted, frustrated, and not knowing how to let their family members know they wish they could be closer to them. Because these feelings are kept hidden and parents may not have any reason to believe they exist, often it takes failing grades, truancy, fights, heavy involvement with drugs, pregnancy, running away, or attempted suicide to prove to parents that their wonderful, seemingly happy child really is yearning for attention and wanting so badly to feel loved.

Sometimes there will be no drastic measure, no inconsistency in a child's behavior, or no hint that inside hurts and feelings of distance from the family are taking their toll. Those hurts may not be acknowledged until years later or maybe never.

The way to deal with this situation is not to find blame or create guilt. Rather, there is a critical need for parents to realize that they mustn't be fooled by the outward appearance of well-being in their children or by the fact that their family does spend time together. Togetherness mustn't be confused with intimacy. You can be with someone and feel even lonelier than when you were by yourself—and many children feel this way. So do adults.

Family closeness doesn't depend on time spent together, or what parents buy their children or what they do for them. It doesn't depend on the frequency of grandparents' visits or on celebrating the holidays together. Rather, it depends on whether your child feels good about the time spent, whether your child is able to express important needs and feelings to the family, whether, you and other family members interact and respond, whether you understand your children, and whether your words and actions tell your child that he or she is accepted, respected, appreciated, and loved.

There are, of course, children who appear happy and who are absolutely happy through and through. They love their parents, get along with brothers and sisters (most of the time), and generally feel wonderful about family life. But, even when family feelings are good, family life is not issue-free. Closeness must always be worked at. Closeness will always be tested.

Children may feel good about their family, but still become frustrated at how a brother or sister acts in front of friends, feel like they'll never get over a cousin's death, or be very uncomfortable visiting a grandmother in the nursing home. They may be upset about having to babysit for their little sister or secretly worry that their favorite aunt and uncle will get a divorce. They may think they'll never measure up to their popular, athletic brother who is always high on the honor roll. There are always issues that are sensitive to confront and always areas where family feelings can be better. But first, these issues and areas need to be identified.

It is my hope that the insights and suggestions offered throughout this chapter will help you and your entire family understand each other better and get closer.

WHAT CHILDREN WISH THEIR BROTHERS AND SISTERS WOULD UNDERSTAND

The following concerns have been shared with me by children of all ages at my programs.

Children often feel frustrated, jealous, angry, upset, hurt, or embarrassed when brothers or sisters:

Show off in front of friends

Ignore them in front of friends

"Hang out" together and leave them out

Borrow clothes, supplies, or anything without asking and don't put them back

Go through drawers, read diaries, invade privacy

"Tattle-tale" to parent to try to make trouble

Don't have to do as much housework

"Hog" the dinner table conversation

Get all the attention

Are seriously ill

Are rarely blamed for what they do

Are free to be with friends while they have to babysit

Tell their secrets to friends

Listen in on telephone conversations and then tell

Smoke; use drugs; are sexually permissive

Get into trouble with police

Say embarrassing things loud enough for person on the telephone to hear

Are emotionally disturbed and act "different" in front of friends

Seem to take friends away

Have a later bedtime or later curfew

Are allowed to watch R-rated movies and they're not

Spend more time alone with parents, and/or seem to be favored

Stay on the telephone for so long that there's little or no time left for them to use it

Get to use the electronic games, pick television programs or generally get what they want

Are favored by relatives

Are better looking, more popular, better athletes, better students, better . . .

Are younger but bigger and more developed

Don't seem interested in listening to problems or sharing theirs

Never have time for them

Never include them with their friends

"Hang around" with another sibling and leave younger sister or brother out

Are mean and tease constantly

Are physically or sexually abusive.

Children sometimes have trouble sharing feelings with brothers and sisters because they are afraid the siblings will get mad, tease, hit, or won't take them seriously, or, as is usually the case, they don't know how to express what they feel. Some children have even said they didn't know how to tell their brother and/or sister how much they love them.

Brothers and sisters also need to be taught how to turn their feelings into words. For example, they could say, "It really hurts when you ignore me in front of your friends." Or "I don't like fighting. And it makes me sad when you always tease me. Can't we try to be friends?"

I don't believe parents can force close feelings to develop between their children. But they certainly can help pave the way for closeness, point out the need for sharing, set the tone for more cooperation and understanding, and encourage brothers and sisters to work at their own feelings together. Parents can also very seriously evaluate and try to correct what they might have contributed to their children's bad feelings about each other. Have they made unfair comparisons? Taken sides? Have they consistently blamed one child without listening fairly?

You might want to approach your children individually before bringing them together to suggest they try to work at their relationship. It is to be hoped that you'll get a positive reaction, but if you don't, you may have to wait until the negative sister or brother decides to cooperate. Talking to them about any resistance might help bring them together.

The time to start this kind of conversation is *not* while your children are fighting, but at a time when they're calm. It's important to have open-ended time to be able to talk about the feelings that might arise.

You might want to make it clear that you're not asking your children to be best friends, even though it would be great if they were. What you're asking is that your children try to understand each other better, get along better and be nicer to each other. Ask them if they would be willing to try.

You might suggest that they make a list of reasons why they think they don't get along or what "bugs" them about each other. A more positive approach might be to ask them what would make them feel better about each other. The more specific they can be, the better. Reading this section of this book themselves can help them realize and consider their concerns about their family relationships.

If they make a list of their concerns, you can ask them to check off what they know they can't change, such as the fact that a younger brother is taller, or a younger sister has gotten her period first. You might also mention other areas of concern they should realize can't easily be changed, such as sports ability, achievement level in school, and particular talents.

This might be a good time to remind all of your children that you're not comparing them to each other. As they learn to trust that you really don't have unfair comparisons, they will be better able to be proud of each other, and more important, better able to be themselves.

Your children may not agree with you on how to handle certain situations on the list. In the process of considering their differences, they can learn that even when people love each other, it's natural for them not to agree on every single thing. They can agree that they don't agree, try to figure out a fair solution, and actually come out smiling!

Concerns such as who gets to choose which television program or how they act in front of each other's friends are areas that certainly can be worked at. Brothers and sisters can make schedules, take turns choosing, and let each other know about hurts, frustrations, embarrassments, or any other differences. Children need to be taught how unfair it would be for them to expect any change from each other if they don't tell each other how they feel. To help initiate conversation between siblings, you might say: "[Adam], would you please tell [Steven] how it felt when he listened in to your telephone conversation and then told your friend what you said?" Adam and Steven can take the conversation from there.

Depending on the age of your children, you may not even need to be present. The more they can work out their own problems with each other, the better. All you need to be is a catalyst. You could help by reminding them not to expect "wonders" immediately. Old habits and reactions will take time to change. But if they can be kind and remind each other of how they feel, they'll begin to realize progress.

At a recent college lecture I conducted, an older woman stood up and shared with us the fact that it wasn't until the past year, when her mother had died, that she found out her brother had always felt their mother favored her. She was amazed because she had always thought she and her brother were close. They probably were, but they probably could have been much closer throughout their lives if the brother hadn't waited fifty or sixty years to admit hurt feelings or resentments. Maybe their mother never realized she was favoring! The more we can teach our children to communicate with each other early on, the closer they might be.

IF YOUR CHILDREN SHARE A ROOM

Your children could make a specific list of concerns related to sharing rooms. Children who share a room often have difficulty dealing with:

Privacy when friends visit

Privacy on the telephone

Studying when the other child wants to do something else in the room

Agreement on lights out, when one goes to bed later or gets up earlier

The stereo volume, the choice of music

Keeping belongings separate and private

Age differences.

By making lists, your children can identify areas that frustrate them and interfere with getting along, and thus try to understand each other and work at overcoming the difficulties.

As in any area of their concern, in sharing a room certain circumstances can be changed, and others must be accepted. Simply changing the arrangement of the room might ease tensions. You could suggest they be creative in placing desks, lamps, and beds to satisfy each. For example, if a desk light is facing away from the bed of a younger sister or brother, an older child may be able to work later without disturbing or keeping up the other; sisters or brothers could agree on days each would like privacy with a friend in the room; or they could set up a schedule of "study hours" and agree when the stereo can be used.

IF YOUR CHILDREN FIGHT

Some children think their brother or sister is "the greatest." They may look up to them, treat them like a little doll, or regard them as a very special companion, and hardly ever fight.

But some fighting is natural, and you shouldn't always feel you should stop it—aside from disagreements where one child is being beaten, scratched, and mauled by another. Many children have expressed to me the desire to handle sibling fights on their own. Some have even said that the fight got worse or lasted longer because their parent intervened. One teenage boy actually told me, "My sister and I used to love to fight. We were so sorry when my mom broke it up every time. We were having fun!"

Often the children will get over a fight and the parent will be sickened for the rest of the day from all the aggravation! Be kind to yourself. But, especially, be kind to them. Keep out if you can and try to let them relate to each other on their own. This way, you can still be wary of the potential for violence and be prepared to step in, separate them, and encourage them to calm down so they can deal with the problem in a positive way.

If your children get along only because you make them, they will have a very shaky basis on which to grow closer. What will happen between them when you're not there if they don't establish their own bond with each other?

If fighting is a problem in your home, encourage your children, when they aren't fighting, to talk about "fighting feelings." You might say:

"It really gets me upset when I hear you fighting with each other. Sometimes I feel like grabbing both of you and yelling *stop!* But I know it's important for you to deal with each other. ———has said [he] really hates fighting so much. And I know you feel the same way. How about if you talk with each other about why you think you fight. Maybe you can figure out a way to get along better."

You can also wait until a particular fight is over, then sit your children down and say, "———, would you please tell ——— why you got so mad?" Let them take it from there, with your guidance, if necessary. The more they discuss their feelings with each other, the better is their chance of getting closer.

How your child can express anger

It's common for children to get so angry at each other that they feel like screaming, smashing, kicking, or worse, just to let their feelings out. Unfortunately, too often those emotions are channeled into a fist directed towards a sister or brother. Rather than tell your child not to feel anger, discuss what they can do with those feelings—how to express them in a way that won't break noses, give black eyes, or leave bruises that take a long time to heal.

You can offer some suggestions, such as smashing pillows (instead of sisters or brothers), screaming "I feel like smashing you!" at least seven times, jumping up and down until you forget why you're jumping, taking a shower, scribbling as fast you can on a blank piece of paper until it's completely covered, running around the block, or shooting baskets. Ask your children if they can add to the list.

IF YOU HAVE TWINS

Both fraternal and identical twins have expressed to me strong feelings about wanting to be considered as individuals. Often they feel frustrated and pressured because people expect them to react, think, and actually "be" the same.

Their differences, such as if one twin gets higher grades, is a much better athlete, gets a driving license first, or starts dating first, can cause the competition between them to be tremendous. This competition may not stem naturally from their relationship with each other, but from how people respond to them and what they expect. Talk to your twins about those feelings in order to ease pressure and encourage them to develop individually in a way that feels good.

Twins also get frustrated when relatives and friends can't tell who is who. Most twins would like people to understand that though they may look alike, they're two different people. They may think similar thoughts but each also has his or her own thoughts, his or her own dreams.

If you also have a son or daughter in addition to the twins, anticipate that he or she may feel uncomfortable and awkward seeking out the friendship of one twin over the other. Remind your other children that each twin is a different person and talk with your other children about their feelings regarding their relationship with the twins.

Brothers or sisters of twins may feel their parents treat the twins specially and may be jealous of the relationship that exists between the twins. They may even feel that the twins love each other more than them. Talk about these feelings to all your children and help them understand that sometimes the bond between twins is just part of the magic of having been born at the same time. Tell them that the bond between twins doesn't mean the twins don't want to be close to other children in the family.

IF YOU HAVE AN ONLY CHILD

An only child might appreciate:

Being able to have private time with his or her parents

Not having to share attention or belongings with brothers or sisters

Being able to go on trips or activities with his or her parents.

Frustrations and concerns of only children usually center around loneliness, boredom, and sadness related to not having a brother or sister with whom to talk, play, and share. Talking about these feelings with your child can provide great relief for him or her.

If you have an only child who is very upset about not having a sister or brother and if a second child is an impossibility, talk with your child about this. Try to find remedies for loneliness or boredom. Your child might be happy at the thought of periodically inviting friends to spend the night. You can also talk about what your child can do, such as develop new hobbies, in order to be more creative with the times spent between school and friends.

I question whether it's healthy to schedule in every single minute for any child. No matter how many children are in a family, it's possible that each will be bored at some point. The more children are encouraged to use their own resources, the better they'll be able to be at adapting to any situation.

IF YOUR CHILD IS ADOPTED

Children who are adopted have expressed to me a variety of feelings about their families, most of which center in on how much they appreciate them. Some have expressed a desire to learn about their "roots," but of course that's a very personal matter between you and your adopted child.

The issue of concern here is whether your child might have negative or perplexing feelings about being adopted, and, if so, the importance of discussing those feelings openly. One seventh-grade boy wrote to me:

> I'm adopted. I know someone who is adopted and takes it really hard. I don't know if I'm taking it too light or if he's taking it too hard. If he's taking it too hard, how should I help him?   Signed, Confused

Depending on how much about the adoption you have discussed with your child, he or she may have unanswered questions about it. Create the chance for your child to ask questions and express feelings openly, and reinforce your love.

Unfortunately, your adopted child may encounter some kids who may not understand what a blessing an adoption can be. They may tease or comment to your child about being adopted and cause him or her to be embarrassed. That's not fair. All children, adopted or not, need to learn about the specialness of adoption for the child and the family.

AGE-DIFFERENCE RIVALRIES BETWEEN SIBLINGS

Age differences between your children may cause specific frustrations and pressures. Sometimes, no matter how parents try to respond equitably with all their children, the middle, oldest, or youngest will still say, "It's not fair!"

If you know you must spend a great deal of time with a younger child, such as assisting with bathing, dressing, or homework, you might ask your older child to help you, or say something like, "I'm sorry to have to spend so much time bathing————, but I'll be finished in about an hour. How about if we plan to have a soda together so we can catch up?"

If, for instance, a child insists that the piece of cake is always smaller, and you know that even if it or anything else were measured by computer, it would still be perceived as smaller, you might say, "What do I need to say to prove to you how special you are to me? It really hurts to know how much you're hurting. You know it has nothing to do with the cake. In fact, why don't you cut the next piece yourself? You think that everyone else is more important. And the saddest thing is that you're wrong and you won't believe it."

Try to spot areas of possible jealousies. Think about which child gets what privileges, which child has what responsibilities. Does one child have to babysit for little brothers or sisters more often? Does one child spend more time with you than another? Does one child consistently get blamed for trouble more than the others? Consider what each child in your family might feel about you and each other and talk about these feelings together.

To start your discussion, you might ask each child to make a list of what he or she likes best and what worst about being the oldest, middle, or youngest child. If they can't write yet, you can take down the lists each tells you.

Ask them to be as specific as they can so that they can better understand their own and each other's feelings.

FAMILY MEETINGS CAN HELP

You needn't wait for major changes, fights, and frustrations to knock you into the realization that your family needs to work together at its internal relationships. Every day each of us learns something new about ourselves. Every day something happens to make our children confident, unsure, scared, stronger, frustrated, confused, upset, pressured, joyous, or sad. There's always something to share, always more to know about the people we love. To start the process of more family sharing, it only takes the recognition that the family can get closer and the mutual desire to try.

A wonderful way of setting aside time to try to learn more about each other is to get together on a regular basis for a "family meeting." You can give the sharing time any name you wish. The concept of the meeting is a provision of a regular forum where everyone shares feelings and discusses individual topics which have come up or continued since the last meeting and where you can confront any specific issues that warrant attention.

You might use the meeting to share tales. You might tell your children what it was like for you growing up, or describe and show pictures of a grandfather whom your children never met. A child might tell about how he or she feels when home alone and the whole family can make suggestions as to how he or she can feel better. There are endless topics to discuss. Start with one.

Family meetings offer a chance to create a very special support system. Sharing at a family meeting may seem awkward at first, especially if this kind of interaction is new. You might encourage or increase response at the meeting by having a "sharing box" where family members can drop in questions and topics they want to bring up at the next meeting.

With young children, it might be easier to start with general questions, such as "What made you happy this week?" "Did anything make you sad?"

If your children tease each other regularly and aren't very close, it may take a while for them to get comfortable enough to chance sharing serious secret feelings. Strict ground rules about not interrupting the person who is talking, not making faces, not making fun, or not intimidating each other in any way, are usually essential. Each person should try to listen to each other without judging. And everyone must agree that whatever is said will remain private.

If you turn off the television, turn off the stereo, take the phone off the hook, close the door, and make it clear that this is your private time together, your family might be happily surprised and forever grateful to find that sincere efforts to share on everyone's part can actually help develop trust and closeness ... in time.

FAMILY STRAINS

Certain circumstances within your family can present pressures and strains that may require extraordinary measures to help an individual or the entire family cope. For instance, if someone or everyone in your family is having trouble coping with pressures and strains due to one of these occurrences within the family:

illness	failure
financial trouble	unemployment
suicide	teenage pregnancy
alcoholism	drug abuse
delinquency	child abuse or neglect

you can anticipate a tremendous need for individuals and the family to address the issue together, and perhaps seek outside help. Often, children react to these issues with a code of silence. Even if they're not told to keep the subject to themselves, they think that's what they're supposed to do. So they don't tell anyone and they cry inside each day.

Children need to be told it's okay to talk about their fears, their worries, their frustrations, their sadness. They need to know that these feelings are natural and that it wouldn't be fair or best for them to handle them alone.

If any of the above concerns exists in your home, evaluate what resources are available to you and your child. Depending on the concern, you might consider family counseling as one way of trying to learn how to cope more effectively with your family situation. Involving the whole family in the matter could take some of the pressure off the specific individual(s) who are having difficulty. The family's involvement allows an outlet for the person(s) directly affected to express concerns so that the whole family can work together at communicating more effectively and giving each other support.

You might also talk with a school administrator, school psychologist, school social worker, guidance counselor, religious leader, Alcoholics Anonymous, Alanon, Alateen, suicide prevention centers, crises hotlines, hospitals, health-care clinics, mental health clinics, drug rehabilitation centers, or any other agency or organization that seems appropriate.

You can ask the telephone operator for information on agencies, look in the telephone directory, speak with a librarian, or call your town or city administration office for a listing of pertinent local agencies or those within reasonable distance.

By letting your child know that, in addition to the family, there are places to go for help, you can encourage him or her to reach out. You might anticipate reluctance, since children may be scared and confused about going for help, or not want to acknowledge that a severe problem does exist.

One girl told me that her mother had been wanting to take her to Alateen because her father's drinking had become a severe problem. This fifth grader was very confused and didn't realize that other children with similar situations would be there to talk about feelings and how to cope.

Another girl knew her father had a drinking problem but she was afraid to let either parent know that she was aware of this. At the time we spoke, she hadn't gone to anyone for help although she had known about this problem for weeks. Parents *must* anticipate how difficult it is for children to acknowledge such concerns. That girl could have been helped if only her mother or father had known to approach her.

Explain to your child the kind of help a given organization or individual might offer in order to ease fears, which may even be unfounded. Many children shy away from reaching out for help because they consider it a sign of weakness. Explain to your child that it takes an incredible amount of strength to acknowledge that the situation is too much to handle on his or her own. The same applies to the entire family.

RELATIVES, ESPECIALLY GRANDPARENTS

Relatives can add a wonderful extra dimension to any child's life. In fact, sometimes children feel closer to a cousin than to their brother or sister, closer to an aunt than their own mother. They may tell secrets to a grandparent that they would never tell anyone else in the world.

Many children love their relatives and feel very lucky. Others wish they could trade them in. How do your children feel about relatives in your family? Do they put up a fight every time the family plans to get together with relatives? Do they stay on the telephone for hours with their friends while an elderly aunt visits downstairs? Do they call their cousins "wimps" behind their backs and feel embarrassed when they have to include them in get-togethers with their friends?

However your children feel, help them to discuss those feelings in the hope that increased understanding can lead to greater acceptance and the possibility of getting closer to their relatives.

Children need to know that it's natural for brothers and sisters in the same family to have different feelings about different relatives. One daughter might *love* an uncle that seems distant and kind of grouchy to another. A little cousin who teases everybody might seem like a pain to most, but may have a special place in your son's heart, especially if he doesn't have a little brother or sister.

Most important for your children to realize is that relatives can't be picked. Your children might smile if you remind them they can't go to a "relative store" and exchange their uncle with the smelly cigar for one that doesn't smoke. They can't trade their aunt for someone who cooks better and asks less questions, and they can't pawn their cousins for others that can play ball. What they got is what they got. That applies to sisters and brothers as well!

The sooner children start accepting their relatives for who they are instead of spending a lot of time judging them and wishing they were someone else, the sooner they'll have a chance to get closer to them. The same applies to relationships with friends, classmates, teachers, the new kid who moves down the block, or anyone.

Getting closer to grandparents

An eighth-grade girl wrote me: "I was so close to my grandmother. I could tell her anything. I am close to my grandfather but not as much. It is just harder to tell him private things. So I just don't. Some things I used to just talk to my grandmother about I just keep inside. I'm not saying I'm not close with my parents. I'm very close with them. But some things that I used to just talk to my grandma about I don't tell anyone and my feelings just get kept inside me."

Children can have a deep, special bond with grandparents that can never be replaced by anyone, including parents. Whether fishing, playing a card game, or sitting in the yard watching them plant flowers, spending time with a grandparent is a treat that children usually remember for a lifetime.

Unfortunately, not all relationships with grandparents are so positive. As much as grandparents may seem magical to many children, they're human nonetheless. They have frailties, hang-ups, and may not have time or interest for their grandchildren.

Circumstances that children have said make it difficult for them to be close to their grandparent include when a grandparent

Favors their brother or sister

Is overprotective

Speaks with a mouthful of food

Has bad breath

Has body odor

Is impatient, short tempered, and gruff

Doesn't seem interested

Is too nosey

Is very frail, ill

Is very senile and hard to relate to

Lives far away and rarely spends time with them

Lives nearby but never makes time to see them.

You could ask your child to make his or her own list about concerns relating to grandparents. Help your child to identify what can be worked at and changed, and what must be accepted.

If a grandparent is ill at home, the hospital or at a nursing home, a child may feel uncomfortable about being close emotionally with them. One boy told me, "My grandfather is very sick and is going to die soon. I'm afraid to get really close to him." Anticipate your child's uneasiness and let your child know it's natural to feel sad or anxious about visiting and natural to be scared of getting too close. The more you can talk together, the more your child will understand, the more he or she might feel comforted by not having to handle the painful secret feelings alone. Even more important, by bringing the feelings out in the open you might free your child from pressures and enable him or her to relate more honestly and get closer to that grandparent in the time that is left.

If a grandparent is living in your home, it's natural for children to wish they had some privacy with their parents, brothers, or sisters, even if they love that grandparent dearly. Your child probably has many feelings about this situation that need to be discussed.

Often, children simply don't know what to say to their grandparent in order to get closer. Here are some ideas. Children often have no idea what it was like when their grandparent was growing up. They probably know little about the schools they went to, or their favorite sports, favorite foods, first boyfriend or girlfriend, parents' dating rules, or first job, or whether they could talk to their parents about sex, dating, or anything. Your child would probably be fascinated by their grandparents' stories, and how inventions changed their lifestyle. They probably would love looking through old picture albums with their grandparent. Most children don't know anything about their great-grandparents. You might even consider taking movies or taping while grandparents tell their life stories.

Children can also talk with their grandparents about school, friends, summer vacation plans, what they think they'd like to do when they grow up, and their favorite music. Grandparents and grandchildren can take walks, go to the zoo, share a pizza, and bake together. There are endless possibilities, only limited by desire, time, and the lack of awareness of how to get closer.

Even young children can be taught to say, "Grandpa, will you take a walk with me . . . sit here with me . . . and tell me about when you were little?" And so it can begin.

If grandparents are no longer alive

You and your child may already have talked openly about a grandparent who has died. You may also have made it clear that you would be happy to answer questions, talk about that grandparent's life, or, in case they never met, tell your child everything you can about that grandparent.

Most children keep their questions about a deceased grandparent very secret. They're scared they might upset a grandmother by asking questions about a grandfather who has died, or vice versa, so they don't ask. They don't want to risk getting their parents any more upset, and so they remain silent, wondering and yearning to know more about who Grandma or Grandpa was.

Sound melodramatic? It wouldn't if you read through all the "sharing cards" that boys and girls have written at my programs over the years. Even if a grandparent died before they were born, there are children walking around with unanswered questions and deeply unsettled feelings about the grandparent they want so badly to know, and always wanting to ask but never having the courage.

If your mother or father died recently or long ago, you could help your child deal with questions about the grandparent by letting your child know it's okay to talk about "Grandma" or "Grandpa." You might take out old picture albums and perhaps even give your child a grandparent picture to "wink at" in his or her room. You can tell your child as much as you can remember about the grandparent's life and what kind of person he or she was. And you can tell yor children that you understand how hard it might be for them to talk about this but that you're really happy they're so interested and hope they'll keep asking any time.

Certain schools have "Grandparents' Day," for children to invite their grandparent(s) to school for the day. Those whose grandparents are no longer alive are likely to feel sad and left out. You might consider suggesting that they "adopt," perhaps from a nearby senior citizen center, a grandparent who would love to have their life enriched by the experience.

You can also visit a nursing home and have your child pick out someone they can visit occasionally, make pictures for, bake cookies for, and talk with about what life was like when they were growing up.

A boy in the sixth-grade wrote me, "My grandmother died in Texas. I only saw her once and never got to say I love you to her." Today, when it's common for family members to live thousands of miles away from each other, it's especially important to the well-being of all for parents and grandparents to remember the children in their life. We all seem to get so caught up with pressured schedules that time just passes. Deep down, most children really care about grandparents. They just don't always know how to show it. You might need to make special efforts to enable your children to know and be with their grandparents before it's too late. I hope this reminder will make a difference for your child.

THERE ARE NO RULES ABOUT FAMILY LOVE

Children often have difficulty accepting the makeup of their family. They compare their family to other families, label their family as "different," and spend a lot of time feeling badly about what they cannot change instead of realizing that they, too, can have feelings of being a "special" family if only they would try.

Perhaps children would be more accepting of their family situation and be more open to getting closer to family members if they understood there are no rules about family love. Whether or not all family members are directly related, they can grow to love each other and feel like they are loved. Being directly related itself doesn't guarantee family members will love each other or even get along.

All children need to understand that boys and girls who are adopted can be raised, loved, and be as close to brothers and sisters as the natural children of the parents can be. Stepfamilies might even be closer than the original family. Foster families, and even orphanages that offer loving, nurturing environments, can help create the kind of family feelings that feel good and are supportive to a child.

Children can learn that, no matter how any family relationship has been in the past, they are capable of saying, "Let's start from today. I really love you and wish we could be closer. Can't we try?"

CHAPTER 11

SEPARATION, DIVORCE, SINGLE PARENTS, STEPFAMILIES

(G) My parents are divorced and my father often puts my mother down. I get very upset but I don't know what to say. I'm afraid to say what I really feel.

How do I cope with telling my friends about my parents' divorce?

B

My Parents Are Divorced I hate the person my moms Dating what do I do

✲✲✺✪✪✪✩ ✩✩✪✩ ✩ ✩ ✩

G

my mom + dad always
have fights, and what
if they get a divorce,
I love both of them.
But if they split
up who do I go
with?

G, 6
Divorce:

How do you cope with
your dad when his
last girlfriend "drained"
the daddy out of him?

Feeling Bad!
My parents are seperated and some times I feel
left out, or not cared for. I always want to be with
both parents but I cant. How can I change it!.

I have not seen my Dad for
4 years and I dont have any
guts to call him and say "This
is your son" and to talk with
him. what should I say and
Do?

The extent to which children at my programs refer to concerns about separation, divorce, single parents, and getting along with stepfamilies is not surprising, but it is incredibly sad.

Even if their parents' divorce occurred years ago, many children sit with tears running down their cheeks when I bring up the subject. The unresolved pain they carry around with them seems unbearable and is often compounded by the fact that they aren't able to let their parents know how they feel—no matter how many times a parent might have told them it's okay to let those feelings out and no matter what your child's age.

Such reluctance is understandable. How can children comfortably tell a parent that they want to live with the other parent? How can they be expected to admit how upset they are when they don't like the person their parent is about to marry? How can they tell their parents not to put them in the middle of a situation, not to pump them for information, or how much it hurts when they forget their birthday or don't call for weeks, months, or years? They can do all of these. But it's hard for them because they're afraid their parents will be angry or hurt, and they want so badly to be loved by both. It's even harder for them because they don't know how to express what they need to say. So, most of the time, they don't say anything.

The information shared in this chapter will help you be more aware of the feelings your child might be holding back. I hope that the more you confirm what your child needs to express and wants to know, the more you will be able to help him or her adjust to difficult family changes.

If this chapter doesn't apply to your own family, please consider discussing the various concerns of this chapter with your child for the purpose of helping him or her to be more sensitive to the feelings of friends who *are* affected. Many boys and girls regularly express confusion as to what to say and how to help friends whose parents are getting divorced. You might also share this chapter with a friend who is separated, divorced, or has a new stepfamily.

CHILDREN NEED TO BE TOLD THEY'RE NOT TO BLAME

Children often feel terribly guilty about their parents' separation or divorce. They think it's their fault. They might also blame their brother or sister.

Children need to know they don't have the power to make their parents' relationship better, just like parents don't have the power to make friends for them. Parents can encourage them to find friends, even give them words to say in order to try to initiate friendships, but they can't make friends for their child. Parents also can't make someone be their child's boyfriend or girlfriend. Unless two people want to make a special relationship, it doesn't matter what anyone else says to or does for them. Each relationship has to be worked at between the two people involved. That goes for parents, too. And that's why children cannot *make* their parents have a better relationship.

If you offer children an explanation of your situation in terms that apply to their own relationships, you can help clarify why separation can't possibly be their fault. You might also add that the way parents get along has nothing to do with whether their children get on the honor roll, do the dishes every night, or babysit without a fuss for their little sister or brother.

If you only say, "Don't blame yourself," with no further comments, your child may not believe you.

WHEN A PARENT MOVES AWAY

If parents' interaction has included frequent angry battles, nasty accusations, and constant vying for a son or daughter's allegiance, a child may well feel a sense of relief when one parent moves out. But that relief probably won't be strong enough to counteract feelings of frustration, fear, sadness, loneliness, hurt, confusion, pain, and guilt, and a tremendous sense of helplessness. Sometimes there's no relief at all.

Once a parent moves out, the questions that children may have long been worrying about will become urgent concerns. Depending on which parent a child remains with, the child will probably wonder:

"What will this mean for me?"

"Is this forever or just for a little while?"

"Who will I end up living with?"

"Am I going to have to move?"

"What if I don't want to live with the parent they make me live with?"

"What if I have to choose between parents?"

"What will I tell my friends?"

"How will we afford to live?"

"When will I be able to see my other parent?"

"How will [Mommy] feel about me if I'm living with [Daddy]? Will [she] think I'm not on [her] 'side' anymore?"

"How can I stay close with the parent who moved away?"

"Why didn't my parents get along?"

"Didn't they love each other when they got married?"

"Maybe I shouldn't get married. I don't want this to happen to me."

"How can I let Mommy or Daddy know how I feel?"

A girl in the sixth grade shared this with me: "My mom and dad are separated and my mom always asks me if I have any questions about their separation. And I always do, but I can't get it out. How can I get my questions out?"

If you are in this situation, try to anticipate the possibility that merely telling your child to feel free to come to you with concerns may not be enough. You might say to your child:

"I know it's very hard and sad talking about our separation [divorce]. And you probably have a lot of worries, like 'What if I have to choose between them?' or 'Is this going to last forever?' Or maybe you're wondering, 'What will I say to my friends?' I know a lot of kids may not think they can tell a parent all the secret feelings they might have. But I want you to know that it's really okay to be honest with me. It would make me very sad to think that you're keeping upset feelings inside and dealing with them alone. Please let me try to help you."

If your child has trouble telling you about feelings, you might also suggest that he or she write the feelings down (spelling doesn't count!). Children need to understand that parents can't guess what they're feeling. The only way that parents can know for sure what children feel is if they tell them.

If your child doesn't come to you with concerns, you can pick any number of the above questions and simply begin to offer answers. Allow and encourage your child to interject responses. But if this doesn't work at first, at least you'll have provided him or her with information that most likely was greatly needed. If what you share with your children is truly not at issue for them, they will probably let you know.

Exploited or forgotten children

I wish there could be strictly enforced rules for separated or divorced parents that would protect children from being put in the middle, used as a pawn or an informer, or exploited for the purpose of getting back at the other parent.

I wish there could be a law that would force an away parent to remember that his or her children want so badly to hear from him or her. I wish these parents could know to tell their children how much they miss them and how much they want to work at staying close. I wish there were a law against forgetting a child's birthday.

Separated and divorced parents throughout the country have

talked with me about their range of feelings in this situation. In many cases it is no wonder that a parent would want to get back at their spouse, especially if the relationship has been terribly nasty. And, unfortunately, a child can be a convenient, prime weapon. But I maintain that the personal animosity between the two parents should not be allowed to involve a child. Children of separated or divorced parents have more than enough confusion and pain to handle. It's not fair to make the situation worse for them.

Rather than bad-mouthing the other parent, asking intimate questions about the other parent, buying boxes of presents to lure a child to your side, and making your child feel guilty for missing the other parent and wanting to keep in contact, it would be kinder to understand your child's need to love both of you and kinder to try harder to keep your own issues separate.

A girl in the eighth grade wrote to me: "My parents divorced when I was about two and I lived with my mother, and I used to see my father every day, then every other day, then every three days, then every weekend, and so on. But I know I haven't seen him since the fifth grade and I know he has his wife and they live far away, but he doesn't even call or send letters. It's like he doesn't know I exist. But I still love him and I can't really talk to my mother about it and I'm scared to talk to my stepdad."

A boy in the eighth grade shared with me, "My parents have been divorced for eight years and I don't get to see my father very much. The last time I saw him was over a year and half ago and I would like to see him, but don't know what to say."

Please don't be fooled by how much time has passed since your separation or divorce. Realize that children still yearn for, still need, and still love the other parent. If you don't approach your children, their feelings may be kept secret for years, forever. They may never know what to say.

SHARING YOUR SADNESS

Many children whose parents are separated or divorced have described times when they've cried in their pillows because they didn't want to upset a parent with their own sadness. Parents, as well, have talked with me about not being able to admit to their children why their eyes were red and swollen.

Even if a parent tried to conceal strain, children usually sense the strain, anyway (see chapter 9). Parents could help ease their children's concern if they would allow themselves to be more human in front of their children. Children are often relieved to see a parent cry. Crying in front of your child may be uncomfortable if you never shared so intimately before, but what are you hiding? Your child is hurting, too. So why not allow yourself and your child to comfort each other?

If you're particularly sad at a given moment, letting your child know could be a special moment for both of you. You might be wonderfully touched by extra hugs and caring attention from your child. Such sharing can bring you closer and encourage your child to be open to express his or her own feelings to you.

Adult children as well as those who are young can be devastated by divorce and have difficulty expressing feelings.

WHEN CHILDREN VISIT THE OTHER PARENT

Children's reactions to visiting the parent who has moved out can depend on such factors as:

Frequency of the visits

Parents' sensitivity to child's feelings

Relationships of parents and whether child is pitted by one parent against the other

Differing values and privileges

"Quality time" spent during visit

Whether parent spends more time with new girlfriend or boy-friend than with them

Liking or disliking parent's new friend or spouse

Brother's or sister's attitude toward the situation.

Each child in the family will probably adjust to the situation differently. Some children vow that they "hate" the parent who moved out and refuse to visit them—a reaction which creates a strain for the child who wants to go. Deep down, the children who "hate" an away parent probably are confused as to whether they should love or hate that parent. What they may hate is the whole situation, and what they may want is to be able to love.

Try to anticipate and discuss with children any differences between your own lifestyle and that of the other parent that might evoke confusions, frustrations, and a sense of competition between you and the other parent. Getting these feelings out in the open and putting the differences in fair perspective can help make your child more comfortable with both parents.

Also, try to anticipate the confusion, strain, and guilt your child might feel if he or she is pressured by a brother or sister to avoid the parent that moved away, or to show interest if he or she is the one who is avoiding the parent. You might ease the pressure and increase the understanding by talking about these feelings with each child individually, as well as getting your children together for a discussion.

WHEN CHILDREN HAVE TO MAKE A CHOICE

Children have shared with me their confused, sad, and wrenching feelings about having to choose whether to live with their mother or father. One of the more upsetting aspects of this choice is that, even when they seem to be told by both parents that the decision is truly their free choice, the choice is so very difficult because they don't want one parent to think they love the other more.

Parents could help their children deal with this monumental decision by being extremely sensitive to what children may want to say but can't. Parents might say:

"I know this is really hard for you. You probably think that the parent you don't choose will be angry or hurt or think you love them less. The whole situation hurts. But we truly want you to choose where you think you'll be most comfortable. Besides us, there are friends to think about, moving, who can take better care of you, who has more time, and so forth."

I don't pretend for a moment that simply reaching out with sensitive statements will diffuse or eliminate the pressure, sadness, and potential trauma involved in this decision for any child. But perhaps such understanding from one or both parents will at least make it easier for each child to decide and to live with the parent of his or her choice.

Some children have even told me that one of their parents has said, "Go live with your father [mother], if you want to." And they really wanted to, but they couldn't admit those feelings for fear of hurting or lessening the love from that parent.

Giving your child what you think is a *totally free* choice may seem "free" on the surface but may be absolutely shackling to the child. Talking about those feelings with your child can help uncover both your and your child's true wishes.

In situations where children are given no choice as to which parent to live with, such as when one parent walks out and absolutely doesn't want custody, it may be excruciating for the children to realize that parent doesn't want to be with them anymore. Rather than walking away in anger or disappearing without warning, parents could help their children deal much better with the situation if they would at least hold their children for a few private minutes, let them know they still love them, and explain that their leaving has much less to do with them and much more to do with wanting to get away, "do their own thing," or whatever. If this can't be said in person, then perhaps the parent can do it by leaving a note.

Of course, there are some people who never really wanted to be parents. No notes, no hugs, and no sensitive words from the parent who feels that way and leaves may serve as indications that will help children understand this terrible truth. If the parent who remains there for those children could just hold them and tell them it's okay to cry and acknowledge that life just isn't fair sometimes, at least the children could take comfort in not being left totally alone.

BEING A SINGLE PARENT

Children need to understand that adjustment to any change may take time. They need to realize that each parent and each child will react differently. No matter how much fighting or ugliness there has been, or how much both parents want to separate, both parents also can feel great sadness. For many, ending a relationship is a painful, significant loss. Everything around the home and every activity that was once shared will be a reminder of the loss.

Talk with your child about the process of this change, about how your being without the other after so many years of being together is probably going to feel strange, and about how you might be sad once in a while and maybe a lot in the beginning.

While parents must adjust to being single, children must get used to the idea of having a single parent. They may not be able to talk to you about how awkward they feel about knowing that only one parent will attend "Back To School Night." They may not let you know how they fear being embarrassed by their friends' noticing that only one parent is present at their ball game or school concert. They may not know how to talk about the change with their friends, and they may be concerned about reactions from friends once they find out.

A young girl said to me, "I live with my father. I'm embarrassed to ask him about a bra." Depending on whether your child is the same sex as you, he or she may be more or less reluctant to ask questions and discuss feelings about intimate personal issues such as wet dreams, getting a period, bras, deodorant, and so forth. (See chapter 2 for ways to approach these subjects.)

The sudden switch from living with both parents to living with one will be an adjustment for any child, even if he or she recognizes the change is a blessing. Talk about these feelings with your children to help them understand their reactions to the changes and to help them with the adjustment process.

IF A PARENT STARTS DATING

When a parent starts dating, children may find the situation difficult to accept or adjust to. Seeing that parent with someone else "hits them" with the reality that their parents are no longer partners. They may feel a combination of resentment, anger, sadness, disbelief, and helplessness at this new situation. They may be jealous that this new person is taking away from private time they would have had with their parent. Their feelings may even prevent them from being civil or nice to the parent or the person the parent is dating.

If your children are responding to you or your date in a very negative way, it might help to talk with them about their feelings.

To be fair, tell them that they don't have to like the person you date, even though it would be nice if they did. But ask them to be respectful. You might add that you realize it's hard for them to give that person a chance if they are hurt to see you go out, but if they did give that person a chance, they might even find that he or she is not so bad after all.

Some children are very happy to see their parents dating. They realize how difficult life has been for them, especially if there has been fighting and long-term bad feelings. Other children might pressure a parent to date even before the parent is ready, especially if the other parent has already started dating. Remind children that each parent is different and has his or her own readiness for dating, just as each child is different and is ready to have a boyfriend or girlfriend at his or her own time, regardless of whether friends have boyfriends or girlfriends.

If your date spends the night at your home, you can expect strong reactions from your children. Some parents try to sneak a date in after their children are asleep and have that person leave before they get up in the morning. Some get away with their efforts, some don't. Many parents simply do what they want and need to do, and hope their children will accept and understand.

Children might relate better to a parent's desire to spend the night with someone if the situation is explained on a basis which they can identify with. For example, you might point out that children often like to invite friends to sleep over so they can spend extra time together and get to know each other in a closer way. A parent might refer to their own experience as a "grown-up sleepover."

A parent might also consider the issue of what bringing different partners home on a frequent basis will do to a child. What does a parent imagine the child will be taught by such behavior? What values must be explained or reinforced?

If you're dating someone on an intimate basis, you should talk to your children about their feelings and questions regarding what this intimacy might mean to them.

Many children have expressed resentment at being disciplined by a parent's date or even by the person a parent intends to marry. Some have told me, "He's not my father. . . . He doesn't have the right to tell me what to do." Ask your children how they feel about this subject.

WHEN A PARENT REMARRIES

While many children feel good about the person a parent marries and are very happy for the parent, others resent and dislike the parent's new spouse. Most often, children keep their negative feelings secret.

Some of the reasons given by children for their difficulty, at least initially, in accepting and feeling good about the new marriage situation include:

"———is mean, doesn't care about me"

"———says bad things about my dad [mom]"

"———doesn't want to get to know me"

"———tries to boss me around"

"I don't want to move"

"My mom [dad] can't spend as much time alone with me"

"Now I can't crawl into my mom's bed in the middle of the night"

"He [she] favors his [her] own children."

It's very hard for a child to feel confident and comfortable enough to tell a parent that he or she doesn't like the person the parent is planning to marry. A great many children keep these feelings secret. This is most unfortunate, since many of the areas of concern could be worked on and changed, providing there's mutual desire to try. Eventually, many issues do work themselves out, but why should children have to wait to feel good?

It might be a great relief to your children to ask them how they feel about your new "partner." Let your children know that you understand that any negative feelings might be hard to share. By acknowledging the possibility that negative feelings may exist, you are encouraging your children to tell what they might otherwise have kept silent.

You can look for clues (as to whether your children are wrestling with feelings that are too difficult for them to share) by paying attention to changes in your child's behavior towards you, your new husband or wife, and anything or anyone.

Stepfamily feelings

To discover and understand your children's feelings about their stepfamily, open your eyes wide, listen carefully, and try to detect any resentments, jealousies, and negative competition, as well as the areas of appreciation.

There are children who have shared with me their feelings of being thrilled to have new sisters and brothers, but the more common concerns from children are those that are kept secret from their family— the concerns that remain under the surface and constantly drain their emotions.

Some of the situations in stepfamily relationships that have caused children sadness, anger, frustration, jealousy, confusion, pain, or feelings of being unloved or left out include the following:

Stepparent favors own children

Stepparent doesn't seem to want to get closer

Stepparent is mean

Stepparent won't listen or try to understand

Stepparent says nasty things about "real" parent

Stepparent has unfair expectations

Stepparent always argues or fights with them

Don't know what to call stepparent (first name? Mom? Dad?)

Stepbrothers/sisters stick together and leave them out

Stepbrothers/sisters have to share rooms that they once had to themselves

Stepbrothers/sisters take out resentment of new parent on new stepsisters/brothers

Stepbrothers/sisters resent them for being more popular, better looking, smarter, better athlete, etc.

Stepbrothers/sisters take attention away from parent

Stepbrothers/sisters get more privileges or never get blamed.

Children are often afraid to love or even like their new stepparent for fear that their parent will be jealous, angry, or feel less loved. They may also be reluctant to get close to a stepparent because of the potential resentment of that closeness from stepbrothers or stepsisters.

Parents need to be sensitive to the possibility that their children are confused about how to relate to their stepparent, and, if there is confusion, they need to confront it. Imagine the positive impact of a parent actually encouraging a good relationship with their new stepparent. A parent could probably help ease much of the strain their children might feel by saying:

"I hope you'll give your new step[mother/father] a chance. Maybe [he/she] could become a good friend. I know you love me and I love you very much. And I hope we'll be close for the rest of our lives. But why shouldn't you be as happy as you can be with your new family? Being close with them doesn't take away your love for me. Please allow yourself to try."

If their parents couldn't stay together, why shouldn't children have a chance to get along in a new family and feel good?

New families might become closer faster if they realize that there is probably no such thing as "instant" intimacy. Stepparents and stepchildren will need time to get to know each other, to become more approachable, and to feel more comfortable. Even if stepparents and stepchildren immediately feel wonderful together, learning about each other and becoming sensitive to each other's needs will take time. It would be unfair to expect otherwise.

But time alone won't guarantee closeness. Family members need to talk about their feelings, acknowledge that they want to get closer, and agree to work actively towards accepting each other. Family meetings (see Family Meetings Can Help, chapter 10, p. 198) can be a wonderful way to help get those feelings out in order to identify and deal more openly with any concerns or differences.

Stepparents can help their own children adjust by letting them know that they needn't worry about being best friends with the new family members. A positive first step in establishing good relations is to simply try to get to know each other in order to get along better. If friendship comes, that's great.

If stepbrothers/sisters are constantly fighting and being nasty to each other, you might be able to help the adjustment by acknowledging (calmly, at a time when they're *not* fighting) that getting used to a new family situation can be tough. There are many emotions, such as sadness and confusion, that can get in the way of good feelings and many memories of how things used to be that probably hurt. This would also be a good time to raise any issues that you feel might be a source of friction between the stepbrothers/sisters. You might check the preceding list of situations to see if any of those apply and offer suggestions on ways to deal with the situation(s). For instance, maybe one child is overweight and the other children are judging that child's outer "package" instead of learning who's "inside" those pounds.

Each child can be reminded that everyone is trying hard to adjust to all the changes and everyone probably has enough difficult feelings to work out. No child need be punished further by being teased or left out, having secrets or rumors told about them, or having to deal with anything else that's mean.

Stepparents can't force their children to love each other but they can teach and demand respectful behavior among them. If stepbrothers/sisters truly don't like each other, they can simply leave each other alone. That's their free choice. But they don't have a right to make the other person feel badly.

Parents can be frustrated by not always being able to know when a child is being teased or otherwise mistreated. The children who are hurtful will probably not be eager to announce how mean they are, and the child who is bearing the brunt of this treatment may be afraid of being labeled a "tattler"—and so he or she may silently feel set apart and unwanted.

At the dinner table or at other times when the family might be together, grab the moments to share and to learn. A good approach to helping adjustments would be to sit everyone in the family down at the outset and let each child know that getting along is something that everyone will need to work at together, and that it will take time to get used to new rules, new values, new responsibilities, new expectations. Children can be encouraged to be aware of whether they're judging each other, and whether they're competing or comparing. No matter how much fighting there has been among them or with you in the past, everyone can decide together that they'd like their stepfamily feelings to be better.

By agreeing and acting on the importance of giving each other a chance, stepfamilies can at least make an effort to learn to live together in a way that allows everyone to feel good. Stepparents also need to do a bit of soul-searching. How kind have you been to your stepchildren? What could they be feeling about you? How can you become more approachable? Softer? Kinder?

Whatever hasn't felt good about the family feelings up until today can be left in the past. Every stepparent and stepchild can decide they want to put the fighting and bad feelings behind them and start again from today to try to get closer. I've never met a child who didn't want to feel good about his or her relationship with a stepparent, stepsister, or stepbrother. But I've met thousands who have been too scared and unsure of how to let anyone in the family know they didn't feel good about their relationship.

When there seems to be no remedy

Sometimes relationships in stepfamilies, as in original families, just aren't good. For instance, when a stepparent has a drinking problem, doesn't care, or is totally insensitive to a child's needs, or when stepchildren truly hate each other, a child may feel miserable about family life throughout the growing-up years and beyond.

If there seems to be no remedy to ill feelings in your stepfamily situation, perhaps someone in the family (parent, grandparent, aunt, uncle, brother, sister), a religious leader, or someone at school (teacher, guidance counselor, school principal or other administrator, school psychologists, social worker) can be a source of strength, advice, and support to help children get through the growing-up years as best as they can under the circumstances. Someone needs to make sure a child knows that it isn't his or her fault that life seems so frustrating or sad and knows that the situation doesn't mean he or she is less special. Sometimes kids just aren't lucky, but they can try to make the best of any situation and set positive goals for the future.

POSITIVE ATTITUDES TOWARD
INTIMATE RELATIONSHIPS

Many college students of divorced parents have told me of their negative feelings toward marriage. One said, "I'm afraid to make a commitment. . . . My mother is on her fourth marriage." Another related: "I'm never going to get married. I don't want what happened to my parents to happen to me."

Remind children that they're not their parents. They're not their sisters or brothers, not their friends, not anyone but themselves. What happened between their parents does not have to have anything to do with what will happen in their own relationships. It would be a shame if the fear of divorce or separation would keep them away from strong attachments.

Depending on the age of your child, you might want to talk about the various positive aspects that can exist in a good relationship, such as mutual trust, caring, sensitivity, respect, and friendship; being able to share fun, be silly, and be serious; accepting the other person for who she or he is, not who you want her or him to be; good communication; attentiveness; compatible values; compatible religious beliefs; common interests and goals; compatible attitudes towards such issues as where to live, sharing incomes, whether or not to have children, how many children to have; and shared hopes and dreams.

Children also need to know that their parents probably loved each other very much and were committed to spending the rest of their lives together when they got married—even though the dreams didn't quite work out the way they had hoped. Children can gain strength from learning that every parent and every child has the ability to dream new dreams and find new, supportive family feelings to replace ones that didn't work.

CHAPTER 12

SCHOOL

G-8

How do you say NO when
somebody wanted to
cheat from you.

B,6

I hate speshle ed

G(8) I hate school I wish I
was popular. I feel lonely. How can
I change that?

My math teacher, and other teachers, used to be my older brothers teachers, and most of them always say things like, "Why aren't you like your brother?" or "I expect you to be good and get good grades since your brother did." I'm sick of that. What should I do? I can't tell them to yes

over ⟶

because they are "superior" and I can't talk back or I'll get in trouble.

G 6

I am new here and it's hard for me to find friends. No one will accept me!

I have a teacher and no matter how hard I try and get along with her she doesn't seem to like me and I make A's in her class

Girl 7th

what can I do?

Some children, looking forward to another terrific day at school, eagerly stride toward the school bus to join their friends. Others, dreading the day, walk more slowly. One of the stragglers may be praying that the kid with the blue jacket will be absent that day. Some may not even be able to think about school until they get through the bus ride, during which they fear being teased or humiliated. Still others have frequent late-night or early-morning stomach aches or other "ailments" which they hope may keep them from making it to the bus in the first place.

There are children who will at some time fall into all of the above categories and everywhere in between. Children's feelings about school are dependent on many different factors, and sometimes the least of those factors is achievement in school work.

High grades can make a child feel very proud and confident, but as a positive factor in creating good feelings about school, the achievement of high grades may not be enough to counteract the negative effects of being teased every day, labeled an outcast, not having any friends, always sitting alone at lunch, being a teacher's pet or pet peeve, not making any sports teams, not having a boyfriend or girlfriend, not being popular, or being more, or less, developed than most kids.

All children, no matter what their levels of achievement, will have some feelings about school that will make them feel better or worse about themselves, more or less motivated, or more or less special. School can be a haven, the only place where a child might feel warmth or even a hint of love, the only place that child is nurtured. Or school can be a living hell from the first day of kindergarten on.

This chapter will discuss aspects of school life that you and your children need to understand better and handle effectively. Attention to these concerns can increase your ability to help your child experience a positive, enriched school life.

FAMILY FEELINGS/ EFFECTS ON SCHOOL PERFORMANCE

First, it is important to consider how family feelings might influence your child's ability to feel good and perform effectively at school. Ask yourself if your child:

Feels pressured by the family to get higher grades?

Feels intimidated by the achievement level of a brother, sister, or parent?

Has extensive household chores to perform that could diminish study time?

Has to babysit frequently, leaving little time for concentration on homework or freedom to just relax?

Has little privacy in which to be able to concentrate on homework?

Does homework, leaves books and papers at different places in your home rather than has one designated, organized area?

Is upset, unable to concentrate due to family stress (illness, fighting, separation, divorce, stepfamily adjustments, death, unemployment, etc.)?

Is pressured to perform well because of being the first in the family to go to school?

Is frustrated due to lack of interest, support, encouragement, and assistance from parents?

Has been neglected or physically or sexually abused by a family member?

Is affected by illness, disability, long-term medication, drugs, or alcohol?

Is living with an alcoholic parent?

Once you identify problem areas from the above list or your own list of family factors that could affect your child's school performance, tell your child you realize certain situations at home might be taking away from his or her ability to concentrate and feel good about schoolwork. You can identify and discuss each area of concern and ask your child to add to the list. Exploring possible solutions together can be an important step towards positive change.

SCHOOL FEELINGS/ EFFECTS ON PERFORMANCE

You can gain further insight into your child's present-day attitude toward learning by considering whether your child's past school experiences have been happy, exciting, successful, troubling, or competitive, or have contributed to a lack of self-confidence, frustration, sense of failure, or feelings of reluctance and resistance to schoolwork.

Some of the important school factors that may affect your child's performance include:

How often your child has been disciplined for bad behavior (sent to principal's office, reprimanded by teacher)

Whether your child has enjoyed good friendships, been well-liked, accepted

Whether your child has been left out, teased, chased, harassed

Whether work has been difficult or easy

Whether your child has been permitted to work at his or her own level (no unrealistic expectations)

Whether your child has been put in a remedial or more advanced reading group (a circumstance that can adversely affect some children's self-images for years)

Whether your child has been nurtured, motivated, encouraged by caring teachers—or the opposite.

While you can't change your children's past experiences, you can help them learn from them and feel better about themselves from today on. For example, if your child understands that difficulties in grasping a lesson in a class may have been caused by his or her relationship with that particular teacher rather than by the actual subject matter, this perspective can encourage your child to be more open-minded towards future classes on that subject. If your child realizes that holding back, or never raising his or her hand, was because a particular teacher was so intimidating, he or she may be encouraged to participate in future classes.

Teaching new, positive perspectives about school performance, such as being careful not to measure self-worth in terms of report card grades or in response to teasing, can open up a world of encouraging possibilities for your child.

TEACHERS

If teachers are kind, loving, consistent, warm, understanding, fun, caring, and fair, children usually feel very good about going to school. If teachers are sensitive to student feelings and needs, there is a greater chance that children will "blossom," become more self-confident, and be motivated to please not only those teachers, but also their parents and themselves. A positive classroom atmosphere encourages creative thought, self-expression, self-respect and mutual respect. Bless the nurturing teachers! Amen.

There is little wonder that children in negative classroom environments, created and perpetuated by insensitive teachers who discipline by fear instead of respect and reason, might buckle under the strain, lose interest in school, "clam up" for an entire year, have falling grades and stifled self-expression, and not feel very good about themselves or school.

Many parents of children who once "loved" and looked forward to school have told me of their heartsickening experiences of watching their son or daughter react to a negative teacher by getting ailments to keep them out of school. In some cases, the resulting damage to a child's self-image, self-confidence, and attitude towards learning may take years to overcome.

I am at a loss to understand why teachers can't at least be fair and nice, even if they're strict. It is an outrage for children to have teachers who are totally unaware of the severity of their impact.

To address the problem of an insensitive teacher, parents can go through the appropriate channels (teacher, guidance counselor, principal/vice principal, on up to the superintendent). If parents find that the teacher or administration won't respond to their pleas for sensitivity and if the class can't be switched, parents will have to help the child find ways to deal more effectively with the teacher.

For example, if a teacher's yelling doesn't lessen even after you have expressed concern, you might encourage your child to put the yelling in perspective as part of the teacher's personality. Like it or not, the teacher may simply be a "yeller!" Try to find out if your child is the only one being yelled at. More than likely, the "yelling teacher" will yell at many students over the course of a day or week. If your child recognizes that fact, he or she will be able to take the yelling less personally.

There may not always be an easy explanation for why a teacher acts a certain way. Children may simply have to recognize that teachers have the right to make certain decisions, whether children like them or not. They may blame unfairly and not listen to explanations, or nitpick about an answer on a test and refuse to raise a grade. Sometimes, a child will have to toughen up and have the ability to walk away respectfully, even when totally frustrated, and hope the feelings go away quickly.

If your child is frequently reprimanded for not bringing pencils, rulers, notebooks, or something to class, he or she has to be more responsible. If the teacher gets sarcastic when your child doesn't know the place in a textbook, or always asks the teacher to repeat the question, then it's a matter of your child needing to pay more attention while the lesson is going on. If your child doesn't give the teacher something to complain about, there is likely to be less complaining!

Children to teachers: Turning feelings into words

Children should be encouraged to turn feelings into words with their teachers in order to talk about how the yelling, or anything that bothers them, makes them feel. They can ask their teachers for some private time to meet (before or after class or school, lunch period, teacher's free period).

According to the situation, they might say to the teacher:

"It's hard for me when you start to yell. I can't think of any answers because I get so nervous and I forget."

"It really makes me feel like crying when you talk that way."

"I don't mean to be disrespectful. But please don't talk like that to me in front of the class. It makes me feel very embarrassed. I know I was wrong. And I'm sorry. I wish you would spoken to me alone."

"I'm very upset that I lost points because of a rule that wasn't announced to the class until yesterday. I was absent and had no way of knowing you changed the instructions. I would really appreciate it if you would reevaluate my paper."

Having a child speak with the teacher is a very good first step to suggest, even before the parent gets involved. But not every child has the confidence to be able to talk so directly to a teacher. If your child has trouble approaching a teacher alone, you could schedule a meeting so that you, your child, and the teacher can confront any issues of concern.

Children need to be informed that as long as they're respectful, it's not only fair but very important for the teacher and for them to let the teacher know how they feel. Should a teacher be faulted for hurting, embarrassing, or frustrating a student, if that student doesn't say so? Should a teacher be blamed for continued insensitivity to a student if the teacher has never been told that student feels the teacher is insensitive?

A few years ago, my daughter was very upset with one of her teachers because he never called on her when she raised her hand. She started believing that he didn't like her or was mad at her. I suggested she speak to the teacher privately and let him know how disturbed she was about this. I also suggested that she ask him if he were upset with her for any reason. After she talked with him, he was very thankful, especially because he hadn't been at all aware that he was avoiding her. The situation got much better after their talk. He never would have known how she felt unless she told him.

If your child is the one who is causing the problems in the classroom, whether the issue is disrupting lessons, too much talking, starting fights, throwing or passing notes, or being fresh, your child can also turn feelings into words to apologize and ask to be given another chance. For example, that child could say: "I'm really sorry for interrupting the class all the time. I would like to try to pay attention more. Would you please give me another chance?"

Judging teachers

Children need to realize that just because a teacher has a gruff voice doesn't mean he or she won't be fair or kind, and just because a teacher is friendly and fools around doesn't mean he or she won't be strict about homework rules or give tough exams. Teachers who may "look" like monsters may really be warm, nice, and very approachable if they're given a chance. Just as it is a mistake for any child to judge another by his or her external appearance, or "package," it is a mistake to judge a teacher by his or her appearance.

Teachers need to be more aware of the extent that their students judge whether or not they're approachable by their looks, tone of voice, weight, height, clothes, physical disability, and/or any other aspect of their outside "package." If teachers were aware how children are fooled by appearances, they might go out of their way to let their students know how human they really are.

Children also judge teachers on the basis of the opinions of friends, brothers, or sisters who have been in the teachers' classes in the past. If your child is about to start the school year with a teacher whose "reputation" is negative, you might be able to help your child have a better relationship with that teacher (and anticipate the start of the school year with less dread) by talking to your child about the reputation before school begins. Since each child's relationship with a teacher will be slightly different, encourage your child not to jump to conclusions and become upset before giving the new relationship a chance.

Some teachers are deemed nasty by students because those teachers caught those students doing something disruptive in class and reprimanded them. If your child behaves, a teacher deemed nasty by others may actually be very nice. Of course, there are some teachers who really are insensitive and harsh even if a child tries to do everything right. But why should your child agonize until concern is warranted?

Positive approach to negative situations

A child of any age needs to be taught that he or she is still entitled to be heard, to have questions answered without being intimidated, to be respected, and to be treated fairly by teachers. If your child is not permitted these entitlements, you and your child have a right to be disturbed and to take appropriate actions.

If a change in the teacher can't be initiated, and if your child can't be placed in another teacher's class, I hope you'll have the patience and wisdom to offer extra nurturing to your child, to be there to listen, talk about feelings, and attempt to maintain a healthy perspective about the experience. You might talk to your child about how sometimes people have to adjust to uncomfortable or unwanted situations. You might explain that not everything in life feels good. Life is not always warm, sweet, and loving. Sometimes it's rotten and crabby. As long as the unfortunate classroom situation can't be changed, a positive approach might be to consider these questions:

What can we salvage from this school year? How can I use this opportunity to help my child learn that he [she] can "hang in," endure, and even become stronger for the experience? What can my child learn about getting along with all kinds of people, anticipating moods and reactions, and knowing when to be careful in thought and action? Can I help my child gain strength from realizing that even the crabbiest teacher doesn't have the power to take away his [her] specialness?

While no child has the power to change a teacher, we can also remind children that they do have the power to control their own behavior and how much effort is put forth in a class. Each child has the power to do homework assignments on time, listen attentively, be respectful of the teacher and fellow students, not pass notes, and try sincerely.

You can encourage your child to go out of his or her way to say hello to a teacher at the beginning of class, goodbye at the end. Your child can ask a teacher about whether a weekend or vacation was enjoyable and can inquire about a teacher's health after a prolonged absence. Your son or daughter can even share with the teacher personal information, such as, "I got a new dog," "I can't wait to go skiing this weekend," "My brother just got engaged," or "My cow had a calf." Such friendliness can add a positive dimension to the relationship.

I'm not suggesting that your child become a candidate for "teacher's pet," nor am I suggesting any invasion of privacy. There's no guarantee that being extra nice will make a difference, but a friendly smile and extra effort to show interest can sometimes go a long way, or at least be a beginning, to more cordial and productive associations.

Appreciating the good

While we must help our children deal more effectively with teachers who are tough or insensitive and cause our children to feel bad, we should not fail to appreciate those teachers who are caring and work very hard to help children grow in a positive way.

We tend to be quick to complain about the negatives and all too often take the good for granted. A deep-felt thank-you to a teacher needn't wait for a special occasion nor be measured by the money you spend on an end-of-the-year or holiday gift. You or your children can write a simple note from the heart, anytime during the school year, to let a teacher know how much the extra help or care was appreciated, or how much it meant that he or she took the time to listen to a problem that had nothing to do with school, or just how good the child feels being in that teacher's class.

As a teacher, I can tell you that it means a lot to me when parents recognize how much effort you put forth and how much you care. But when you hear such appreciation, unsolicited, from a student, that means the most. It would be a wonderful lesson to teach children to express their appreciation to teachers, and not take what teachers give for granted.

CLASS CATEGORIES

Advanced classes

Being in an advanced class may make your child feel important, proud, and challenged in a very positive way. He or she may even feel part of an elite, special group in a higher "class" than the rest of the students. Or being in an advanced class may make your child feel pressured, if he or she is only taking advanced courses because of your wishes or the fact that most of his or her friends are at that level.

Regardless of the degree of difficulty in each subject area, children in advanced classes will likely be highly motivated, focused, and "self-winding." As teachers, parents, and advanced students themselves tend to have high expectations for performance at the advanced level, your advanced-class child may be very pressured and disappointed if his or her achievement level is lower than expected. The attitude often is that advanced students *should* get very high grades because they're "advanced." Competition is usually very high and can add to your child's pressure positively and negatively.

A boy in the eighth grade once told me, "I'm getting an F in advanced math. I really think I'd be better off in regular math. But my parents won't let me switch and they'll 'kill' me if I fail." How good could that boy have felt about himself and his studies? What could his parents have thought he was gaining from the class experience under those circumstances? What price are those parents making their child pay for the label "advanced"?

If your child is in an advanced class, how pressured do you think he or she is to stay there? What part do you play in helping to create that pressure? Might your child feel much more comfortable "shining" in a regular class than struggling constantly in the advanced? If your child is very bright and always brings home honor-roll report cards, do you simply acknowledge those grades as if they are expected, or do you tell your child you appreciate his or her ability level and efforts to achieve? If you're not sure how your child feels about being in advanced classes or how he or she feels about your responses to achievement, please *ask*. And talk together.

"Regular" classes

If your child is in a regular class, he or she may feel good or bad depending on the subject, teacher, and friends in the class. Competition among regular-class members is usually less pronounced and apparent than among advanced-class members but may be very keen between a particular friend, "the class brain," or smart sisters or brothers.

Regular classes are by no means pressure-free. There are children at every level who strive for 100 every time and are deeply disappointed and upset when they don't earn it.

Many students might feel that as a group, "regular" students aren't as "good" as advanced students. To counter such attitudes, discuss self-worth, judgments, comparisons, and "labels" with your child. It would be unfortunate if your child had a lesser sense of self-worth due to not being in an advanced class. If you consider how many of your son's or daughter's close friends are in advanced classes, you might discover an indication as to whether your child has concerns about his or her achievement level and class placement.

Special education

Many children in special education classes are very thankful to be able to learn at a pace that is comfortable and caters to their special needs. Others there feel good in their classroom, but once they walk out into the halls, they may have a tough time dealing with stares, whispers, and taunts from students who don't understand what special education means.

If your child is placed in a special education class, talk to him or her about any feelings he or she might have about such placement.

Whether or not your child is in a special education class, you could talk with him or her about putting such class differences in perspective and about sensitivity to others. You can reinforce the idea that a person won't be any more trustworthy or a better friend because their class finished the unit in February instead of March. How a person learns has little or nothing to do with who that person is. A person is *not* a label. That's not *who* the person is. If someone is liked or not simply because he or she is in a special education class, then what kind of a friendship would that be?

IF YOUR CHILD MUST REPEAT A GRADE

An eighth-grade boy recently talked with me about how he felt about repeating the grade. He said that he and a few friends felt set apart even more because they were about two years older than anyone else in their class. He mentioned that the situation was not only awkward because of his age and how other kids related to him, but also because of his "older" interests.

I could only hope that he would be able to gain strength from realizing that everyone has his own time of readiness. I hope that the school administrators and teachers were providing him with the necessary guidance to help him approach his studies more effectively. More than anything, I hope that his parents and teachers know to remind him that failure in school doesn't mean he's less special as a person.

Some children have expressed to me that they regard kids who have been "left back" because of failing grades as "losers." One ninth-grade boy said, "People don't give them much of a chance." Many children seem to have a different, more accepting attitude towards those who have been held back a grade due to an illness or injury that forced them to miss much of that year's schoolwork.

Children who must repeat a grade because of illness also need an outlet for their special feelings, frustrations, fears, pressures, and concerns. Since children miss being in touch, the more contact they can have with friends, the better. Such involvement with friends will help ease any concern about how long-term absence might affect their relationships. They may be overwhelmed and very troubled about the potential consequences of their prolonged absence. Those who continue to be sick might also be scared about the illness itself, scared of not recovering soon, or at all.

If your child has had to repeat a grade and you have already had extensive discussions about the related feelings and the hope for new direction, keep in mind that the issues, changing relationships, and classmate attitudes involved in your child's situation are ongoing. You could help your child deal with any problems by periodically asking him or her how things are.

Since feelings of self-worth can be seriously damaged by failure, parents and teachers need to work extra hard to find non-scholastic areas in which these children can excel, to nurture positive self-esteem and keep the experience in healthy perspective.

IF YOUR CHILD "SKIPS" A GRADE

Children who advance or "skip" a grade also have feelings that need to be discussed at the time of the decision and also during the transition year and beyond.

Essential to include in the discussion are such issues as acceptance by new classmates, making new friends, and how the change might affect old friendships with children in the grade below. Since chronological age will not necessarily coincide with social maturity or physical development, a child who skips a grade may find difficulty "meshing" with many of the kids in that new grade. Remind your child that making friends in any situation requires having patience.

Another area you need to consider is your and your child's expectations of performance. After all, this child is not only an "advanced" student, he or she is considered "super advanced!" You need to be aware of whether your expectations for achievement are still fair and realistic, and of the fact that many social and emotional adjustment factors must be considered.

Remember, just because your child has the scholastic ability to skip a grade doesn't mean it would be the best thing for him or her. Do not skip a child unless ALL signs point to "success."

HOMEWORK

Most children would probably vote to outlaw homework! But since outlawing homework is not possible, we need to consider what can we do to help our children plan their work more efficiently, reduce last-minute pressure, and gain the most out of assignments.

If your child is old enough to have homework, he or she is old enough to learn to check assignment pads, make sure the right books and papers are brought home, and be responsible for at least trying to complete assignments on time. But it is a mistake for parents or teachers to take a child's awareness of these necessities for granted.

Some parents, in what they think is the "best interest" of their children, nag about assignments and make sure their children start their work early enough to finish when due. If you are a "homework nagger," please think about the potential effects of your nagging. Nagging can prevent children from having to take the responsibility for remembering on their own. The more you nag, the less your child has to bother even thinking about assignments, knowing you'll signal the amount of time left to finish. If you stop nagging, your child will have no choice but to pay more attention to homework if he or she wants to avoid zeroes.

If you feel responsible for reminding your child about schoolwork, remember there is an important difference between constant nagging and an occasional reminder balanced with helpful guidance.

It's not enough to tell children, "Please be more responsible." Children need to be shown specifically how to put their notes in order, approach their work, and balance their time in a more effective manner. A step-by-step approach can make it easier for your child to organize homework. For example, your child can:

Write down assignments on a special homework pad

Next to each assignment, write down approximate time needed for completion ("a lot" or "a little" may suffice for young children until they learn how to figure time requirements)

Next to each assignment, put a special mark for date due, a special mark for test date

Write down starting date to read a book for a book report and minimum number of pages needed to be read per day

Write down a starting date necessary for a project to be completed in time without rushing

Cross off assignments as they are completed

Make a new assignment list for each day.

This is a very simple way for your child to figure out and organize daily time for work and time for friends, sports, or television. Be sure to reinforce the idea that they need to plan ahead and pace work so that their assignments, reports, and projects won't have to be "thrown together" at the last minute.

Teachers usually expect their students to write assignments down correctly and complete them according to instruction. How many times has your child forgotten to write an assignment down? How many times has he or she not realized there would be a test tomorrow? How many crumpled pieces of paper containing homework assignments copied from a friend in the lunchroom have been misplaced? And how many times have you had to drive your child to the home of a classmate in order to "copy the notes" or "get the list"? If you identify your child's work patterns, you can determine what corrective steps would be most meaningful to discuss.

Even if your child remembers to copy the assignment and a reasonable amount of time is set aside to do work, the homework effort can be undermined by poorly arranged or incomplete notes and uncertainty about how to follow instructions. Also, consider whether books and homework papers are in one area or strewn around your home. Does your child have a special place where homework can be done? What is his or her work area like? Is it well lit? Comfortable? Is there enough storage area so that books and papers can be neatly put away? Determine which of these areas need to be improved.

No matter what your child's age, you still need to talk about establishing priorities, balancing time, organizing notes, and how to study effectively for a test. A college sophomore once told me that it wasn't until the current year that he felt he finally understood how to organize his notes and assignments in a way that lessened the pressure and brought more positive results.

If your child has left homework for the last minute and is under pressure, don't yell—this isn't the time for an "I-told-you-so." Help him or her calm down, help if you can, and at a later time or day, discuss how to plan more effectively.

DOING YOUR CHILDREN'S HOMEWORK

Children often feel a sense of relief when parents do a major portion of their homework assignments for them. With parents in charge, they feel confident that "their" work will be more acceptable and earn a higher grade than if they did the assignment on their own.

I worry about this. Children need to learn that they have their own resources. They also need to know they don't have to be perfect and can learn a great deal from their mistakes. Every picture, every paragraph, or every wire on a science project may not be as perfect as a given teacher had hoped. But children have the ability to learn from their efforts, grow from the work experience, and try to do better next time.

If a parent does most of the writing, most of the wiring, most of the drawing, what will his or her child learn? If the resulting grade is higher solely because of a parent's efforts, how honest will that child's average be? How realistic will a teacher's future expectations for performance be? How panicked do you think that child might feel when an assignment is given when parents are out of town and that child has never been given a chance to work on his or her own? How embarrassed and guilty might a child feel among classmates who know only too well that his or her parent did most of the work?

If children feel comfortable working on projects only when they're masterminded by parents, what will happen when that child attends an out-of-town college? Will the parents have to commute to that child's campus in order to continue this pattern? How many years will it be before that child has the freedom to come face to face with his or her own ability level and grow from there, instead of feeling pressured to perform up to standards that were never his or her own?

What if children fail because their parents stop doing homework assignments for them? Isn't it important for children to learn that it's part of life to sometimes fall flat on their faces? Isn't it essential for children to prove to themselves that even if they fail, they can find the strength to pick themselves up and go forward on their own?

Think about your own involvement with your child's work. Guidance is certainly tremendously important. Your child's confidence and ability can be strengthened if you occasionally check finished assignments in order to indicate errors and suggest which answers he or she might need to reconsider. "Being there" to give support and "bounce" ideas around will probably be very helpful and greatly appreciated. But actually doing your child's work warrants serious reconsideration.

MOTIVATION

Gumdrops, earrings, and gold stars

Many parents bribe their children to reach higher scholastic goals with such enticements as earrings, vacations, higher allowances, stereos, or more privileges.

It's not so surprising that some children respond to these enticements quite well. They tend to work harder, sincerely try for the goals their parents have set for them, and often succeed in qualifying for their rewards. But then what? Another stereo? When will the inducements stop motivating and personal goals take over? How many years into the children's adulthood will parents buy presents in order to "encourage" their children to advance themselves?

If your child isn't very motivated, you may feel compelled to reward initial successes with "certificates," or small prizes that you might even allow your child to choose. As long as you're careful not to take your reward system too far, and as long as prizes don't interfere with your child's attention to schoolwork, you can gradually encourage and support your child's internal motivation. Hugs and telling your child you're proud of his or her achievements, or attempts, can work every bit as well as gumdrops (and the flavor lasts longer!).

To my knowledge, twenty-year-olds don't have charts with gold stars and thirty-year-olds don't get gumdrops for working towards promotions. In all probability, once your children become adults, no one will be around to hold their hands and whisper over their shoulders, *"Do it now!"*

For the child who doesn't reach the goal that brings the prize, there will probably be disappointment and frustration. But for what reason? Because he or she didn't get the earrings, or because he or she didn't satisfy personal achievement goals?

Fear

Instead of trying to motivate with presents, some parents use children's fears: fear of punishment, fear of parental wrath or disapproval, fear of being "grounded" (not allowed out with friends), fear of losing telephone, stereo, or television privileges, or fear of being physically beaten. It is no wonder why some children think they have no choice but to cheat in order to survive.

Parents might argue, "Well, fear works! My son's grades are higher than they ever were. He's afraid he won't be allowed to go to parties on the weekend, so he has been working very hard." Students might even agree that they definitely wouldn't be putting as much time in their studies if it weren't for that "outside" threat of losing something that's important to them.

Such fear-induced constant stress over performance is likely to take its toll. Children have expressed to me that they feel very pressured and find it harder to concentrate knowing that they *must* get that certain grade or else!

Although fear is more stressful than bribery, the results are potentially the same. If a child is trying to achieve only in order to keep the telephone or the stereo, what are the effects on that child's actual learning and development of self-motivation?

Positive and negative pressure

Often, parents are quick to respond to anything negative and forget to praise their children until something extra special happens. Rather than wait for your child's occasional accomplishment, you can encourage your child by realistic, more frequent praise about his or her efforts, attitude, or anything else. Look for the opportunities to say such things as, "I really feel so good about how hard you're working," "I'm so proud of you; I know you're really trying."

Each parent needs to try to establish that delicate balance between positive encouragement and negative pressure. Once you've found it, your child will likely feel freer to concentrate and more comfortable approaching you for school-related advice. Remember to talk with your child about unfair comparisons and judgments of classmates—the fact that each person can only do his or her best.

Rather than blaming or taking away party privileges because a child didn't make the honor roll or earned another 70, you could give a more productive response by sitting down with your child and saying something positive, such as, "Let's talk about how you studied for this test. What did you do? How much time did you spend? How about getting your notebook so we can see if maybe there's a better way to organize your notes. Maybe I can make some suggestions so you'll feel better about trying next time."

Children who are working below capacity

Children work below their capacity for a variety of reasons. Perhaps they are bored, truly don't care, or are afraid to achieve because friends don't and they don't want to be labeled a "brain." Perhaps they're trying to get needed attention in any way they can. Perhaps they are bitter over not being in the advanced class again this year and have decided not to work as hard. Maybe they have learning disabilities as yet unidentified. Maybe they don't like the teacher.

Maybe they simply aren't ready to perform up to their capacity. Maybe they don't know how to organize their work or ask for help—or maybe they're a little lazy. No matter what the reason, you need to talk to your child about the reasons for the work being below capacity and about his or her feelings—not from the blaming standpoint, but from the positive standpoint—in order to help your child understand the problems and to offer your support.

Rather than concentrating on what you *expect* your child to accomplish, you'd be more understanding and supportive by accepting your child's current status and encouraging improvement from there. I'm not suggesting you hold back your own feelings. In fact, a positive step would be to let your child know that you're frustrated as a result of thinking he or she can do better but just doesn't seem to be trying. You could follow by asking if he or she is sincerely trying, and, if not, you could suggest your child think about why. If your child can't come up with an immediate answer, you can ask that he or she think about the question and any related feelings in order to talk with you later about them. This approach can reduce the pressure and gently, but directly, zero in on the important issues.

In order to stimulate motivation in a younger child, you might suggest that the two of you can be secret partners working together in a secret plan to help the child try harder to improve in school. The secrecy involves not letting the teacher know how hard the child is trying—and then surprising that teacher with the child's improvement. You can vow to help your child get more organized in work habits, promise to offer guidance, and help explain concepts where necessary. Your child's part of the deal is simply a sincere pledge to make extra efforts and to let you know when he or she needs advice.

For an older child, you might have better results by talking about what interferes with his or her interest or studying ability and what can be changed to enhance performance. In addition to expressing your frustration about your child's achievement levels, ask if there is anything specific going on at school or home that is interfering with his or her ability to concentrate. Making a list can help pinpoint areas of negative influence and provide an agenda for change. Talking with your child out of concern has the potential to accomplish much more than yelling out of anger. Besides your own involvement with your child's learning habits, it would be important to talk with your child's teacher in order to gain further insight and advice.

EXTRA HELP FROM TEACHERS

Although teachers may tell students, "I'm here for you; come in after class, before class, on my free period, before and after school, and I'll be happy to help you," there are many children who have said they wish they could go for extra help, but they're too embarrassed to let the teacher know they didn't understand the class lesson. Many are worried that the teacher will think they are inadequate or "dumb." Others are often uncomfortable with the teacher's manner . . . or even their outside "package," the way they *appear* to be.

Children are entitled to approach their teachers for additional explanations, clarifications, or whatever the particular need. Be wary not to take for granted your child's ability to make this approach even if the teacher has stated that help was available and the child really wanted it. Here, too, asking for help would be easier for children if parents suggested words for them to use in order to express their needs to teachers.

Some suggestions:

"I don't want you to think I didn't pay attention. I really did. But I'm not sure of a few things. Could you help me understand them better?"

"I tried very hard to understand what you were saying in class . . . and I know I didn't raise my hand when you asked if there were any questions. But I felt funny because no one else raised a hand. Could you help me?"

"Do you have any time to explain the——to me today? I studied but I still have some questions."

TAKING TESTS

Some children don't mind tests. Others panic, no matter how high their grades are in the courses. Most often, the pressure of being tested is what makes it hard for children to concentrate. Parents and teachers could help ease this pressure by identifying and talking with children about "test feelings."

To help your child reduce pressure and increase concentration during tests, you might acknowledge that it's very natural to be nervous before a test, and offer the following suggestions:

The night before a test, get right amount of sleep; the morning of a test, have a good breakfast.

Bring to the test the appropriate supplies (pencils, pens, tissues, erasers, calculators, etc.)

Before starting the test, scan to see if you have the correct number of test pages; read the instructions.

Ask questions about the instructions even if no one else does. (You can also signal teacher to come to your desk privately, but that depends on test policy.)

Be sure to be able to keep track of the time. If there is no clock, you can ask the teacher to periodically write the time left on the chalkboard.

Read through test to get a quick sense of how much time to leave for each section.

Don't be fooled by how quickly others start writing or how quickly classmates finish. (Everyone works at their own pace. Fast answers aren't necessarily correct. Neither are long answers.)

If you're stuck on an answer, come back to that question later.

Make sure you've answered all questions before handing in test.

Know your teacher's rules on avoiding cheating. (Some teachers will think you're cheating if you wiggle a little in your seat or roll your eyeballs. To avoid unnecessary confrontation for unintentional motions, find out the rules ahead of time.)

Aside from helping your child approach test taking more effectively, try to nurture a positive attitude about test results. If you regularly pounce on your child for poor test grades, he or she is going to be very upset while taking a test—in anticipation of having to deal with your reaction over possible poor grades.

Rather than blame your child for grades that are lower than you (or your child) had hoped, a more positive approach would be to examine the test together, and to try to help figure out where he or she went wrong and in what ways chances for improvement can be increased. If your child made a sincere effort, don't forget to comment positively on how much you appreciate that effort.

IF YOUR CHILD HAS CHEATED

If you learn that your child has cheated, try to find out the reason he or she felt the need. Children may cheat because they don't study sufficiently, don't trust their ability to do well even if they study, are scared of doing poorly, don't want to be humiliated by classmates' higher grades, or don't want to lose privileges at home if grades are low. Low grades are especially embarrassing if a teacher's policy is to read all the grades aloud.

Talk with your child about the "false achievement" of cheating. If your child cheats and doesn't get caught, how long will the cheating continue? How fair can a measure of his or her scholastic ability be if the only way grades are attained is through cheating—whether it's copying work during a test, copying assignments during lunch, or having parents complete projects at home. What if he or she is accepted by a college based on grades that could never have been earned alone—how pressured would your child be to cheat to stay in that college? And what about the stiff penalties for cheating at colleges, some of which call for instantly being "kicked out"?

Children are usually very aware of their own ability. They know when they're being praised falsely and, if they've cheated, they may well have guilt for praise that is unearned.

With all the extra pressure to achieve on competitive levels— nationally, statewide, and within each classroom—it's that much more important for us to remind children that we'll still love and respect them, and appreciate their efforts, if they sincerely try their hardest to do their own work.

CONCERNS ABOUT THE LOCKER ROOM/ PHYSICAL EDUCATION CLASS

If your child is comfortable with his or her size and is happy with friends, chances are that changing in the locker room and playing sports in physical education class will be a fun, social time of day, something to look forward to that will break up regular class routines.

Children's feelings about changing in the locker room are directly related to self-image—body size in comparison to classmates, how much teasing or whispering they're subjected to, and whether or not they have good relationships with many of the students in the class.

Indications of children's embarrassment over changing in front of everyone can be detected in a number of their approaches to p.e. classes. A variety of tactics they use to avoid embarrassment might include:

Reducing the "audience" by walking very slowly to class, arriving after most have changed and started going into the gym

Changing in the bathroom

Facing the lockers without turning around until ready

Changing in the most private area; for example, in the back of the locker area

Trying to think of every excuse possible not to participate in physical education class.

If you anticipate that your child is experiencing discomfort changing clothes in front of others, you might let him or her know that such feelings are quite natural. Your son or daughter should know they certainly have the right to change in the bathroom instead of the locker changing area. It might help to mention that more than likely many of the other children also have secret "butterfly pangs" of embarrassment while changing.

If your child is concerned about his or her physical development, you can talk to him or her about the "package" concept discussed in chapter 2 (see p. 9). Remind your child that each person's body is slightly different and will grow on its own time schedule, and that if friendship is based only on size or stage of development, what kind of friendship could that be? You can suggest comments your child might make in response to anyone who makes fun of his or her size or development.

Performance in physical education class itself is another related concern. Depending on your child's size, relationship with classmates, and athletic ability, and the sensitivity of your child's teacher, he or she may feel more or less free to try, more or less pressured to perform, more or less wonderful about the class, or more or less devastated by it.

A girl in the sixth grade wrote to me, "I'm not so good at some things like forward summersalts and I don't want nowon [sic] to laugh at me or tees me and I have gym today." If your child is constantly nervous, frustrated, embarrassed, or humiliated by having to participate in gym class, discuss these feelings with your child, and also with the physical education teacher.

MOVING TO A NEW SCHOOL

If your child is moving to a new school, a new town, or has graduated from one school and is moving to another where there will be many new children to meet, it's natural for him or her to feel excited, happy, nervous, and unsure. Although telling your child these feelings are natural will not necessarily ease them, such confirmation will probably be appreciated.

The scary feelings stem mainly from the unknown. Children don't know if they'll be accepted, don't know the "rules," don't know the teachers, don't know if the work will be harder than what they're used to, and are worried about having to deal with older kids who might try to pressure them into doing what they don't want to do.

Some children who are new to a school end up latching on to whoever seems to show interest in them. In order to "belong," they might even find themselves having to behave in ways that are against what they believe. Discussing this possibility with your child can help the adjustment.

I suggest you also consider the perspectives and specific approaches to making a friend and dealing with crowds offered in chapter 4. Be sure to remind your child to investigate what activities are offered after school. If you leave enough time for discussion prior to the first day of school, your child could be helped to feel more ready and confident even if the jitters won't go away. No one ever said new situations would be easy! It's the anticipation that is sometimes worse than the actual experience.

A girl recently told me how difficult it was for her when she changed to a new school and didn't know anybody. She waited months for someone to come up to her. Every day, she hoped and waited, feeling very alone. She said her loneliness was especially hard at lunch, when everyone else seemed very involved with each other and she had no one. The fact that she wasn't told that she didn't have to wait is terribly sad. She could have approached others starting on the very first day.

Once your son or daughter walks into that new school, he or she has the ability to try to trade any lonely, left-out feelings for an exciting challenge. Your child can actively start looking for that first potential friend to approach as soon as he or she leaves your home. Looking forward to making new friends can be part of the fun of the move.

Your extra support during your children's initial "search" and adjustment period will help them a great deal. Finding that first new friend may take time for them. They'll need to be patient. Help them by acknowledging these feelings and by offering realistic encouragement.

In situations where children are moving together to a central school in a district, your child might feel confused and torn between wanting to hold on to old friends and wanting the freedom to make new ones. Talk with your son or daughter about being sensitive to the feelings of old friends and being careful not to "burn bridges" too quickly, but also about having the right to explore other relationships. To help ease your children's possible confrontations with old friends who may not understand, you might suggest ways and words for your children to use.

Most important, encourage your child to "be yourself" and to realize that he or she has the personal resources and ability to make the transition positive. Waiting for that first friend may require some patience, but the fact that your child can take charge of looking beats waiting around!

P.S. No matter what their report card average, all children are entitled to a classroom experience that feels good, builds confidence, nurtures self-acceptance, and fosters respect for differences in others. Every single child is entitled to be respected for who he or she is, not who teachers or parents expect him or her to be. But first, we've got to teach children to believe in themselves.

CHAPTER 13

ILLNESS, DEATH, SUICIDE

A friend of mines grand mother just died and I have a herd time talking to her. Should I talk first or should I let her talk first?

G 7

My Grandma died before I was born and I want to find out more about her. But I don't know how to ask my Dad about her.

G 6

My brother died a few years ago and we used to go to the park together with my mom and dad. How can I cope with having my brother dead and me going to the park alone without him?

G.

10 years ago my sister died. Now I'm the only girl. I really cant talk to my mother. Theres a space that only my sister can fill. How can I get closer to my mother?

7. my grandmother is in a wheelchair and she stays in a nursing home. I really don't know her that well and I'm not sure I wan't to. Whenever my ~~xxxx~~ father visits her I think of some exuse not to go. What should I do?

What do you do when you feel like you just don't want to live any more? On the outside I try to look like everything is okay, but inside I feel like crying all the time & I feel like I want to end it all. Everything in my life is wrong, I have 2 of the greatest friends but it aint enough. There are to many wrong things, I really just can't handle it

female

On the anonymous sharing cards children have written at my programs, child after child has acknowledged deep feelings about illnesses and deaths that they wanted so badly to share with their parents, relatives, or friends but couldn't.

EVEN IF NO ONE IN YOUR FAMILY IS ILL/NO ONE HAS RECENTLY DIED

Even if no one in your family is ill and no one has recently died, you might anticipate that your child will have secret thoughts or fears about death. Students from the elementary-school level through college age have written to me their specific concerns about the eventuality of a mother or father dying and about wondering how they'll survive without either one of them.

If you create an opportunity to deal with these natural concerns at a time when you don't have to rush, your discussion with your child might prevent much confusion and anguish when they eventually have to confront serious illness or death.

It is my hope that the information shared in this chapter will enable you to be more aware of what your child needs to know to better understand, discuss, and handle these difficult experiences.

WHEN A LOVED ONE IS SERIOUSLY ILL

To help your child deal more comfortably with serious illness, offer honest, age-appropriate explanations to the relevant questions he or she will need answered but probably keep hidden. By considering the specific nature of the illness, how family life has been interrupted, how much information your child already has, and your child's relationship with the ill person, you can determine what your child needs and wants to know. For example:

> If chemotherapy will cause the ill person to lose his or her hair, explain this to a child prior to its occurrence.
>
> If the ill person will probably lose a lot of weight, talking about this beforehand will help ease the shock of seeing the person look frail and weak.
>
> If the ill person needs long recuperation at home, all family members could gather and discuss how this might change family life and what each person can do to help.
>
> If the ill person needs an operation, explain why surgery is needed, how it will help the person recover, and what the recovery will involve.

Visiting

> If the hospitalized person has tubes inserted, let your child know this *before* going to visit. (You might say it's normal to feel a bit uncomfortable looking at these tubes, explain why they're necessary, and encourage your child to try to look past the tubes to the person who will be very happy to see him or her.)
>
> If the hospitalized person might doze on and off, explain that such a pattern is normal. (A child might wonder why anyone should bother visiting if the person is sleeping most of the

time. You might explain that, for the few moments that person's eyes were open, it will be very meaningful for your child to be there to show care and concern.)

If the ill person is in a nursing home, you might talk with your children about their possible discomfort in seeing older people in various states of ill health. (You might mention that many of those people will be very happy to see them since they don't often get to see children anymore.) The nicer your child can be to all the people there, the better it will make everyone feel.

If you suspect that your children may dislike the smell of a hospital or nursing home, you might discuss this in the "briefing session" prior to a first visit.

Often parents only superficially explain the ramifications of an illness, thinking that details might cause the child to be too upset and too sad, and to not know how to handle the information. Sometimes, it's the parents who have difficulty acknowledging the truth, because they can't handle what it means.

Most children can sense strain. If left uninformed, they'll probably think "the worst." The overriding fear most children have is that the ill person will die, especially if a parent. Children can't imagine living without one or both of their parents. These feelings are essential to discuss in order that children can realize they will be able to go on.

If such concern over death is warranted, is it fair for your child to handle such fear alone? If the illness is not life-threatening, why not let your child know? Talking honestly with your child not only might reduce unnecessary anxieties, but also can help strengthen the bond of trust between you. Such interaction can also add to your child's sense of security in knowing that you will not hold back if any changes in the ill person occur, and that, until you say so, he or she needn't worry.

Talking about illness/
talking with a person who is ill

It's usually not enough to tell your children that they can come to you with any questions about the illness of others. Your child may be concerned that he or she will upset you by bringing up the subject, especially if you have been visibly disturbed. And, as with any emotional issue, your child may not know what words to use in order to express inner feelings.

You might help to dispel your child's resistance by saying:

"I know I've been upset lately. All of us have been. But I hope you won't hold back your questions thinking you'll upset me more. I'd be the most upset if you couldn't come to me. It would be sad for you to have to deal with your feelings alone. Maybe we could even hold each other and give each other strength."

Help your child turn feelings into words to encourage communication. You can say:

"I know how hard it might be to figure out how to let me know you're so sad about————. If you are sad, that's just what you can say. Or, if you don't really know what to say but you want to talk, you can start with, "I really don't know what to say but I want to talk with you about————.""

Children as well as adults are often uncomfortable being with a person who is ill. They aren't sure what to say, don't know whether or not to let the person know how upset they are about the seriousness of the illness, and may end up talking about everything but their emotions, keeping "in" everything that yearns to be expressed.

Very often, children and adults mask how deeply upset they feel because they're very uncomfortable about losing control and crying in front of the ill person. They're also concerned about making the ill person cry. Although it may be very difficult to do, crying together with the ill person may be very comforting and special to both. Adjustment to the situation can be aided by "letting those feelings out." Your child and the ill person might even feel much closer because they didn't hold back.

In situations where the ill person has not been informed of the extent of the illness, let your child know. If the person is aware of how ill he or she is, you might encourage your child to share those feelings of sadness. If the patient is terminally ill, your child might even talk about how much the person will be missed.

While it can be painful to acknowledge the truth about someone's serious condition, it also can be a relief to the ill person to know that he or she no longer has to pretend that everything will be fine. Perhaps your child's honesty will open the door for sharing between the two that would never have otherwise been expressed.

Thoughtful expressions can be very meaningful

If your child visits a loved one who is ill, or is too young or too uncomfortable to visit, he or she can show concern in many ways. Your child might:

Draw a picture

Send a picture of himself or herself alone or with the ill person

Write a poem

Write a letter

Send a card

Make a specially created tape of music that the ill person likes

Speak with the ill person on a tape

Write a story.

If your child feels too uncomfortable to talk openly with the person who is ill, your child may find it easier to write feelings in a note that could be sent or handed to that person.

IF YOUR CHILD IS THE ONE WHO IS ILL

Among the variety of concerns children may have about the extent of their own illness, they may worry that they'll never recover, worry about not keeping up with schoolwork, and worry that their friendships may not be intact upon their return (the longer the absence, the greater the potential worry). The more you keep your child informed about the progress of the illness, anticipated side effects, and expected recovery time, the better.

Encourage your children to express inner feelings and concerns, not only to you but also to your physician or the person in charge of their recovery.

FALSE HOPE

If you give false hope to a loved one who is ill or to your own child, seriously evaluate your reasons. Is it your inability to cope? Denial?

Being honest about painful reality is tough. More than tough. It can be excruciating, especially when dealing with illness that might be terminal or permanently debilitating. But at what price will you mask the truth? At what price will you deny your child the right to learn that life is not always fair, not always kind? How else will your child learn to cope with and accept situations that are beyond control if you shield him or her from reality?

HELPING YOUR CHILD DEAL WITH DEATH

The following are questions children have asked me:

"How do you prepare to face a parent's or grandparent's death when you know it will hurt so much you want to die yourself?"

"My brother died a few years ago and we used to go to the park together with my mom and dad. How can I cope with having my brother dead and me going to the park alone without him?"

"My father died three years ago. How do I talk about it with my mother?"

"My grandmother died last year. I want to talk with my parents. But I feel inbarest [sic] to talk about it. What should I do?"

"One of my friends' father died last spring and he didn't tell me & I can understand that but I don't know how to tell that I'm willing to talk to him if he wants. Should I try to help or would that be butting in?"

No matter who the person is who died, children will likely have feelings that are difficult to handle and even harder to discuss. To realize that a child who has lost one parent can't find comfort in the other parent is to realize the need to openly control this subject. It doesn't seem to matter how long ago a loved one has died or if a child has ever met that person, boys and girls regularly admit that they have questions that have been gnawing within for years, waiting to be answered, if only they knew how to ask them.

If you bring this subject up with your child and sense resistance, you might acknowledge that you know it's painful to discuss. You might also say you hope that no matter how hard it is to talk about this, he or she won't let the discomfort prevent a sharing of these important concerns.

Offering words and specific sentences for your children to use can help them express feelings that might otherwise have remained hidden. The following represent examples of basic sentences your child can consider as guides to expressing their feelings (your own examples might be structured around feelings that you think your child might be holding inside):

"I'm so sad about Daddy. I can't stop thinking about him. I wake up crying almost every night."

"No one ever talks about————. I really want to talk about her. But it's very hard. I loved her so much."

"I wish you would tell me about————. It makes me very sad when all my friends talk about their grandparents."

"I'm really scared that someone in our family is going to die. I don't know how I will be able to cope."

To a friend, your child might say, according to the situation:

"I'm so sad about your mother."

"I know we never talked about your father dying, but I want you to know that if you ever want to talk about anything, I'm here for you. And if you just want to sit quietly together and not talk, I'll be happy to keep you company. Let me know. I really care."

Besides learning how to express feelings about death, children need to understand that death knows no age. To prove to your child that death takes infants, children, teenagers, and adults of all ages, all you need to do is read about the deaths in a newspaper. At the same time, you might talk about health care, caution when crossing the street, good nutrition, good sleeping habits, and sufficient exercise. During these discussions you might also make your child more aware of safety measures that could prevent them from being seriously injured, abused, and possibly killed.

You might also mention to your child that if he or she ever doesn't feel well, no matter how silly the complaint may seem or how much he or she thinks it's "probably nothing," he or she should tell you so you could check it out yourself.

Obviously, this kind of discussion can be expansive and may not be presented in one sitting. The important point is to be aware that your child can gain from realizing that he or she can actively make decisions that can help contribute to a longer, healthier life.

The "finality" of death

Children need to understand that death is final, that after someone's death, there will be no more letters from that person, no phone calls, no surprise visits on Thanksgiving.

If you try to avoid making such a strong statement about never seeing the deceased person again, your child may have false hopes about his or her return. If you simply tell your child that person has "gone away," he or she may always be looking out the window, waiting for that phone call. I question how fair it is to skirt the truth on this matter.

If you try to avoid the issue by offering the explanation "He went to sleep," imagine how fearful your child might be about his or her own bedtime. Make the distinction for your child between sleep (when all the organs of the body are working, even if a person is resting with their eyes closed) and death (when all of the organs of the body have stopped working forever).

Death can teach children to appreciate life more fully

Telling children the truth about the finality of death can put life in a different perspective for them. By helping them realize there is a limit to life, you can encourage them to appreciate each day more fully. Maybe they'll try harder to work at getting closer to the important people in their lives. We can try to teach this perspective even to young children.

Grief/expressing emotions

When talking about death with your child, you should include the topic of grief. Even if no one in your family has recently died, talking about grief will not only prepare your child for when death takes a loved one in your own family, but also will help him or her become more sensitive to how a friend who has lost a loved one might feel.

Explain that each person will grieve in his or her own way, even in the same family. Often, children have told me about their concerns relating to not wanting to cry when a family member died. They wondered if their relatives thought that, because they didn't cry, maybe they didn't love that person as much. Talk to your child about how different people express and deal with grief—some people are very vocal, others are more private; some may scream or cry and not try to hide their emotions from anyone, others may seem very controlled in front of friends and family but may cry for hours when alone; still others may not cry at all. No matter how a person expresses his or her emotions, it's not a measure of love.

Your son or daughter might be surprised that family members and friends will talk openly about the person who has died. You could tell your child that such talk is not only acceptable but also might be very comforting and important to those who are left behind. People who are grieving might be happy to remember special times spent with the deceased. They might even laugh at the memories. The more your child understands that a range of reactions is natural, the more comfortable your child might be to simply be "himself" or "herself."

At the time of a relative's death, explain any traditional practices that will follow, such as services, ceremonies, visiting at a designated home to pay respects, and any others that may apply.

It might also be helpful to your child's adjustment to explain, within the week or so after the death, that as friends and family go back to their normal schedules and visits are less frequent, the reality will probably start sinking in. It will take a while, sometimes many months, sometimes much much longer, to get used to the fact that a loved person won't be around. The knowledge that it's natural even to wake up in the middle of the night thinking of the deceased person may help your child to reach out to you. Let your child know it's okay to wake you up, if he or she feels sad and wants to talk or just wants to be held.

FUNERALS

Many parents have talked with me about their confusion over whether to allow their child to attend the funeral of a loved one. Naturally, this is a very personal decision. That decision might be aided by considering this: if the child is old enough to care and old enough to ask to be included, that child might be old enough to go. Also think about how your child might feel if you refused to allow him or her to attend.

Perhaps my son's first experience at a funeral can help put the situation in better perspective:

Several years ago, when my son's closest friend's grandmother died, my son asked to attend the funeral in order to "be there" for his friend. My husband and I felt it was very special that he felt this way and gave him, as well as our daughter, permission to go with us.

Since our children had never before experienced a funeral service and had never gone to a cemetery for a burial, we felt it was very important to explain exactly what they might expect. Besides letting them know what the service might be like, we specifically described the cemetery experience. We also felt it important to give them options in case they felt very upset. For example, they knew that, if they got too sad, they could walk to the side, get back in the car, or stand closer with us.

In this particular ceremony at the cemetery, the casket was lowered into the ground while everyone in attendance watched. Dirt was then shoveled over it. As the last shovelfull of dirt was pitched, the casket disappeared. At that exact point, my son was hysterically crying on my shoulder. He turned to me and said, "She's gone!"

I don't know if any book we could have read about death together or any conversation in the abstract could have hit home the message about death's finality as did that moment. My son didn't "break" or crumble. He eventually stopped crying. And, after a few moments, he said, "I want to spend more time with Grandma." He was twelve at the time.

While some children want to attend funerals, others would rather not. One thirteen-year-old girl described her feelings about funerals this way: "A funeral is even more depressing than the actual death because it's so final. What I mean is that, it's the end. You will never see them again. Seeing your loved one lying in the coffin, the one who had read you a story last week, can be a deep cut of hurtness that will never be healed. Funerals are just a slap in the face of reality."

In making your decision over whether to allow your children to attend the funeral of a loved one, please consider that, with funerals, there are no rehearsals. You have to know your own children and to anticipate how difficult the situation might be for them to handle.

If your child's feelings are strong about attending the funeral with the family, it may be important to his or her emotional well-being for you to make an extra effort to give appropriate explanations, offer support, and help your child to be a part of the experience. If you deem his or her attendance inappropriate, you should, at the very least, explain why. If your child doesn't want to go, please be careful not to associate this response with how much your child loves the person who died. In that case, you could help ease or prevent your child's guilt over not attending by talking about feelings and letting your child know you know it has nothing to do with love. This decision to attend a funeral is a very personal one, for you as well as for your child.

DEATH CAN BE A BLESSING

If a loved one has been very ill, in terrible pain, and/or hooked up to machines that kept him or her alive, you might consider explaining to your child that death can sometimes be considered a blessing, especially if the condition has existed for a prolonged period. This does not mean that anyone wishes someone they love would die, but your child might be better able to accept the death if you explained how much the person suffered and how kind it might be that he or she is finally at peace.

THE DEATH OF A PET

When dealing with the death of a pet, talk with your child about his or her feelings of sadness, loss, and grief, and about the fact that each person in the family will probably react to the death slightly differently. Children need to realize that it's natural to think sometimes of the deceased pet and to occasionally become filled with tears for months, even years.

If, because of the death of a pet, your child gets up feeling sad in the middle of the night, and taps you on the shoulder, you might want to let him or her know that it's all right to not want to be alone.

Rather than try to sneak to replace a goldfish, canary, or other small pet that could be "impersonated" easily by another of its kind, a better learning experience for your child could result from your honesty about the death and your understanding of the need for time for grief. In order to let your child say a final goodbye, you might even plan together a "shoebox burial" in your yard or some special place.

If you decide to get another pet, teach your child that the one that died can never be replaced, that each animal is unique, just like each person is unique and can't be duplicated. The new animal may even look like the old one, but it will have its own personality, its own appetite, and its own ability to respond to your child's love.

Allowing your child to be involved in and to learn to cope with the death of a pet can help prepare your child for when a person he or she loves might die.

SUICIDE

The vast numbers of teenagers who commit or attempt to commit suicide confirms parents' need to discuss this topic with their children as early as possible.

If you're saying to yourself, "Not my child!", or if you are waiting for a warning signal to prove that such a discussion is warranted, you might be making a sorrowful mistake. Even if your own child is not thinking of suicide, the information you share with your child may help save a friend or classmate.

If you have never talked about suicide with your children, it might be less threatening to them to approach the subject generally before turning the conversation toward them specifically. Begin by asking them for their opinions on why kids commit suicide. Common reasons that might be suggested and discussed include: feeling that there's no other way out; failing grades in school; wanting attention; difficulties at home; or breaking up with boyfriend or girlfriend. Talk about the reasons that many kids are reluctant to approach anyone for help, as well as about the devastation felt by family members when a child commits suicide.

After exploring your child's general feelings about suicide, you can then address specific concerns. Even if you have said it to your child many times before, make it clear that, no matter what the situation or what the difficulty, you hope he or she knows you are there and want to help. You might also say that, if he or she is angry with you, it would mean a lot to you to know. If he or she is frustrated because you seem to be distant, preoccupied, not understanding, or totally oblivious of his or her pain, you also would want to know.

You might acknowledge that you know how difficult it can be to admit there's a problem. Many people think that not being able to cope is a sign of weakness. By emphasizing to your child that admitting an inability to cope is *not* weakness but takes a great amount of strength, you will be encouraging your child to reach out for help when needed.

Always encourage your child to turn his or her feelings into words. Mention that it would be a sad mistake to think that no one cares just because no one has noticed how much he or she is hurting. Often, people assume that close loved ones will automatically be able to sense their pain. I wish this were so. Your child needs to know that the only way to be sure that you know he or she has feelings that are tough to handle is to make sure to tell you. Remind your child that using a suicide attempt as a call for help could be a fatal mistake. Suicide is forever.

Help your child turn feelings into words by suggesting topics and ways to talk about critical situations that have the potential to be difficult to confront (pregnancy, drugs, alcohol, failure in school, suspension, etc.). Remind your child that whatever he or she is feeling—the desperation, the pain—is going to pass in time. You might even refer to a difficult past experience that did ease. Confirm your willingness to be there and to talk about *anything*. And to *listen*.

Warning signs and hot lines

Some of the warning signs of suicide are increased talk or concentration on the topic of death; saying, "I'm going to kill myself"; using alcohol or drugs; changing behavioral patterns (personality changes, less care about appearance); changed eating and sleeping habits; less involvement with family or friends; and giving away something that is important, such as a record collection. Naturally, if a friend has committed suicide or your child has made previous suicide attempts, those would represent serious warning signs.

The above changes may not definitely mean your child has thoughts about suicide. However, if you even think there's a hint of a warning signal, be very attentive to anything concerning your child that could indicate clearer signs. Going out of your way to spend some private time to try to find out what's bothering your child may be helpful. Approach your child by saying, "Are you okay? You seem very strained lately." Or "You seem really depressed lately, just not yourself. Would it be helpful to talk about anything that is bothering you?"

Of course, your child may not let you in on the truth. But if you believe something is wrong, even after being told by your child that things are fine, don't back off. You might try a different approach, such as saying, "I know you said everything is fine, but I have this gnawing feeling that it's really not. I'm not trying to invade your privacy. But I'm worried about you and it makes me upset to know you might be dealing with difficult feelings alone. If you don't want to talk to me, would you at least think about talking with someone else who might be able to help you?"

You can then offer a list of people and places to go for help. Naturally, if there is even a hint that your child might be considering suicide, it would be essential to seek help. You might talk with your child's teacher, guidance counselor, school psychologist, principal, school social worker, or family doctor; a child psychologist or psychiatrist; family therapist, religious leader, or friend. In this matter, family counseling can be very helpful.

You can also contact crisis hot lines, specific suicide hot lines, suicide prevention centers, and mental health clinics in your area. If you aren't sure where to go for help, you can check with your child's school, your family doctor, a local hospital, and your librarian. If one choice isn't satisfactory, choose another—and keep choosing until you feel that the situation is in hand.

When advising your child about where he or she can go for help, be sure to mention that it is important not to give up trying to find the person or place that seems right. Remind your child that, if you don't hear or don't respond to his or her cries or hints for help, he or she should tell you again. And keep telling you until you respond.

Parents would be wise not to ignore possible warning signals because they believe their child is very popular and good looking, has high grades and close family relationships, and dreams of becoming a doctor. None of us can turn our backs. We can't deny any possibility that these warning signs might apply to our own children. Suicide doesn't give us a second chance to respond.

In all fairness, just because something upsetting happens to your child, such as failing a subject or breaking up with a girlfriend/boyfriend, this doesn't mean that you should be alarmed. The most important thing is for you to be *aware*.

Be sure your child understands what could represent suicide warning signs. Many warning signs are taken in jest because friends and classmates weren't taught to recognize their potential significance.

At my programs for children, I've received an increasing number of (anonymous) written comments on concerns about what to do in regard to a friend who keeps threatening to commit suicide. Teach your child to take seriously signs and specific threats to "kill myself." Children need to tell someone of these signs, whether they tell you or a responsible adult at school who can follow up from there.

If you or the other adult(s) don't listen the first time, children need to be advised to approach again and again until someone believes them and responds.

Helping children tell of suicidal thoughts

If your child is contemplating suicide, offering hotline numbers and lists of people to approach for help may not be enough. Even if a child wants badly to get help, he or she may not have the inner strength to pick up the phone or walk through that door.

Besides offering those important hotlines and alternatives, we need to give children the words to express their feelings. What exactly can they say if they're hurting and have been thinking of suicide? They can turn feelings into words and start by saying, "This is really hard for me to say. Please help me."

Because these words seem so simple, often adults take for granted a child's ability to know what to say. Most children don't.

Preventative measures

One of the best ways to prevent suicide is to prevent the conditions that could cause it and thus promote the conditions that would nurture self-acceptance and a positive attitude. Preventative measures we could take with and for our children include:

Teach them to put differences into healthy perspective (size, achievement, athletic ability, race, religion, financial status, looks, etc.)

Teach them how to express difficult inner feelings

Anticipate and attend to concerns that might be too hard for them to mention

Teach them ways to make friends

Teach them realistic perspectives about cliques and the power of cliques

Help them learn to deal with changing relationships

Help them learn to handle disappointment, frustration, pressure, failure, success, and day-to-day ups and downs

Help them understand that life is not always happy, fair, or exciting; down times are normal and expected

Help them develop responsibility, compassion, and respect and appreciation for family

Teach them that everyone makes mistakes but everyone also has the ability to learn from mistakes

Teach them how to cope with family strains, illness, death, or other traumas

Teach them how to cope

Teach them to appreciate each day, realizing there is a limit to life

Be realistic about our expectations

Be wary of pressuring unfairly, and pitting one child against another, or your child against yourself

Teach them how to make decisions, explore choices and evaluate possible consequences

Teach them that asking for help is not a sign of weakness but of tremendous strength, of awareness of resources

Accept and love them for who they are; realize they can only be themselves

Teach and *remind* them of their specialness, their uniqueness

Listen without judging and convince them of our sincere approachability, our love, and our own fallibility.

If parents took these preventative measures, perhaps kids would never reach the point of even contemplating suicide.

But there's just so much that any of us parents can do. We can only try our best. If our child commits suicide, in spite of our awareness and all the life skills we've tried to help them learn, then I hope we would have the strength to move forward without feeling guilty.

We can't be there to hold our their children's hands every single moment. We can only try to teach, guide, nurture positive feelings, be there, and show we care . . . and add prayers and hope for good luck—the rest is up to our children.

ENJOYING LIFE FULLY

A sixth-grade boy whose father had died three years earlier told me he still didn't know how to cope with the loss. I asked him if he had been close to his dad and he said, "Yes, we always went fishing together. He spent alot of time with me."

I said, "How special. I'm glad you spent the time you had together in such a wonderful way. It means so much that you were able to be so close to your dad. And, although I know you'd rather he was here with you right now, we both know that there are some things we just can't control. At least you can always hold on to all that your father gave you of himself, all that he taught you, all the love that was between you. You can carry a part of your father with you for the rest of your life. No one can ever take that away from you. I hope those special memories can give you strength."

After our conversation, he seemed to be a bit more settled. I hope he was better able to appreciate and remember that he had taken full advantage of the years he had had with his father. I don't know that there are any magic words to take away the pain of his loss, but understanding can help ease it.

If your child is very afraid that someone in your family will die, you might help diminish the fear by explaining the importance of sharing all the time in all the meaningful ways possible. If, for example, your child thinks only about death when with a grandparent, your child might miss the "life" that could still have been shared.

If children can learn to appreciate the limit and value of time spent with others, they can work even harder at getting closer in their relationships with parents, family, and friends and at sharing life as fully as possible. Then, when death takes a loved one, at least they will be able to hold on to special memories and be comforted as well as strengthened by the knowledge that they made the most of the time they had with that person.

CHAPTER 14

BEING DISABLED

G8

Sometimes people make fun of my brother, because he was born without ~~the~~ part of his arm. It makes me feel really sad because I know deep inside he's not really different!! I don't understand how they can make fun of him about something he can't control !!

Children often respond to disability in others with confusion, discomfort, and fear, or with extreme curiosity. They usually aren't sure how to act with someone who is disabled and don't know what is "okay" to say. Many mistakenly believe that a disabled person (for example, someone who has lost a limb, loss of hearing, loss of eyesight, or loss of muscle control) is less adequate, less whole than others. They commonly fail to realize that a disability has little to do with a person's *ability* to be a good friend, need to love and be loved, and pursuit of challenging goals and dreams.

Since disability can be a difficult topic for children to confront, many of the misconceptions and discomforts it can cause may exist but remain secret, sometimes for years. The unfortunate result for children who are disabled might be lowered self-image, greater obstacles to achieving self-acceptance, and increased difficulty in relating to others. Among children who are not disabled, such misunderstanding can increase their distancing, insensitivity, and cruel teasing of the disabled.

This chapter should help you better anticipate what would be important for your child to understand about disability. The more thoughts and feelings about disability that you know to examine, the more questions you'll be able to answer, even if they are unexpressed by your child. The more answers your child has, the better he or she might feel about himself or herself and others, regardless of differences.

MORE THAN AN EXTERNAL "PACKAGE"

Children can usually learn to overcome discomfort with disability in others by understanding that a person is *not* a disability, not a leg that doesn't work, not a hearing aid, not a wheelchair.

You might explain that if a child loves someone who has an arm amputated, the love shouldn't lessen just because the arm is no longer there. It's not the arm that your child has loved, it's the person who was attached to that arm. The person inside will still be there, even after the amputation. Limb after limb could be removed and the *person* will live on inside, capable of loving, hoping to be loved, and very whole—and more than likely a much stronger person than ever.

Many children don't know any better than to believe that person isn't whole. They mistakenly think that a disabled person is his external "package." Children need to be taught not to be fooled by outside appearances.

ACCEPTING AND COPING WITH BEING DISABLED

If your child is born with a physical disability or becomes disabled due to illness or accident, he or she will probably need help in reaching a point of self-acceptance. This maintaining or bolstering of a positive self-image may be very painful and difficult, not only because of any limitations that are involved, but also because of peer pressure, judging, and the media's attention to idealized beauty.

It may be agonizing to know of your child's difficulties in dealing with the acceptance of his or her disability, and even more frustrating to know that there's only so much nurturing you can do. Your child will have to make peace with his or her own "body." There may be screaming, depression, anger, more depression, moodiness, silence, and many tears before your child reaches that point of peace.

As described by several people who became disabled, eventually the depression seems to level off. It's hard to say how long it will be before any given depressed child will be able to reach a leveling-off point. After that point, rather than having all bad days, there are good days and bad days.

If your child becomes disabled, you could help your child tremendously by emphasizing that there's hope. If your child can just "hang on," try to understand and work through the feelings, a day will come sooner or later when he or she will be able to adapt and move forward in a positive way.

You can't make the personal adjustment for your disabled child. No one can. But you can be there to show you care, offer support, and *listen*. Eventually, your child will need to make a personal decision to accept his or her disability—and go on.

You could remind your child that the disability is not his or her fault. You could acknowledge that you understand that he or she might be scared especially if he or she must adjust to a dramatic change in appearance or ability to function. Family support is essential, but it should not be allowed to be overbearing or to foster self-pity or pity.

Help strengthen the capacity of your child to accept his or her disability, and its impact on others, by offering positive perspectives. It's more positive and much more productive to dwell on what he or she *can* do than to lament over limitations that can't be controlled or changed. You could make the point that if kids only like or dislike you for looks or abilities, they are not basing friendship on who the real person inside is.

A man who became a paraplegic from a car accident sixteen years ago at the age of seventeen said that his adjustment was greatly helped when he was forced to go back to school, because he found that being around people was very supportive. Until then, he had been avoiding friends, afraid of how they would react to him. He came to realize that the stares, especially from small children, were more from curiosity than anything else. The looks he got became less intimidating and more understandable.

It might be relevant for a child who has become disabled to know that one of the turning points in that man's ability to accept his permanent changes was when, at the rehabilitation center, he realized that there were people much more severely disabled than he was. Then he started being thankful.

If your child is giving up on himself or herself, and feeling so confined and limited that life might as well be over, you might share with your child, as a way to offer hope and challenge, this man's story. After his rehabilitation, he started an organization offering paraplegic children and adults the opportunity to get involved with outdoor activities such as camping, scuba diving, and kayaking. He even received media recognition as well as a call from the President of the United States praising his efforts to plan and actually climb a mountain with several others in their wheelchairs.

On this climb, they moved forward in their chairs, dragged their chairs behind them, and crawled on their bellies at least half the time. The climb took five days and a few made it to the top.

This man told me that although he wasn't one of the people to make it to the top of the mountain, the fact he had tried was all important and made the whole experience worthwhile. All who were involved felt that the experience alone, and the fact that some were able to reach the top, made an important breakthrough for those who were disabled.

Yes, there are limitations, and each disability will have slightly different restrictions and ramifications. But if your child can't move one way, he or she can be taught and encouraged to move another. If your child can't speak aloud or has difficulty forming words, he or she can learn sign language. If your child is unable to use sign language, he or she might be able to use a typewriter, even if with one finger.

While it's fair to caution your child about those who will always say, "You can't do that!", you can always encourage him or her to try new activities and dreams. Often the mind and heart, not the disability, can interfere with acceptance of a disability and the ability to move forward in a more positive way.

If the adjustment process is still very difficult and you're concerned about your child's self-image or ability to cope, it may be wise to seek help. An ideal confidant for your child would be an older, more experienced person with a similar disability.

You might find it helpful to read or give a book to your child about being disabled. You can also arrange for your child to speak with a counselor or teacher at school. You can contact a child psychologist, mental health clinic, youth service, local hospital, religious leader, or family physician. You can also call for information or ask a librarian to help you locate the nearest chapter of a national organization relating to your child's specific disability. Depending on your circumstances, you and other family members might also find comfort and positive direction from talking with someone who is trained to help. Support groups for parents of disabled children, as well as the children themselves, can be very helpful.

ARE YOU AN OVERPROTECTIVE PARENT?

Try to evaluate how overprotective you are with your child. Some parents are truly afraid their son or daughter will be hurt, taken advantage of, or lost. Others are driven by guilt to do everything for their child. While many children might appreciate the security of such protection, a parent has to be concerned about how well prepared a disabled child will be to cope as an adult.

One of the best things you could do for your child is to help him or her become as independent as possible. This belief was expressed by a young man who works with disabled children and is himself confined to a wheelchair:

"One of the most harmful things that is happening in the handicapped world is overprotection, overlove. It was easy for me to say to my mother, 'Bring me a cheeseburger.' I didn't have to do a thing for myself as long as my mother was there to help me. It's the easiest thing to ask for help when you're handicapped. In a way it's good that parents are so protective about their kids, but in a way they're killing them. Lots of parents don't know how to let their kids take some risks. If they keep protecting their little babies, they'll find that they're still little babies at twenty-five."

Just as with children who are not disabled, those who are might gain a great deal from falling flat on their faces and then proving to themselves they have the resources to pick themselves up again, even if that means climbing back into a wheelchair. Of course, only you can determine how much assistance must be given to your child and how much he or she can do alone.

You might ask with your child if he or she feels you're being overprotective, but don't expect a completely truthful answer. Kids often know a good thing and they may not want you to stop doing the wonderful things you always do.

HELPING YOUR CHILD
UNDERSTAND REACTIONS TOWARD
THOSE WHO ARE DISABLED

Even if your disabled child is very popular, he or she will still need to be helped to understand the differing reactions of others toward those who are disabled.

Understanding teasing

If a disabled child is teased, even by a renowned bully, it's very possible that child will blame the disability as the reason for being teased. The more negative attention your child receives because of his or her disability, the greater the chance your child will feel worse about himself or herself and the disability. If, for example, a child is frequently teased about crippled legs, he or she might end up hating those legs even more.

Unfortunately, teasing may be hard to avoid. The more prepared your child is to put teasing in perspective, the better. You could remind your child that he or she may have to "look out" for kids who just don't understand. It's *not* your child or your child's disability that's the cause of nasty reactions but it is the misunderstanding and discomfort of others. You can refer to chapter 3 for suggestions on what your child can say or do if teased.

If parents of able-bodied children confront the topic of disability, dispel misconceptions, and talk about being sensitive to the feelings of others, children should be able to relate to each other in ways that feel good, regardless of whether they are disabled.

Besides teaching your child how to handle nasty remarks, teach him or her not to be the one to tease. Disabled children aren't necessarily exempt from needing to learn sensitivity for others. Disabled children have certainly been known to tease other disabled children, and they also might tease those who aren't disabled—whether out of anger, anticipation, or disposition. *All* children need to be taught how much teasing can hurt; all need to learn to handle it.

Understanding "slips"

Help your child learn to distinguish between an insult and an accidental "slip of the tongue" that is said innocently. An example would be saying "See if you can do it" to a person who is blind.

If your child makes a slip, he or she could quickly respond to let that person know not to be upset by what was said and to help ease that person's possible embarrassment.

Humor can be a great defuser. Your child might even choose to be the one to make a "slip" about his or her disability in order to help that other person be more comfortable.

Understanding the discomforts of others

Disabled children need to understand and know how to deal with the discomfort other children may have about referring to physical activities in which your child can't participate. If a friend of your child has to "watch" every single word, such as be careful not to say how great she did in the tennis match or how much he loves his new jogging sneakers, the conversation could be very strained—and so might the relationship.

Anticipating a friend's discomfort, your child might say, "It's really okay to talk about the track meet. Come on, I want to hear how your race went." Or your child could say, "You don't have to worry about telling me about things I can't do. Just say what you want to say and that will be better for both of us!"

Such a response on your child's part might not only help ease the conversation, but also may pave the way for a closer relationship with that friend.

Understanding stares and pointing

You might be able to ease your child's discomfort about a disability if you discuss the natural tendency of young children to stare and point at someone or something that seems different. They may simply be reacting out of curiosity. While people of any age might stare at someone who is disabled, most young children don't know any better.

If your child can learn to smile back, acknowledge with a wave, a nod or some kind of gesture, that will also help to dispel the other person's discomfort. If your child is close enough to the person staring, especially if that person happens to be a small child, he or she might say, "It's okay if you want to look at my leg braces. They're kind of neat! They really help me walk better." Such a response will leave the child who stared with more comfortable, positive feelings about disability and the person who is disabled.

Understanding others' desires and hesitancy to help

Many people have told me about being confused about whether or not they should have offered help to a blind student walking across campus or a person in the wheelchair ready to cross a busy street. Although the disabled person may seem to be in control, there is a tendency among many people to reach out and offer assistance. Some do and some don't. The ones who don't usually don't want to risk questioning the disabled person's ability to function independently.

If your child might need any kind of help, it would be wise to emphasize that it's a sign of strength, not weakness, to ask. If someone offers your child help and he or she doesn't need assistance, he or she could thank that person for being so thoughtful. If your child is capable of helping others, you might suggest that there's no harm in offering. That person can either say yes or no. At least your child will have been sensitive enough to ask.

THE NEED FOR INFORMATION ABOUT SEXUALITY

It would be a tremendous mistake not to talk with your disabled child about physical changes, sex, reproduction, relationships, and sexuality in general. All children, disabled or not, will physically develop and need to understand the changes and deal more comfortably with the related feelings.

You can talk to your child in an age-appropriate way, with consideration of concerns based on your child's specific condition. If you're waiting for your child to ask questions, remember: you might be waiting a lifetime.

Sexual functioning

The fact that so many children don't relate to a disabled person as a sexual human being makes it that much more important to tell your child the truth, and to be specific. For example, if your son is unable to have an erection because of his disability, he may worry about whether he'll be able to share sexual feelings with a woman. If your child is missing a limb, or is partially paralyzed, he or she may worry about whether he or she is attractive, is considered whole, and will be able to share in a sexual way.

Children usually believe that there's only one *right* way to have sex. A disabled child who believes this may worry about being able to have sex with body parts that don't work. But you could explain to your child that there is no one way for sexual sharing. Body parts don't love each other, people do. The love is expressed from the inside. No matter what your child's disability, the capacity and need for love will still be inside.

Children with impaired vision need to be taught that they will be able to "see" a loved one with their hands. If their disability involves their hands or arms, they can touch with other parts of the body. If most of their body is paralyzed and it's very difficult to move, the person they love can lie close with them and feel the special warmth inside that comes from trusting someone who truly cares.

All children would gain from realizing that intimacy is very personal, very special, and can only rightfully be defined by the two people who are sharing it, in whatever way they can. There aren't any rules.

There are books that deal with sexual functioning concerning specific disabilities. Some of these may be found at your local library. If they're not available, you might call a nearby medical institute, your physician, a health clinic, a local college library, or college department of health and human sexuality, as well as asking the telephone information operator for the national organization for your child's specific disability.

If you are extremely uncomfortable about confronting sexual topics, please respect your child's needs for accurate information and a chance to talk about sexual feelings. If you can't or don't wish to be involved in this discussion, you might ask a relative, teacher, religious leader, older brother or sister, or one of your friends to speak with your child.

DEALING WITH BOYFRIEND/GIRLFRIEND RELATIONSHIPS

Children who are disabled may need extra encouragement to take a chance in first relationships. For fear of rejection, they may be very confused about whether or not they should even try to show an interest in someone.

A disabled child may believe a rejection is due to the disability. Rejection can make the disability harder to accept and may reduce self-image significantly. After being rejected, it may take a disabled child a long time to take another chance.

Try to help your child put rejection into perspective. First of all, not everyone "connects" with everyone else, disabled or not. A rejection may happen simply because the "chemistry" was wrong, and have nothing to do with your child's disability. Or, it may be that the other person truly was uncomfortable with your child's disability and didn't know how to respond. It's also possible that rejection was spurred on by the person's concerns about how other kids in the school would react if they learned he or she was "going out" with someone who was disabled. While being honest about causes of rejection may be painful, it would be more painful for your child if he or she wasn't prepared to deal with realities.

In boyfriend/girlfriend relationships, it may be very helpful for your child to acknowledge any awkwardness because of his or her disability. If the disability can be confronted in the beginning of the relationship, that will help ease the interaction.

RELATING BETTER TO THOSE WHO ARE DISABLED

Help your child understand that children who are disabled are still children, still human. It's not their fault that they are disabled. No matter what disabled children look like or sound like, their disabilities don't make them less special. It just means that your child will have to make a decision to try to "get past" the disabled person's "outer package" in order to learn who that person is on the inside.

If your child is to get closer to someone who is disabled, he or she should honestly confront the disability rather than making believe it doesn't exist. Dealing with the disability openly, your child has a better chance of going forward in the relationship. In case your child doesn't know what to say, you might suggest that he or she ask the person whether they were born with their disability or if they became disabled because of an accident or illness.

Also, help your child understand that not everyone has been taught to be sensitive to differences. Classmates and other friends might make fun of your child's new friendship and this can lead to embarrassment, humiliation, anger, and resentment.

You might offer suggestions of comments for your child to make to answer friends who don't understand. Encourage your child to continue to be strong about the personal right to choose to be friends with anyone, regardless of what anyone else thinks.

FAMILY MEMBERS OF A DISABLED CHILD

Depending on your child's disability, you may have to spend a great deal of time taking care of that child's needs. No matter how much other children in the family might comprehend that this need is legitimate, they may still be jealous and resentful of the time you must spend on that need. It will help to talk to all your children about any such personal feelings. You might say, "How about keeping me company so we can spend some extra time together?"

Many children have expressed sadness, frustration, and sometimes embarrassment about how friends react to their brother's or sister's disability. This would be an ideal topic to discuss at a "family meeting." Talk with your children about what would be important to say to those friends in order to let them know how they feel—talk about turning feelings into words!—and talk about the need for sensitivity.

If appropriate, your child could also be encouraged to let his or her disabled brother or sister know how sad he or she is about how friends have been acting. Your child might mention his or her efforts to do something about such behavior.

You might discuss the range of reactions encountered by disabled children that I mentioned earlier in this chapter. These reactions are not only difficult for disabled children to deal with, but are also difficult for other children in the family who see those reactions. For example, if a child could understand why people stare at his or her disabled brother or sister, such awareness could prevent embarrassment.

A girl who has a sister who is deaf told me that her mother always seemed to take her sister's side when they were arguing. She guessed that her mother was being protective because she believed her non-hearing daughter wasn't capable of responding as an equal. But that wasn't true. The girl felt she and her sister certainly were able to communicate with each other. The interference of the mother prevented them from working at their relationship with each other and caused unfortunate resentment.

A FINAL PERSPECTIVE

Whether or not your child is disabled, you can point out the special facilities, such as wider parking spaces, railings, ramps, lowered telephones and water fountains, and public bathrooms with larger stalls and railings, that are provided to accommodate disabled people. You might tell your child that those changes are society's way of saying, "I care. You have a right, just like everyone else, to be a part of society instead of staying in the background."

As your children see more disabled people, you can help to foster their understanding by making an effort to offer explanations and to deal with feelings whenever an opportunity arises.

Children need to be taught specifically that "disabled" is not a negative label that automatically sets people apart, although, unfortunately for some of the disabled, many people do look at those who are disabled that way.

You can also point out to your children that some people who became disabled later in life have found they have been challenged to accomplish goals they may never have otherwise pushed themselves to reach.

One very wise comedian who has been wearing leg braces since he contracted polio at age four told me that he doesn't like referring to himself as disabled. He'd rather say he's "differently able." Perhaps if we could teach our children such a perspective, our children would be more accepting, sensitive, and understanding.

CHAPTER 15

DIFFERENCES

G.?

Why do people pick on me just because I'm a different Nationality

B-(7)

1. What do you do if someone makes fun of your religion.

What do you do if some person grown up! in your family is predjudice and you are not allowed to see these people or have them over? I've asked but just got yelled at!

G - 7th

I can't tell my mom I'm
going with a Mexican

2. What if I couldn't be a
persons friend because
of my color

I feel left out of the group of (G)
people that I sometimes hang around
with because they are all rich
and I'm not, and they are all
smart and live in big houses. I also
feel that if I don't do everything
just like them that they won't
like me.

While some children who differ from the majority of their peers in racial, religious, or economic backgrounds are accepted by them, many are teased, harassed, beaten, or shut out.

Based on the painful responses from children who are the target of such treatment, as well as cries from parents who are extremely disturbed that their child can't even walk home from school in safety, it is clear we need to do more to teach sensitivity and respect for differences in others.

DIFFERENT "COLORS"

"It makes me feel hurt when the American kids make fun of me. They told me to go back to Laos. And some even spit at me or threaten. They said I don't belong in the United States. Sometimes I even cry or get scary. No one very like me either."

This sharing note from a child in the seventh grade gives me the chills. Never having actually experienced those feelings, I can only try to imagine how deeply hurt any child would be from such treatment. It's not fair. *All* children have a right to feel good about themselves, no matter where they come from, no matter what the color of their skin. No one has the right to deny anyone else's good feelings by piercing prejudicial remarks, which have no basis in understanding and are usually potentially fueled by the need to seem "tough" in front of peers.

You might want to talk to your child about the "package" concept (see chapter 2) in an effort to aid your child's understanding about differences in color. By talking about the real person as being what's inside rather than outside, you can teach your child that it's not a boy's or girl's decision to be born a certain color. Color doesn't change a person's ability to be a good friend. Color doesn't change whether that person can be trusted with a secret. Color alone doesn't make a person cruel.

Children need to realize that they are sometimes quick to judge, and that often they avoid people they don't even know just because they're a different color. While it's each child's right to choose to avoid someone because of differences, no child has the right to be mean to, to make fun of, or otherwise be disrespectful to someone else, for any reason.

Usually the parents of a child who is persecuted will talk about these concerns to their child, but parents of children in the racial majority may forget the need to confront these issues. *Every* parent and teacher needs to talk with their children about being more sensitive to the feelings of others. If your child doesn't want to have anything to do with someone, fine. But please teach him or her to at least leave that person alone.

Children need to understand that their own feelings about racial differences may be "colored" by parental prejudices. You, as a parent, certainly have the right to teach whatever standards and attitudes that you wish. I would only hope that you give some serious thought to the impact of your teachings.

I have spoken with many children who have shared their frustration and sadness with me about not being allowed to bring "different" friends home. If you are imposing such rules, consider that your child may have questions and confusions about them that are just too difficult for them to mention. If you could explain your feelings to your child and offer him or her a chance to respond, that could represent an important step in helping your child to bring hidden concerns about the matter to the surface.

Children who are constantly being judged and avoided because of their color may have difficulty feeling good about themselves and may even have trouble feeling good about their race. It's not surprising that they may feel angry, sad, confused, and frustrated.

Try to take the edge off those negative feelings by explaining that the insensitive children probably haven't been taught to be sensitive about differences, and explain that what those children may say or do doesn't take away from your child's specialness. Acknowledge that you understand how painful it might be to be set apart and treated terribly because of something over which you have no control.

DIFFERENT RELIGIONS

After one of my parent programs, a mother talked with me about her son who was constantly persecuted because of his religion. She was anguished over the fact that he regularly had been chased home after school by a group of kids who taunted him with denigrating names referring to his religion. On several occasions, he was beaten up by this group of boys.

What could those boys have been taught about respecting differences? The mother said that talking with their parents didn't seem to help. And, while school authorities tried to be aware of the situation during school hours, the taunting took place almost exclusively off school property. At that point, the mother couldn't think of any other alternative but to drive her son home from school every day.

It is essential to talk with your child about religious differences and how powerful those differences can be in regard to how people treat each other. You might also mention that religious beliefs are not a child's decision. Usually, a child's feelings about religion and the way he or she has learned to worship depend on the religious beliefs of one or both parents. As with racial differences, "beliefs" won't change a child's ability to be a good friend. But not every child has been taught to realize this.

A girl in the seventh grade talked with me about how religion had affected her friendship. She had made a new friend at the beginning of school that year. She was invited to her home on many occasions and spent a great deal of time with her—until she mentioned her religion. According to this girl, immediately after her "good friend" found out she was of a different religious faith, she lost interest in the friendship. The girl told me, "We were such good friends. I know she's not being with me because of my religion, because we were so close before I told her. I can't understand how my religion would change our friendship."

Countless other stories shared with me by parents and children confirm the misunderstanding, distancing, and cruelty that often exists because of differences in religion. *Talk* to your child about differences in religious beliefs, whether or not your child is the one that is "different."

I'm not suggesting that just because your child is among the religious or racial minority, there will be antagonism. Certainly, there are children in the minority who have always been accepted, popular, and felt terrific about themselves. But it would be important to be aware of the possibility of insensitivity on the part of others.

DIFFERENT HOLIDAYS AND OBSERVANCES

If there are to be holiday preparations, celebrations, and assemblies at school that do not represent your religious beliefs, you might anticipate that these experiences may cause a variety of stressful feelings in your child. Create the opportunity to talk about such feelings. If your child has no concern in this regard, he or she will probably tell you. If he or she has unexpressed feelings about being different and left out, you will have opened up an important avenue for their expression.

If your beliefs dictate that your child not participate in certain school activities, specifically because of your religious beliefs, anticipate how your child might feel about being set apart and how the classmates might react. Children often suffer when their religious beliefs dictate that they need stay in the principal's office while the rest of the class is involved with holiday preparations.

Your child's feelings about being in the minority needn't be negative. In fact, if he or she feels "funny" or left out, you might try to turn the focus of being different around by encouraging your child that it can be very interesting to learn about other religions (if your beliefs allow).

Adults as well as children have expressed confusion over whether or not it was right for them to learn those holiday songs which were based on religious beliefs that weren't theirs. Learning songs related to the religious holiday that most of the kids celebrate and singing along with the class doesn't have to mean that your child is betraying his or her religion. Encourage your child to share in the spirit of the holiday preparations; this participation can keep your child involved rather than set apart.

Your child might speak with his or her teacher about having the opportunity to share information or articles about the religion of the majority of classmates. Perhaps your child might also wish to teach his or her class songs that are related to his or her own religion.

If such sharing is awkward for your child, you might join your child in meeting with the teacher in order to discuss how your own religious music or practices can be incorporated into class preparations. To be considerate of the teacher's plans, you should have such a meeting well in advance of the holiday. You might also speak with the music teacher directly in order to provide copies of the words and music related to your own holiday. Such direct action might help incorporate your holiday songs as an integral part of the curriculum rather than a supplement.

FOSTERING RESPECT FOR DIFFERENCES

Parents and teachers don't have to wait for holidays in order to create the opportunity for classmates to share information that can ease misunderstanding about religious differences. The library has many books that explain all religious practices. This information can be fascinating and exciting, and add to your children's realization of the many different religious beliefs all over the world.

You might add that while each child may feel his or her own religion is right for them, it doesn't mean it's right for anyone else. It's just different. The differences are natural. Taking the time and making the effort to foster better understanding and respect for these differences is essential.

The library also has books that explain the different races of people throughout the world. Such information can help increase understanding among children.

You and your child's teacher might look for "teachable moments" to introduce and reinforce the need for accepting differences, moments such as a news report describing the bombing or defacing of a religious house of worship or fighting or mistreatment because of racial differences. News reports make the point vividly. By acknowledging the painfulness and devastation of persecution because of their beliefs or nationalities, you can introduce a discussion about any possible disrespect among students at your child's school. This discussion would be also a good time to introduce the idea of scapegoating.

DISCRIMINATION IN YOUR CHILD'S SCHOOL

If there is discrimination in your child's class or school, discuss this with the teachers. If you don't get any satisfaction, you might talk again with the teachers, or then with the vice principal, principal, guidance counselor, school social worker, and on to the superintendent, if necessary. You might need to seek out the advice of your own religious leader. You might also arrange to speak with the school psychologist, depending on the extent and nature of your child's mistreatment.

In order to share your concerns about any religious or racial discrimination that may have affected your child or others, you could contact officers of the parent/teacher/student organization. Getting involved in your school organization will give you the chance to establish a rapport with other parents who can offer support. Parent education programs can be helpful in guiding parents to help their children deal with discrimination. Sometimes, it's the parents who need to be more aware of how *they* are fostering the disrespect and distancing.

Teacher in-service programs dealing with these concerns can also help in determining how to more effectively handle discriminatory behavior in and out of the classroom. Rather than waiting for a formally arranged "course," teachers, parents, and school administrators can arrange to meet informally to brainstorm over how to help the children better understand each other's differences and learn to be kinder to each other.

You needn't wait for a school district or classroom ruling for encouragement. You can start at home. Suggest your child invite one or several friends to share your holidays or religious ritual, or any other religious experience that might be important to your family. Such sharing will not only increase understanding, but it can also add an extra special bond between your child and those friends who might otherwise have felt distant.

HOPE FOR THE FUTURE

We can hope that the children in your child's school will accept your child for who he or she is and not make prejudicial judgments that have nothing to do with *who* your child is.

When children are not accepted, especially young children who don't understand, they may feel that something is wrong with them. They certainly may have a lowered self-image or a lack of self-confidence. It's hard for children to feel good about themselves and to realize their specialness if everyone around them sends negative messages and avoids them.

If you know your child is among the minority at school, be on guard for signals that might indicate discrimination against him or her. Stomach aches and headaches may be some of the indications.

You should also consider that, even if your child is victimized by frequent discrimination, he or she might be reluctant to tell you for fear that you'll come to school, call up an offending kid's parent, and make conditions even more difficult. Unfortunately, sometimes parental intervention does make the situation worse. But only you can decide how serious the discriminatory confrontations are and whether or not it's safe to allow your child the time to try to work out the differences on his or her own with your guidance.

Anticipating your child's concern, you might address the issue of your intervention and let your child know you won't approach the teacher or another parent without first discussing it with him or her. I'm not suggesting that you should hold back, if that's not what you deem appropriate. But at least your child will be able to trust that the plan of action has been initiated jointly.

If your child has talked with you about experiencing racial or religious discrimination, discuss safety measures and potential responses. Besides offering your child words and ways he or she can use to deal with name-calling and people who want to fight, you might make specific safety-measure suggestions, such as not walking home or standing around on the playground alone, being more aware of antagonizers at school or anywhere, and standing closer to the teacher in charge if trouble is expected.

If your child had been mistreated in the past because of differences, please remind him or her to let you know if there is any further trouble so that you can together develop a new way to handle any difficulties. Even if nasty remarks and problems occurred several years ago, make sure your child remembers and understands that such behavior has nothing to do with who he or she is inside.

All parents need to help children understand that no matter how a person is different, each one has a right to feel good about who he or she is. Children need to be given information and a positive perspective to turn negative attitudes and misunderstanding into acceptance. And again, they need to be reminded that if they don't like someone, to leave him or her alone. Many wonderful friendships could blossom if people could only get past the labels that make differences seem so monumental.

IN ALL FAIRNESS

It's only fair to mention that there are some minority children who taunt others with or without provocation. They may be "lashing out" against a history of injustice against their race or religion. They may be responding to very derogatory name-calling or justifiably intolerable actions, or they may simply want to pick on someone.

This behavior isn't necessarily confined to one race or religion and sometimes children of one minority band together to taunt or beat up other kids in the majority or a different minority group. This kind of behavior can perpetuate negative feelings about an entire race or religious group.

If someone of a different race or religion picks on your child, let your child know it was *that* child, not necessarily the race or religion, who was involved and at fault.

How good it would be if all children could have the chance to confront feelings about differences at a time when emotions are not high, when there's no fighting, and no plans to fight. If parents at home, teachers at school, and teachers in religious classes could confront these feelings ahead of time, perhaps *all* children will learn to work through the attitudes and misunderstandings that might prevent them from relating peacefully with each other.

Why not step up our efforts now?

OTHER ISSUES

Other issues children have difficulty discussing with their parents include concerns about dating and marriage. If you refuse to meet the person your son or daughter is dating, because of racial or religious differences, you ought to be aware that your child may feel forced to withhold the truth about the seriousness of the relationship.

I've talked with college students who were seriously dating people of a different racial or religious background. They were concerned that their parents would disown them if they learned about their marriage plans. Some parents had actually made such threats, but most of the students anticipated this kind of reaction from their parents, having never spoken with them about their relationships.

No child wants to be disowned by his or her parents. More than anything, children of any age want their parents' approval and "blessings" for marriage. If your child senses that telling you the truth will distance you and incur your wrath, he or she may do anything to avoid such confrontation.

You have the right to react any way you choose to whomever your child dates or wishes to marry, but try to anticipate your son's or daughter's confusion and sadness if you disapprove of his or her choice and refuse to allow that person in your home. Talking with your child about these feelings and concerns might help you get closer.

BEING RICH OR POOR

No matter what your child looks like, what your religious beliefs or racial backgrounds may be, or whether or not your child makes the high honor roll, there's still one more difference kids have to reckon with—money.

A girl in the seventh grade wrote to me: "I feel left out of the group of people that I hang around with because they're all rich and I'm not, and they are all smart and live in big houses. I also feel that if I don't do everything just like them that they won't like me."

Many children judge themselves and others by money, clothes, where and how they live, and the vacations they take, so it would be very important for you to talk with your child about attitudes, judgments, and the need to develop a sensible perspective about money and what it can buy.

Have you ever heard your child make an excuse to a friend about your home? Have you noticed that your child always goes to the homes of friends, and rarely, if ever, invites friends to your home? Consider who your child's friends are, and where they live, in comparison to you. What could your child be feeling and thinking in that regard?

Beware that your child's self-esteem, self-confidence, and sense of belonging may be influenced by the desire to measure up and keep up with friends who "have more." Often, children feel inferior if their families can't afford to go on vacation or their room is smaller or simpler than that of a friend.

It may be hard for your child to listen to friends talk about ski vacations, summer trips, tours, and camps when you can't afford to offer your child such choices. It may also be hard for your child to feel great about how he or she looks if most of the kids at school can afford more clothes.

The judgments might be less harsh if all parents could teach their children that it's not a kid's fault how much money his or her parent(s) has. And, less money doesn't mean less special, nor does it affect the ability to be a good friend. It would also help if parents who do have comfortable incomes could teach their children not to brag, tease, or otherwise try to intimidate those who have less.

I realize that all the perspectives we adults can offer still may not lessen our children's yearnings to take a trip on an airplane "like everybody else," or to have a room of their own to be proud of. It's probably unfair of us to expect that reasoning and discussion could eliminate jealousy completely. It's natural for children to want luxuries flaunted by friends and the media. But, acknowledging and discussing your child's feelings may help ease any frustration about what they cannot have and increase the ability to appreciate what they do have.

We'd be lying to our children if we didn't admit that comfortable homes, vacations, clothes, or other things that *can* be bought are nice to have. But we need to teach them that these are not the most important things in life. What is really essential cannot be bought. In fact, it can't even be seen. It can only be felt.

I like to tell children that many boys and girls have confided to me that even though their parents have a lot of money and they live in a "huge house," they would trade it all for the love they feel they are missing. There are children who would trade their vacations for a friend, and give away their designer clothes if it meant they would feel good about themselves instead of believing they were accepted because of what they wear. Money can't buy family love, meaningful friendships, or self-acceptance. It can't buy good health, either. How wonderful it would be if we could teach our children what is really important—early.

All we can do is try our hardest to give our children as much of ourselves as possible. We can't do more than that. And it would be unfair for any parent to feel guilty about not being able to give a child more. The most important things parents can give their children can't be bought.

CHAPTER 16

GETTING CLOSER

S|

As clichéd as it sounds, I wish I could be emotionally closer to Mom + Dad. Last year, I gave my father a hug for the first time in 4 or 5 years and it felt good for that was a step in the right direction, but I'd like to be closer.

Sometimes I wish they'd LISTEN to what I'm saying, understand my confusion about "growing up" and advise but not preach.

Getting closer is a process of unfolding that continues throughout a lifetime. It's exciting to realize that no matter how close you are with your child, you can always be closer. No matter how much distance or misunderstanding has kept you and your child apart, it's possible to initiate positive change. No matter how old you are or what your child's age, it's never too late to start down the path towards closeness.

Simply knowing that you want to be closer with your child won't guarantee instant intimacy. Getting closer takes time. It's a process that requires a great deal of patience, along with the conscious effort to open up, reach out, and share.

The more you understand about your child's world, the greater your capacity will be to reach out and be there in a way that neither of you may have thought possible. But the reaching out can't be only one way. You must make a *decision* to get closer and so must your child. If your child isn't responding as you would wish, at least you have the capacity to keep reaching, and hoping that someday you'll strike the right nerve.

Getting closer involves taking chances, risking vulnerability, testing trust. It is a process of actively working to let your child know the real you and encouraging your child to do the same. It's sharing

tears as well as laughter, failures as well as successes, fears as well
as dreams.

Be careful not to judge unfairly your progress towards closeness.
If you find yourself thinking, "I *should* have been able to feel a change
by now," remind yourself that it may be months, even years, before
you start feeling closer. You can't rush intimacy. And trying to rush
your child might push him or her further away from you. Just try to
appreciate each new step you take on the road to getting closer.

As you move forward on life's path with your child, you'll be
met with many challenges, ups and downs. Through it all, if you can
trust the love between you and if you are able to talk honestly with
each other, then you've got the strength and the resources to deal with
any situation, any change, any misunderstanding—even if it means
agreeing that you disagree, in order to understand and communicate
and work at trust.

I hope that all I shared in this book will aid you in your ability
to understand and feel closer to your child, and not only during the
growing-up years, but also throughout your lives together.

For information concerning Ellen Rosenberg's
Programs and Audio Cassette Tapes for
 Parents,
Teachers and Children, write:

GROWING UP FEELING GOOD
Box 659
Rockville Centre, N.Y. 11571

About the Author

Ellen Rosenberg is one of the nation's most articulate and respected experts on the concerns children, parents, and teachers have about the day-to-day experiences related to growing up. Her Growing Up Feeling Good, Getting Closer, and Enriching The Classroom Experience programs have helped thousands of people feel better about themselves, improve their relationships, and deal more effectively with life issues. Ellen created these programs in response to the staggering number of college students in her classes who lacked self-confidence, felt distant from their family and friends, and had difficulty expressing their feelings. Since her first program in 1976, she has answered and discussed hundreds of thousands of questions gathered anonymously from audiences of children, parents, and college students throughout the United States. She is the author of *Growing Up Feeling Good,* the first complete handbook for children about the pressures, confusions, and decisions that are a part of growing up. Her audio cassette tapes include Getting Closer and Talking to your Child about Sex and Puberty.

Ellen has appeared on numerous television and radio talk shows, and has been featured in newspapers throughout the United States and Canada. An educator since 1965, she has taught Health, Family Life, and Human Sexuality at the college level for twelve years. She received a B.S. from Tufts University and an M.S. in Education from Hofstra University, and is certified as a Sex Educator by the American Association of Sex Educators, Counselors, and Therapists. Ellen lives on Long Island, New York, with her husband and two children.